Rolf Kreyer

Introduction to English Syntax

PETER LANG
Internationaler Verlag der Wissenschaften

Bibliographic Information published by the Deutsche Nationalbibliothek
The Deutsche Nationalbibliothek lists this publication in the Deutsche Nationalbibliografie; detailed bibliographic data is available in the internet at http://dnb.d-nb.de.

Cover design:
Olaf Glöckler, Atelier Platen, Friedberg

ISSN 1862-510X
ISBN 978-3-631-55961-1
© Peter Lang GmbH
Internationaler Verlag der Wissenschaften
Frankfurt am Main 2010
All rights reserved.

All parts of this publication are protected by copyright. Any utilisation outside the strict limits of the copyright law, without the permission of the publisher, is forbidden and liable to prosecution. This applies in particular to reproductions, translations, microfilming, and storage and processing in electronic retrieval systems.

www.peterlang.de

To Jürgen Esser,

    for many years of advice, support and friendship

Preface

This book provides an overview of basic syntactic categories, analytical methods and theoretical frameworks that are needed for a comprehensive and systematic description and analysis of the syntax of English as it is spoken and written today. It is therefore useful for students of the English language but also for teachers who are looking for an overview of traditional syntactic analysis. In addition, the book explores various aspects of variation, instability and fuzziness in the syntactic system, including syntactic differences between writing and speech and stylistic variation in syntax. It discusses the relation between syntax and semantics and provides an overview of some major models and theories, including, *inter alia*, generative grammar and construction grammar as well as psycholinguistic approaches. One focus throughout is to introduce the reader to the 'art' or science of syntactic argumentation: Why does it make sense to posit a particular category?, Are there any alternative models?, What are advantages and disadvantages of one framework in comparison to another? Almost all of the examples that are found in this book are drawn from language corpora – each syntactic concept, therefore, is exemplified by authentic language data.

I would like to thank my dear colleagues Jürgen Esser, Sebastian Patt and Sharmila Vaz for many insightful discussions and many comments on the manuscript. I would also like to thank Joybrato Mukherjee for inviting me to write this volume in the TELL Series and Viveka Velupillai for proof-reading the whole manuscript and for her help in formatting it. Finally, I want to thank my beloved wife Anna for many discussions and comments, and so much more.

Bonn   Rolf Kreyer
January 2010

Table of Contents

	Introduction	**1**
1	**From Language Data to Syntactic Description**	**7**
	1.1 Identifying the constituents of a sentence	7
	1.2 Different schools, different analyses	16
	1.3 Categorisation, form and function	18
	1.4 Outlook	24
	1.5 Further reading	26
	1.6 Study questions	26
2	**Words and Word Classes**	**29**
	2.1 The term 'word'	29
	2.2 Word classes	31
	2.2.1 Open and closed classes	31
	2.2.2 Descriptive parameters – the example of the class 'noun'	32
	2.2.3 Main verbs	36
	2.2.4 Adjectives and adverbs	38
	2.2.5 Closed word classes	43
	2.3 Further reading	48
	2.4 Study questions	48
3	**The Verb Phrase**	**51**
	3.1 The structure of the finite verb phrase	51
	3.2 The operator	63
	3.3 The non-finite verb phrase	65
	3.4 Further reading	66
	3.5 Study questions	66
4	**The Noun Phrase**	**67**
	4.1 The notion of 'head'	67
	4.2 The structure of the noun phrase	69
	4.2.1 The determiner	70
	4.2.2 Premodification	74

	4.2.3 Postmodification	80
	4.3 Further reading	87
	4.4 Study questions	88
5	**Adjective, Adverb and Prepositional Phrase**	**89**
	5.1 The adjective phrase	89
	5.2 The adverb phrase	94
	5.3 The prepositional phrase	97
	5.4 Three sample analyses	99
	5.5 Further reading	104
	5.6 Study questions	104
6	**Clauses and Sentences**	**105**
	6.1 The clause elements	106
	6.1.1 Verb	106
	6.1.2 Subject	107
	6.1.3 Direct and indirect object	111
	6.1.4 Complement	113
	6.1.5 Adverbial	115
	6.2 The structure of the clause	120
	6.3 Non-canonical order and secondary clause patterns	123
	6.4 Complex and compound sentences	130
	6.5 Two sample analyses	132
	6.6 Further reading	135
	6.7 Study questions	135
7	**Indeterminacy: Multiple Analysis, Fuzziness and Gradience**	**137**
	7.1 Multiple analysis	138
	7.2 Fuzziness	141
	7.3 Gradience	147
	7.4 Further reading	149
	7.5 Study questions	150
8	**Same Same but Different? Spoken and Written Syntax**	**151**
	8.1 Does spoken language have structure?	151
	8.2 Two modes, one descriptive apparatus?	152

		8.3 Principles of online production and their consequences	156
		8.3.1 Disfluency	157
		8.3.2 Structural differences	158
	8.4	Spontaneous spoken language as interaction and its consequences	166
	8.5	Further reading	167
	8.6	Study questions	168

9 Syntactic Variation — 169

9.1 Kinds of syntactic variation — 170
9.2 Factors that influence syntactic variation — 173
    9.2.1 Syntactic complexity — 173
    9.2.2 The distribution of information in the clause — 176
    9.2.3 Emphasis, text structuring and artistic concerns — 180
    9.2.4 A note on interactions and interdependencies of individual factors — 184
9.3 Further reading — 186
9.4 Study questions — 187

10 Syntax and Meaning — 189

10.1 Generative syntax and semantics — 189
10.2 The open-choice principle and the idiom principle — 192
    10.2.1 Collocation — 193
    10.2.2 Colligation — 196
    10.2.3 Semantic preferences and prosodies — 198
10.3 Constructions — 200
10.4 Further reading — 205
10.5 Study questions — 205

11 Major Approaches to Syntactic Description: An Overview — 207

11.1 The standard theory of generative-transformational syntax — 207
11.2 X'-Theory — 214
11.3 Construction Grammar — 221
11.4 Further reading — 225
11.5 Study questions — 226

12	**Psycholinguistic Aspects of Syntax**		**227**
	12.1	The derivational theory of complexity	229
	12.2	The psychological reality of syntactic units	233
	12.3	Parsing	237
	12.4	Further reading	245
	12.5	Study questions	245

References — 247

Index — 255

Introduction

The present book provides an introduction to the description and analysis of English syntax. Syntax can be defined as follows:

> The term 'syntax' is from Ancient Greek *sýntaxis*, a verbal noun which literally means 'arrangement' or 'setting out together'. Traditionally, it refers to the branch of grammar dealing with the ways in which words, with or without appropriate inflections, are arranged to show connections of meaning within the sentence. (Matthews 1981: 1)

The units of syntactic description occupy a central position among the units that linguistics is concerned with: in syntactic units, individual words are combined with each other to form larger units of communication, namely phrases (e.g. *The President*), clauses (e.g. *The President ate a pretzel*) and sentences (*Because the President ate a pretzel he fainted*). Sentences, on the other hand, are the building blocks of texts. This grants syntax a central position among the other disciplines of linguistics, as shown in Figure 0.1.

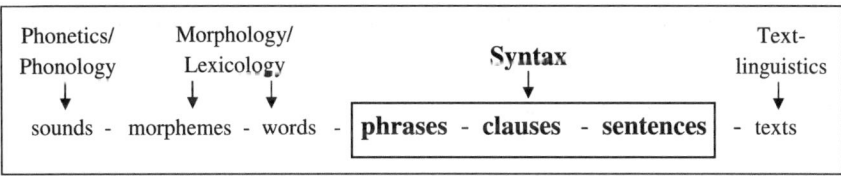

Figure 0.1: The central position of syntax and syntactic units.

The main concern of syntax lies in the structural description of the units in bold print in Figure 0.1. Syntax explores and describes the rules and principles according to which words are arranged in phrases, phrases are arranged in clauses, and words and phrases are arranged in sentences. One of such rules, for instance, is that in present-day English the subject, typically representing the doer of an action (or 'agent') should be expressed first (i.e. *The President*), the verb that refers to the action itself second (i.e. the verb form *ate*), and the object, typically referring to the entity that undergoes the action (or the 'patient') third (i.e. *a pretzel*): therefore, the sentence in (1) is in line with the rules of English syntax (i.e. it is grammatically well-formed), while the sentences in (2) and (3) are not (i.e.

they are grammatically ill-formed): examples (2) and (3) are thus marked with an asterisk (*), which indicates the lack of grammatical correctness.

(1) The President ate a pretzel.
(2) *The President a pretzel ate.
(3) *Pretzel President the ate a.

Note that it is of course possible to re-arrange the items so that other grammatically well-formed sentences with different orders of the words of example (1) are achieved. For example, the passive variant of (1) would have the patient of the action in front position, a form of the verb *be* and the past participle of the verb *eat* in second position and the agent of the action in final position (with the agent being no longer an obligatory element, but an optional 'by-agent' that can also be left out):

(4) A pretzel was eaten by the President.

Syntax is devoted to the description of the set of rules that produce all the grammatically well-formed sentences in a language – e.g. sentence (1) but not sentences (2) and (3) – as well as the analysis of the operations by means of which we can derive certain (and more complex) syntactic structures, e.g. sentence (4), from other (and more basic) structures, e.g. sentence (1).

In addition, syntactic structures also make reference to aspects of meaning. Consider example (5).

(5) ?A pretzel ate the President.

This sentence is marked with a question mark because it is dubious. On the one hand, it is grammatically well-formed as it represents the same syntactic structure (subject – verb – object) as sentence (1) using the same verb. On the other hand, the sentence in (5) is not meaningful as the action that is described (i.e. eating) is not compatible with the agent of the action: inanimate entities like pretzels cannot eat anything. That is, although the sentence is grammatically well-formed, it is not meaningful – at least not in its literal sense and according to our shared world-knowledge.

This makes clear that an introduction to syntax will also have to take a look at the units below the units of syntax, i.e. words. In addition to the aspect of 'meaningfulness' discussed above, words are relevant since they are the building blocks of syntactic units and influence their structure. Phrases, for instances, are classified with regard to the word class of the most important word in the phrase, e.g. the phrase *The President* is a noun phrase, because the central word (*President*) is a noun. On the other hand, syntax is partly concerned with texts, since clauses and sentences are the building blocks of texts and, often, textual requirements influence the form a clause or a sentence takes. For instance, the choice between active and passive, as in (1) or (4), can be motivated by the structure or function of the text in which a sentence occurs. The relation of syntax to neighbouring disciplines and their units is shown in Figure 0.2.

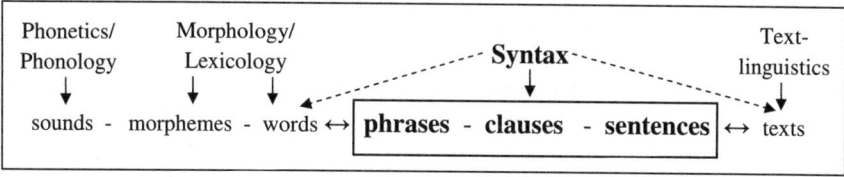

Figure 0.2: Syntax and its relation to elements of linguistic description.

The influence of textual requirements already hints at the fact that syntax is not only about grammatical well-formedness but also about the acceptability of a sentence in a given situation, context or genre. Acceptability does not capture the correctness of a sentence but whether it is an appropriate, idiomatic and, thus, generally accepted utterance in a particular setting. Often, sentences are acceptable in certain contexts even though, strictly speaking, they are not grammatically well-formed or at least grammatically deviant. Consider sentences (6) to (8).

(6) Gotta be joking.
(7) They're enough funny, innit?
(8) !A pretzel the President ate.

The sentence in (6) is perfectly acceptable in informal spoken language, although it does not conform to written English syntax. This example illustrates that what one finds in English grammar books has traditionally been restricted to written and formal language. The sentence in (7) is not in line with standard English grammar rules either because, firstly, the tag question *innit* (as a variant of *isn't it*) is not the negative equivalent of the verb in the main clause (that is, the tag question should be, according to standard English grammar, *aren't they*) and because, secondly, the word *enough* is used to premodify the adjective *funny*, which is not possible in standard English grammar either. Both deviations from standard English are, however, perfectly acceptable in certain contexts, e.g. in the informal speech produced by teenagers in and around London. The sentence in (8) provides yet another example of the clash between grammatical well-formedness and acceptability: while this sentence is not in line with the basic word order of English (which requires the subject to be in first position and the object in postverbal position), this variant with a 'fronted' object is acceptable in certain (spoken) contexts, for example if the speaker wants to stress that the President ate an pretzel and not, say, a doughnut: "A pretzel the President ate, not a doughnut". The exclamation mark in front of example (8) shows that this structure is unusual and only acceptable in certain situations. What examples (6) to (8) illustrate is the need for a description of English syntax to also accommodate for sentences that may not be admissible in formal writing but that are acceptable in spoken language, given that speech is prioritised over writing in modern linguistics for various reasons (cf. Lyons 1981: 11-17): for example, every human being acquires speech before writing, and virtually all language users produce much more spoken language than written language.

In addition to the situation- or genre-related acceptability of sentences, sentences can also be (non-)acceptable from a psychological or cognitive point of view. The sentence in (9), for example is grammatically well-formed and meaningful but sentences of this kind will usually not be found in authentic language data, since they are too difficult to understand.

(9) The dog the cat the rat bit chased died.

This example illustrates multiple reduced relative clauses. Note that reduced relative clauses are grammatical and that a single reduced relative clause is easy to understand. That is, the sentence *The dog the cat chased died* does not cause any difficulties. Problems arise when the noun *cat* is postmodified in a similar way together with a postmodification of *dog*, as example (9) shows. In that case, it is difficult to understand the sentence, i.e. that a particular dog died, namely that dog which chased this one cat that was bitten by the rat. Examples of the above kind hint at psychological processes relevant for the production and reception of syntactic units. These are explored in the field of psycholinguistics, which is also concerned with the psychological reality of the units of syntactic analysis.

The aim and scope of the present book follows from the core ideas and key concepts that have been sketched out above. The book provides an overview of basic syntactic categories, analytical methods and theoretical frameworks that are needed for a comprehensive and systematic description and analysis of the syntax of English as it is spoken and written today. In addition, the book also wants to introduce the reader to the 'art' or science of syntactic argumentation. In some cases, therefore, a particular result may not be that important but the focus will be on the arguments that lead to this result. In those cases, the reader is invited to follow the argumentation and increase his or her awareness of pitfalls and possible alternative explanations.

Introduction

The book falls into two major parts. Part I (chapters 1 to 6) focuses on syntactic analysis proper. This involves a general discussion of syntactic categories and methods used in syntactic analysis, as well as an introduction of a particularly useful descriptive apparatus for the analysis of syntactic structures; this apparatus is largely based on the framework suggested by Quirk et al. (1985) and covers all grammatical structures from the word level to the sentence level. Generally speaking, we can say that the first part of the book deals with syntax of the written norm of Standard English, and depicts syntax as a stable and largely invariant system. Part II (chapter 7 to 12) widens the scope and discusses various aspects of variation, instability and fuzziness in the syntactic system, including syntactic differences between writing and speech and stylistic variation in syntax. The second part will also put into perspective the relation between syntax and semantics, discuss whether and to what extent syntactic structures have meaning, and provide an overview of some major models and theories that have exerted an influence on the description and analysis of English syntax over the past few decades, including, *inter alia*, generative grammar and construction grammar. The book will conclude with an exploration of psycholinguistic approaches to the study of syntactic units, syntactic structures and syntactic processing.

Almost all examples that you will find in this book are authentic language data drawn from two major corpora. namely the British component of the International Corpus of the English language (ICE-GB) and the British National Corpus (BNC). Since most of the examples are taken from the first corpus, the source just provides information on the text-document and the line in ICE-GB, e.g. 'sa1-006:130' instead of 'ICE-GB: sa1 006:130'. Tokens taken from the BNC are marked as in the following example: 'BNC-J13: 3398'. In some cases examples have been slightly altered, for instance shortened. For the sake of readability, such changes have not been marked in the text.

1 From Language Data to Syntactic Description

1.1 Identifying the constituents of a sentence

In the previous chapter syntax was described as the study of the linear arrangement of word forms, i.e. syntax is concerned with strings or chains of word forms. Word forms occurring within such a chain are related to each other and also to other word forms of the same language. Linguists speak of syntagmatic relationships and paradigmatic relationships. The first concerns the relations that obtain between words (or more generally: elements) that occur within the same string or syntagm (from Greek *syntagma*), hence the name 'syntagmatic'. Syntagmatic relations become most obvious in those cases in which one element influences the form of another element in the same string, as in example (1) taken from a discussion of the film *Back to the Future*:

(1) But he knows it's his mom. (Sa1-006:130)

Firstly, the form of the verb *knows* depends on the number of the subject noun phrase *he*, which is singular and third person and therefore demands a third person singular ending with the present tense form of the verb. Secondly, the form of the possessive determiner *his* is also dependent on the subject, as it has to be in line with the number (singular) and the gender (male) of the subject.

Paradigmatic relations are those between one word or string of words in a given syntagm and other words or strings of words of the same language. Although being the term that is most widespread, it is not very telling (as opposed to 'syntagmatic' which becomes self-explanatory given the Greek word). Maybe de Saussure's (1959 [1916]: 122-127) original term 'associative relations' is more accessible: the language user can associate any string of words that actually occurs in a given syntagm with a large number of other strings of words which could fill the same position in that syntagm. Syntagmatic relations, then, are relations between elements that are 'in front of us', either in writing or in speech, whereas paradigmatic relations obtain between one of these given elements and a number of elements in our heads. Lyons (1981: 96) uses the term 'substitutional' instead of paradigmatic or associative, which expresses the insight that any string of words in a syntagm can be substituted with a large number of other strings, as example (2) shows:

(2)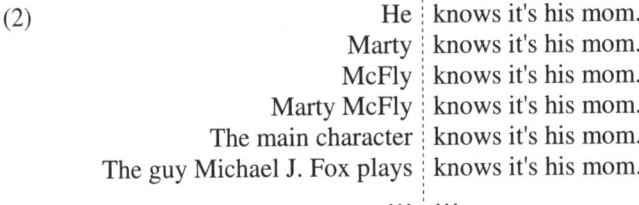

The element *He* in the original example can be substituted by any of the other strings on the left-hand side, since all of them can fill the same slot in the syntagm without any loss of grammaticality. Accordingly, all of these strings stand in a paradigmatic (or associative, or substitutional) relationship. In the following we will see that paradigmatic relations play an important role in the identification of the constituents of a sentence.

A constituency analysis (often referred to as 'Immediate Constituent Analysis' or 'IC-Analysis') of a sentence is concerned with two main questions, namely (a) which units belong together, and (b) how closely they belong together. Keeping these questions in mind, we can compare a sentence and its structure to a necklace consisting of beads on a chain, with the beads representing the individual words. Are these beads just lined up on this chain or do we find that some beads are closer to each other than other beads, i.e. do we find groups of beads? These two possibilities are shown in Figure 1.1 below.

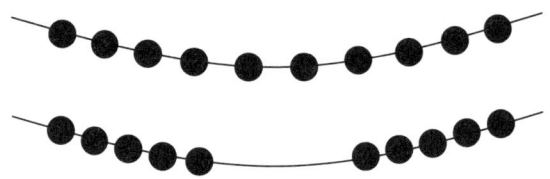

Figure 1.1: Which units belong together?

In the top case there does not seem to be any structure in the necklace whatsoever, whereas the bottom half clearly shows two groups of beads consisting of five beads each.

Obviously, we can also think of a more intricate necklace with one main chain and other smaller chains connected to this main chain. In addition to groups of beads, we now can draw a distinction between (groups of) beads on the main chain and (groups of) beads on the smaller chains. With regard to question (b) above we would say that we still have two groups of five beads each, but that within each group there is a smaller group of three beads (those on the smaller chains). We could thus say that these three beads belong together most closely; at the same time they are also part of the bigger five-bead group. Note that while we are still dealing with the same number of beads and the same basic groups as in the bottom of half of Figure 1.1, the five-bead groups on the right and the left are more intricately structured.

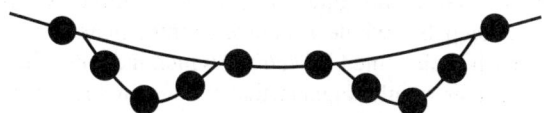

Figure 1.2: How closely do the units belong together?

Admittedly, this simile (as all similes) has it weaknesses, but we will see in the following that the arrangement of words in a sentence is not too different from that of the beads in Figure 1.2.

Let us begin with the simple sentence *The coal trade provided work* (s2b-022:047). Intuitively we would all agree that this sentence consists of three main parts or constituents, namely *The coal trade*, *provided*, and *work*. While this is intuitively clear, it is obvious that a scientific approach has to substantiate intuitive claims by objective arguments. One set of such objective arguments is what is usually called 'constituency tests'. These tests are designed to make explicit which words belong together and how closely they belong together. One of these tests is the 'replacement' test (also known as 'commutation' or 'substitution' test). Other tests discussed here are the 'coordination', the 'movement' and the 'question' test.

First of all, a replacement test can show that each of the words in this string is a constituent, since each of the words can be replaced by another word without leading to an ill-formed or ungrammatical sequence.

(3) The coal trade provided work. (s2b-022:047)
(4) **Their** coal trade provided work.
(5) The **skin** trade provided work.
(6) The coal **market** provided work.
(7) The coal trade **offered** work.
(8) The coal trade provided **income**.

This procedure may seem unnecessary; after all, words are clearly demarcated by spaces or a space and a period. However, we have to keep in mind that this only works with written language (or with beads on a necklace). In the spoken medium, clues as to the constituency status of words are usually not given, since we do not mark individual words by pauses or distinct sound signals. To make things worse, even the written code is not fully reliable with regard to words. To give but one example consider the string *in front of* in (9) below.

(9) He is standing there in front of Mason (s2a-009:030)

You would be hard put to find a substitute for each of the three 'words' in the above example and still keep the whole sentence grammatical. On the other hand, *in front of* can easily be substituted by *behind*, which indicates that *in front of* forms one constituent. This would suggest that we are in fact dealing with what is often called a 'multi-word unit' (see, among others, Sinclair 1991), i.e. a sequence of 'words' separated by spaces which, however, cannot sensibly be split up into its individual 'words'. This short discussion already hints at the fact that the concept 'word' is not an easy one. It will be discussed in more detail in chapter 2 below. For now, let us use the term 'word' to denote a string of letters demarcated either by spaces on each side or by a space and a punctuation mark.

The next step is to try to determine how closely words belong together. With the replacement test, we usually try to replace a sequence of words by another word, preferably a pro-form, e.g. *he*, she, *it* or *there*. Let us take a slightly more complex sentence to illustrate how this works.

(10) The man had locked the briefcase in the boot. (w2f-018:006)

In constituency analysis, it is often useful to try to identify the main constituents of a sentence first. In the present example, pro-forms show that *the man*, *his briefcase*, and *in the book* all form constituents, since we can replace them by *he*, *it* and *there*, respectively.

(11) The man   had   locked   the briefcase   in the boot.

      He   had   locked   **it**   **there**

The structure of a sentence like this can either be described by a tree diagram or by bracketing. Both ways of representation are completely isomorphic, i.e. they provide the same information and can be mapped onto each other, as shown in examples (12) and (13) below.

(12)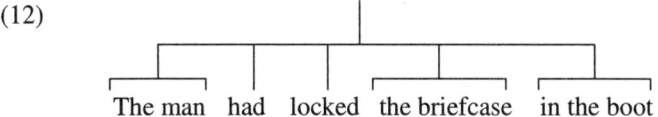

(13)   [[The man] [had] [locked] [the briefcase] [in the boot]]

Each opening bracket and its corresponding closing bracket in (13) relates to one node in the tree diagram in (12). The two bold brackets on the left and the right represent the top node in the tree diagram or the 'root' of the tree. Each of the other bracket pairs corresponds to exactly one of the nodes in the middle of the tree diagram.

So far, our string of words resembles the necklace at the bottom half of Figure 1.1. Further tests show that the structure of this sentence is slightly more complicated. Firstly, the constituent *in the boot* has an internal structure, since we can replace *the boot* by a pro-form, e.g. *it*, and not violate the grammaticality of the sequence (although it may sound clumsy). The structure of the clause, then, is as follows:

(14)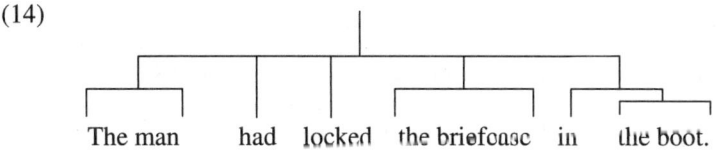

(15) [[The man] [had] [locked] [the briefcase] [in [the boot]]]

While the constituents so far seem to be fairly obvious a less obvious constituent is *locked the briefcase in the boot*. This sequence can either be replaced by *done so* if we keep the original order of the sentence or merely by *so* if we swap some elements.

(16) The woman had locked the briefcase in the boot and the man had **done so**, too.
(17) The woman had locked the briefcase in the boot and **so** had the man.

The status of the word form *had* is slightly problematic. It could be argued that *had* cannot form a constituent with another word or string of words. *Had*, thus, would be regarded as a constituent of its own, leading to the following analysis.

(18)
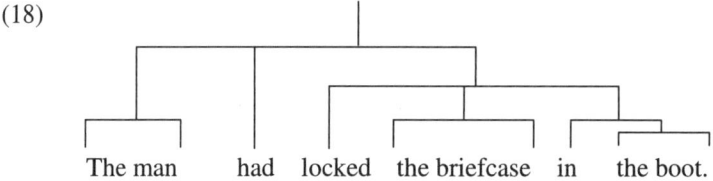

(19) [[The man] [had] [locked [the briefcase] [in [the boot]]]]

Others would argue that the string *had locked* could be replaced by the word form *locked*, i.e. *The man locked the briefcase in the boot*. Note that this analysis also contradicts the constituent status of the string *locked the briefcase in the boot* which was demonstrated in (16) and (17) above: the verb form *locked* cannot form a constituent with *had* and, at the same time, be grouped together with *the briefcase in the boot*. As a result we arrive at a completely different and less hierarchical analysis.

(20)
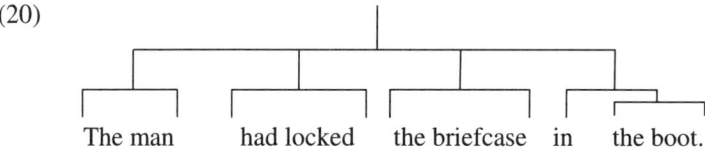

(21) [[The man] [had locked] [the briefcase] [in [the boot]]]

The problem of such conflicting analyses will be discussed in section 1.2.

With the next test, the 'coordination' test, we coordinate the sequence under scrutiny with a similar sequence and see if the result is a grammatical sentence. Consider the examples below; the coordinated elements are in bold print.

(22) **The woman** *and* **the man** had locked the briefcase in the boot.
(23) The man had locked **the briefcase** *and* **the suitcase** in the boot.
(24) The man had locked the briefcase **in the boot** *or* **in the house**.
(25) The man had locked the briefcase in **the boot** *or* **the house**.
(26) The man had **locked the briefcase in the boot** *and* **taken the suitcase from the room**.
(27) The man **has** *and* **had** locked the briefcase in the boot.

As you can see from the six examples above, the coordination test identifies the same constituents as does the replacement test. Note again, however, that arguably the following sentence would also work, leading to the conflicting analysis discussed above.

(28) The man **would lock** *and* **had locked** the briefcase in the boot.

The intuition underlying the next test, the 'movement' test, is that if we can move a string of words to another place in this sentence, this string of words must be a constituent. This test is a bit more restricted than the other two: we have to create a particular context in which the new sentence makes sense, as the examples below make clear.

(29) I thought the man had locked the briefcase in the boot.

As you can see, the sentence under analysis is part of a larger sentence. This is the only way to move the string *the man* out of its position in the original sentence, as is shown in example (30). The string that is moved occurs in bold print, the added context is put in brackets.[1]

(30) **The man** (, I thought,) had locked the briefcase in the boot.

Similarly, we need specific contexts to identify most of the other constituents in the sentence under scrutiny. Sentences (31) to (34) are preposed constructions, i.e. sentences where a constituent that usually occurs postverbally is preposed to initial position. In (31) below, for instance, the direct object *the briefcase* is preposed. The effect is that the preposed constituent is emphasised. This makes preposed sentences a useful means of expressing contrasts (among other functions). In (31), for instance, this contrast is between the briefcase and the suitcase.

(31) **The briefcase** the man had locked in the boot (, but not the suitcase).
(32) **In the boot** the man had locked the briefcase (, but not in the house).
(33) **The boot** the man had locked the suitcase in (, but not the house).
(34) (The man had wanted to lock the briefcase in the boot and) **locked the briefcase in the boot** the man had.

The question in (35) shows that the verb form *had* can be moved to initial position, thus indicating its status as a constituent.

(35) **Had** the man locked the briefcase in the boot?

---

[1] This could also be interpreted as the application of another test, the 'insertion' test: if one or several elements, in this case *I thought*, can be inserted somewhere in the string, the resulting strings to the left and to the right of this or these element(s) are constituents. We will not discuss this test further here.

The next test, the 'question' test, is similar to the movement test and to the replacement test. A constituent is replaced by a *wh*-pronoun and then moved to the beginning of a question that contains the same proposition.

(36) **Who** had locked the briefcase in the boot? **The man** had locked the briefcase in the boot.
(37) **What** had the man locked in the boot? The man had locked **the briefcase** in the boot.
(38) **Where** had the man locked the briefcase? The man had locked the briefcase **in the boot**.
(39) In **where** had the man locked the briefcase? The man had locked the briefcase in **the boot**.
(40) **What** had the man **done**? The man had **locked the briefcase in the boot**.

The identification of constituents automatically leads to a hierarchical description of the sentence structure. The tests above have shown that one plausible analysis is to assume three main constituents namely *the man*, *had*, and *locked the briefcase in the boot*. The latter itself consists of the three constituents *locked*, *the briefcase*, and *in the boot*. Finally, *in the boot* was bipartitioned into *in* and *the boot*. This hierarchical structure is mirrored in the tree diagram in (19), repeated here for convenience:

(41)
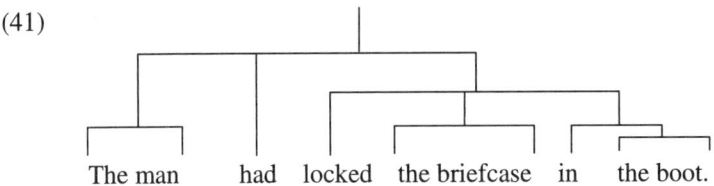

This way of representation (resulting from our constituency tests) provides an answer to the two questions that we posed above, i.e. (a) which units belong together? and (b) how closely do they belong together? Words or strings of words belong together if they share a node in the tree diagram, e.g. *The* and *man*, *the* and *briefcase*, or *in* and *the boot*, etc. In addition, the tree diagram makes explicit levels of hierarchy of syntactic structure. *The boot*, for instance, forms a constituent on the lowest level. At the same time, the whole string is part of a larger string *in the boot*, which again is one constituent in a string consisting of three constituents *locked the briefcase in the boot*, and so on. It is through this hierarchical organisation that the notion of closeness of constituents becomes most apparent. If we climb down the branches of our syntactic tree we find that those words that belong closest together are separated last: *boot* belongs more closely to the final *the* than to any other word or string of words, since it is separated from *the* at the very bottom of the tree. Following the analysis under (41) *locked* belongs more closely to *the briefcase* or *in the boot* than to *had* or *The man*, because *locked* is separated from the latter two before the former two, etc. Note, however, that other analyses might also be possible (see section 1.2 for details).

The discussion of the status of *had locked* above has already shown that constituency tests need to be applied with care, since they can lead to conflicting analyses. Another question is the number of positive test results that are needed to establish constituent status for an element or a string of elements. If one test identified a constituent that the others fail to identify, would we assume that we have a new constituent or not? From our example above consider the string *the briefcase in the boot*. We cannot replace this string by a pro-form and we cannot apply the question test. The result of the movement test sounds very unnatural.

(42) ?**The briefcase in the boot** the man had locked (but not the suitcase in the house).

Only the coordination test seems to yield a perfectly acceptable sentence.

(43) The man had **locked the briefcase in the boot** *and* **the suitcase in the house**.

But even here it could be argued that sentence (43) is an elliptical version of sentence (44).

(44) The man had **locked the briefcase in the boot** *and* **(locked) the suitcase in the house**.

The question that arises concerns the constituent status of *the briefcase in the boot*. If we follow the analysis in sentence (44) we arrive at the tree diagram in (41). Accepting the result of the coordination test in (43) yields a different tree diagram and, thus, a different syntactic analysis of our sentence, which is shown in (45).

(45)

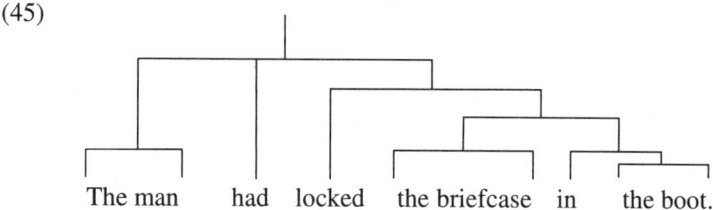

Note, however, that this analysis is highly questionable and would be rejected by most researchers. But the above example makes clear that constituency tests need to be applied with care. It is always advisable to try and corroborate the results from one test with the help of other constituency tests. Even then, different syntactic schools may come up with different solutions for the same sentence, as we have seen in the discussion of the constituent status of the string *had locked*. The same tests may lead to different results. In the next section such aspects will be discussed in more detail.

1.2 Different schools, different analyses

There is a large number of different syntactic schools and approaches. Although most of them would agree on the validity of tests like the ones discussed above, we can still find discrepancies between the analyses of individual schools. These are due to different aspects of description that the individual schools regard as central.

Most traditional descriptive grammars, for instance, seem to lay a focus on logical and functional aspects of sentence analysis. An example is a distinction that dates back to Aristotle, namely that between the 'subject' and the 'predicate' of a sentence (see, among others, Quirk et al. 1985: 78-79, or Huddleston & Pullum 2002: 25-26). The subject refers to what a sentence is about, and the predicate tells us something about the subject. Accordingly, our example would be bipartitioned into the two major constituents *The man* and *had locked the briefcase in the boot* and not into the three constituents that our constituency tests yielded (see example (47) below). Another analysis (e.g. the major clause patterns advocated in Quirk et al. 1985) would focus on the function that different parts of the sentence fulfil with regard to the verb form *locked*. The verb *to lock* (in the sense above) demands three specifications, namely someone who locks (*The man*), something that is locked (*the briefcase*) and the place where this something is locked (*in the boot*). As a consequence the sentence would be divided into four main parts, namely the subject, the verb, the object, and the adverbial (see example (48)). Finally, many theories in the generative framework follow a rigid binary branching strategy, i.e. each constituent on any level is considered to consist of two parts (e.g. Radford 1997: 98). As an example let us consider the structure that one version of what is called X'-theory (see chapter 12 for details) would assign to the sentence under scrutiny, as shown in (49) below. Each node only has two branches, as opposed to the structure given in (46), where the whole clause is partitioned into three elements, namely *the man*, *had*, and *locked the briefcase in the boot*, the latter of which is analysed as a three-element chain consisting of *locked*, *the briefcase*, and *in the boot*.

From Language Data to Syntactic Description

In addition to our original analysis given in (41), here repeated as (46) for convenience, we arrive at three additional analyses, shown in (47) to (49).

(46)
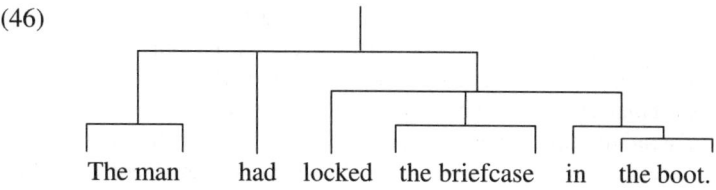

(47)
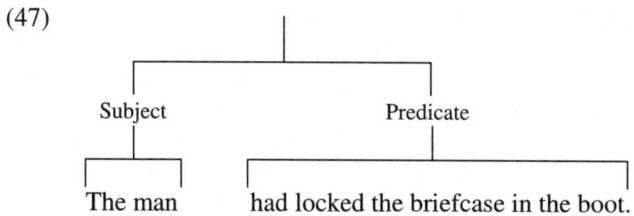

(48)
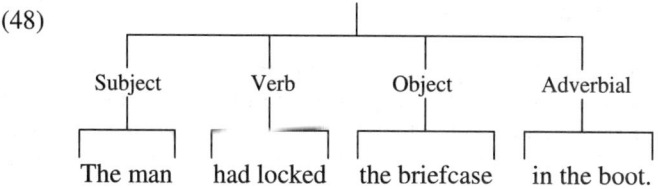

(49)
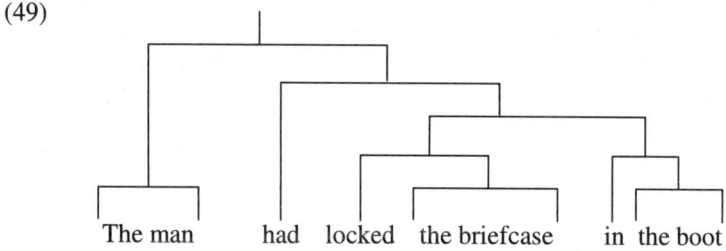

Despite the obvious differences, these analyses are not fully incompatible. For instance, the binary distinction of subject and predicate in (47) also shows up again in (49). Similarly, apart from (47) all analyses agree on the status of the elements *the man*, *the briefcase*, and *in the boot*. Finally, (46) and (49), apart from the number of branches a node might have, provide a fairly similar description.

It is important to note that none of the above analyses is more correct than the other; Quirk et al. (1985: 90) speak of 'multiple analysis' in this respect: "There are occasions [...] when [...] alternative analyses seem to be needed, on the grounds that some of the generalizations that have to be made require one analysis, and some require another". The differences that become apparent are either due to different aspects that are focused on, or to theoretic assumptions underlying a particular approach. The binary branching, for instance, that is often found in generative approaches is at least partly motivated by questions of child language acquisition (see Haegeman ^{2}1994: 138-144). Another important criterion may be the elegance of theoretical description, also referred to as Occam's razor: models are favoured which are simple and reduce the descriptive apparatus to a minimum. From this perspective, the structural description under (49) would have to be preferred over that under (46) simply on the basis of the fact that the former only needs one descriptive element, the binary-branching node, whereas with the latter two descriptive elements are applied, namely binary-branching and ternary-branching nodes. On the whole, it is necessary to be aware of the aspects focused on and of the underlying assumptions in order to assess the validity or plausibility of a particular syntactic analysis.

1.3 Categorisation, form and function

Syntactic theory, and linguistics in general, not only is concerned with the description of structures but also with the categorisation of these structures and of the elements within them. Note that categorisation is a natural and everyday process. It serves to reduce the complexity of the world to manageable portions by grouping together those things that share a number of features. For instance, all members of the category BIRD have two legs, two wings, a beak and feathers and lay eggs. Most birds, in addition, sing and can fly. The advantage of a category like BIRD lies in the fact that those bits of information that characterise the whole category do not need to be stored for individual members of that category. That is, if somebody tells you that a sparrow is a bird, you know that it sings, can fly, etc., even though you may never have seen a sparrow. In addition, there may be many kinds of birds you do not know but still, you will be able to recognise them as birds and, thus, deduce a number of characteristic features that are relevant for them.

The same is true for syntactic and linguistic categorisation. These categories, too, reduce the complexity of elements and structures that occur in a language and make it manageable, for the linguist as well as the language user. Before we describe syntactic categories more closely, we will first discuss the nature of categorisation more generally.

From Language Data to Syntactic Description

Categorisation, first and foremost, has to do with abstraction. Every phenomenon in the world can be regarded as a bundle of features which co-occur. In the process of abstraction, one or more of these features are regarded as relevant, whereas other features are ignored. As a consequence, phenomena that share the same relevant features will be treated as identical, even though they may differ in irrelevant features. The symbols under (50), for instance, have a particular shape, a particular size, and a particular pattern on the surface, and none of the symbols, obviously, is identical to any of the others.

(50) a) ☐ b) ⇔ c) ▲ d) ○ e) △ f) ☐

However, these six symbols can be assigned to groups of (in a given respect) identical elements, if irrelevant features are ignored. A focus on the shape, for instance, would group together (a) and (f), (c) and (e), and assign (b) and (d) to individual groups. Focusing on the surface pattern, in contrast, would result in a group consisting of (a), (d), (e) and (f), and another group containing symbols (b) and (c), and so on, as shown in (51) and (52) below.

(51) a) ☐ ☐   b) ▲ △   c) ⇔   d) ○   (focus on shape)

(52) a) ☐ ☐ △ ○   b) ▲ ⇔   (focus on surface pattern)

It is important to note that each of these categories is based on abstractions: in the first case, by focusing on the shape, we have abstracted away from the features 'size' and 'surface pattern'; the different sizes in group a) and the different patterns in group b) are regarded as irrelevant. It is important that the elements within one group have the same shape. In the second case, only the feature 'surface pattern' is regarded as relevant, the other features are disregarded.

In syntax we are usually not only concerned with categorising individual elements but also with the categorisation of sequences of elements. Let us assume the following four sequences.

(53) a) ☐⇔▲   b) ◇▦▲   c) ○▨◇   d) ⊕△▦

If we abstract away from size and surface pattern and just focus on the shape of the symbols, these sequences can be rewritten as shown in (54).

(54) a) ☐◇△   b) ◇☐△   c) ○☐◇   d) ○△☐

A look at these modified sequences makes it clear that they can conveniently be grouped together under three different classes if the focus is on the position of the square in a given sequence, namely a square in initial, in medial, or in final position. In this case, (54b and c) fall into the same class, namely (55b).

(55)   a) □+X   b) X+□+X   c) X+□

A look at examples (53) to (55) illustrates that abstraction and categorisation are powerful tools when it comes to identifying patterns and structures. Note that the patterns under (55) become much more obvious in the sequences shown in (54) than in those under (53), where the wealth of additional information provided by the different sizes and surface patterns is likely to distract the observer.

In many respects, syntactic description is similar to what has been illustrated in examples (50) to (55). Consider the sentences under (56).

(56) a) I hate this. (s1a-001:019)
    b) Did you catch it? (s1a-004:022)
    c) We had a very good turnout. (s1a-005:212)
    d) What's he doing? (s1a-005:097)

These four sentences do not show any similarities, there is no word that occurs in any two of the sentences. However, if we abstract away from the individual words and focus on the form of these words and on the function that they have in the sentence, similarities become apparent.

With regard to form, we can distinguish pronouns (PN: *I*, *this*, *you*, *it*, *we*, *that*, *what*, *he*), nouns (N: *turnout*), articles (Art: *a*), verbs (V: *hate*, *did*, *catch*, *had*, *'s*), adverbs (Adv: *very*) and adjectives (Adj: *good*), which yields the description under (57)

(57) a) I hate this.   PN+V+PN
    b) Did you catch it?   V+PN+V+PN
    c) We had a very good turnout.   PN+V+Art+Adv+Adj+N
    d) What's he doing?   PN+V+PN+V

This is only a first step. As you can see in (57) above, the sequences on the right of the example sentences do not show any similarities yet. As in the case of (50) to (55) above, such similarities only become apparent if we abstract away from the form of the individual words and focus on what is called 'phrases'. Phrases are a level of description that is in between the level of words and the level of sentences: Words combine to form phrases, which combine to form sentences. Note, however, that phrases may consist of one word only, as the following example by Quirk et al. (1985: 41) nicely illustrates.

(58) a) The weather has been very cold just recently.
   b)   It   was   cold   recently.

Both sentences above consist of four phrases, all of which are realised by one word only in sentence (58b).

With regard to example (57) above, the pronouns and the string *a very good turnout* would be considered as realisations of a noun phrase, in short: NP. Leaving the verbs as they are for the moment, we arrive at the following formal analysis:

(59) a) I hate this.   NP+V+NP
    b) Did you catch it?   V+NP+V+NP
    c) We had a very good turnout. NP+V+NP
    d) What's he doing?   NP+V+NP+V

On this level of abstraction, it becomes obvious that a) and c) are similar.

Further similarities become apparent if we look at the functions of the words in the examples above. More specifically, we can identify three syntactic functions, namely those of subject, verb, and object. Without going into too much detail now (syntactic functions are discussed in more detail in chapter 6), a short description of these functions is in order here. The subject in many cases denotes the 'doer' of the action described in the sense, usually referred to as the 'agent'. The object is that part of the sentence which refers to the element to which something is done, the 'undergoer' of the action or the 'patient'. The verb describes the action itself. On the basis of these functional elements the sentences in (57) can be described as is shown in (60).

(60) a) I hate this.   SVO
    b) Did you catch it?   VSVO
    c) We had a very good turnout. SVO
    d) What's he doing?   OSV

Again, abstracting away from the given word forms and focusing on their function in the sentence makes apparent patterns that otherwise would have remained hidden. As in (59) we find that a) and c) are similar and can be distinguished from b) and d). Note, however, that the functional analysis under (60) provides more information than the formal one under (59). While both analyses yield identical subsets of patterns, the description of the patterns is more detailed in (60). The formal analysis can only distinguish between verbs and NPs; a functional perspective reveals that some of the NPs function as subjects (S) while others function as objects (O). This shows that formal identity does not necessarily entail functional identity.

Another look at the functional description under (60) provides further insights. All of the sentences are similar in that they contain functional elements of the types S, V, and O, and no other elements. All sentences are instantiations of what we call 'monotransitive clauses' (see chapter 6). In addition, we find that two of these sentences do not begin with the subject but with a verb and the object, respectively. These two sentences are of the interrogative type, whereas the other three are declarative sentences. On a very basic level, i.e. if we only regard the clause type as relevant and ignore the order of elements as an irrelevant feature, we can say that all of the five sentences are identical, because all of them are monotransitive. If order is treated as relevant we would have to come up with two different classes, namely monotransitive declarative clauses and monotransitive interrogative clauses. From this it becomes clear that syntactic description involves different degrees of abstraction: what is identical from one point of view may become different if further aspects are taken into account.

The distinction of form versus function of syntactic elements is extremely important and deserves some further discussion. Form and function are the two basic ways in which syntactic strings and their elements can be described. It is important to note that there is usually no one-to-one mapping between these two descriptive dimensions, i.e. a particular phrase may fulfil several functions (see Quirk et al. 1985: 60). Above we have seen that a noun phrase may function both as subject and as object of a sentence. Another frequent function of NPs is that of complement (C). A complement "applies some attribute or definition to the subject [... or] the object" (55), as shown in (61a) and (61b), respectively.

(61) a) That's *the challenge*. (s1a-001:042)   SVC
    b) She called Ian *an ugly bastard*. (s1a-036:021)   SVOC

In the first case, the attribute 'being a challenge' is applied to the subject of the sentence, *that*; *the challenge*, here, is a subject complement. In the second case, the noun phrase *an ugly bastard* functions as an object complement, i.e. the attribute it denotes is applied to the object, *Ian*.

Conversely, a given function may be implemented by different kinds of phrases. A case in point is the complement function. In addition to an NP (as in the example above), complements are often realised by adjective phrases, i.e. a phrase which has an adjective as its most important element, such as *well known* or *extremely large*. A complement may even be realised by a whole sentence, e.g. *he is not like Louis*.

(62) a) But his own position is *well known*. (w2c-003:047)   SVC
    b) The danger is *he is not like Louis*. (s1a-020:118)   SVC

The necessity to keep formal and functional categories separated is most obvious when concepts sound similar and are likely to be confused, as in the case of the formal categories 'adverb' and 'adverb phrase' and the functional category 'adverbial'. The first describes a phrase that contains as its most important (and often only) element an adverb, such as *quite*, *very*, *slowly*, or *there*. With regard to the second, a distinction needs to be drawn between obligatory and optional adverbials. The former category describes a function that is similar to that of the complement in providing necessary spatial or directional information on the subject or the object of a clause, without which the clause would not be grammatical; hence the term 'obligatory'; the verb *to send*, for instance, demands a location, otherwise the sentence would be incorrect.

(63) a) You wouldn't be sending her *there*. (s1a-054:132)
b) The man had locked the briefcase *in the boot*. (w2f-018:006)

Optional adverbials supply additional information, usually on the circumstances (time, manner and space) of the action described in a sentence; if they were missing, the sentence would still be grammatical, as in the examples below.

(64) a) I haven't really taught them *directly*. (s1a-002:019)
b) *Behind her back* they'd polish the wood. (w2f-020:123)

In (63a) and (64a) the adverbial functions are fulfilled by adverb phrases which are realised by adverbs. The following examples show that adverbs not only function as adverbials on the level of the clause, as in (63) and (64) but also on phrase level, as modifiers either to adjectives or adverbs, as in (65).

(65) a) But that's not *always* available. (s1a-003:027)
b) We *very* rarely at that time worked with disabled. (s1a-002:064)

We see that there is only a partial overlap of the formal category 'adverb phrase' (or adverb) and the functional category 'adverbial': Many adverbials are not realised by adverb phrases and in many cases adverb phrases do not function as an adverbial. The complex interaction of formal and functional categories will be discussed in more detail in chapter 6. Suffice it for now to emphasise, again, that syntactic description works with formal as well as functional categories. In both cases, description can make use of varying degrees of abstraction, which will highlight or veil similarities or dissimilarities. For the student of linguistics it is important to be familiar with the formal and functional categories that are applied to the syntactic description of language data, to be able to identify the criteria that a description or an analysis is based on and to recognise the level of detail or abstraction that is applied.

1.4 Outlook

The sections above have already hinted at many of the aspects that will be discussed in the first part of this book. As syntax focuses on the combination of word forms it is necessary to start with a discussion of the term 'word' and the many meanings associated with it. We can then proceed to categorise and describe the main classes of words that are found in English. All this is done in chapter 2.

On the basis of this discussion, chapters 3 to 5 deal with the description of phrases, i.e. the structures that are intermediate between the level of words on the one hand and the level of clauses and sentences on the other. Many of the aspects hinted at in the present chapter will be discussed in greater length there.

Chapter 6, the final chapter of the first part of this book, deals with the syntactic analysis of clauses and sentences.

Taken together, chapters 2 to 6 aim at providing a useful descriptive apparatus (largely based on the framework suggested by Quirk et al. 1985) for the analysis of all elements and structures that are relevant for syntactic analysis. This will enable the reader to analyse English phrases, clauses and sentences in a traditional fashion.

The second part of this book, in a way, aims at putting into perspective the descriptions and analyses discussed in part one: The concepts and methods introduced by then will be subjected to a more critical review.

For instance, much of the first part of this book is about introducing and describing categories of syntactic description. Chapter 7, in part II, will provide a critical discussion of the nature of categorisation and categories with a special focus on syntax. All of us have an intuition that some birds are 'birdier' than others: a robin or a sparrow, for instance, would usually be regarded as a good example of a bird. Penguins and ostriches would be treated as rather unrepresentative of the whole category. What is true for categories of natural objects also holds for syntactic categories. To give but one example: just as it is typical for birds to be able to fly, it is typical for adjectives to be gradable, as we can see with the forms *happy, happier* and *happiest*. However, birds like penguins and ostriches cannot fly and adjectives like *alive* or *utter* as in *an alive presence* and *utter horror* are not gradable. We can see that, similar to the natural category BIRD, the syntactic category ADJECTIVE has more and less representative members. This feature of natural language is discussed under headings such as multiple analyses, fuzziness, and gradience and will be explored in chapter 7.

Chapter 8 will deal with an aspect that is usually not given that much attention in many other introductions to syntactic description, namely the syntax of spoken English. One point of interest will be the question of complexity in spoken as opposed to written language. It is usually assumed that written language makes use of complex structures and constructions, whereas spoken language is rather simple and lacking in complexity. This seems to become evident when we consider the fact that it is usually difficult for us to understand a written sentence when it is read out to us: it is difficult to keep in mind what was said at the beginning of a sentence while trying to concentrate on and process those bits towards the end of the sentence. However, as Halliday (1989) has argued convincingly, it does not make much sense to claim that written language is more complex than spoken language. Rather, each is complex in its own way and in some respects, written language has a less intricate structure than spoken language. Chapter 8 will explore the structures typical of spoken language, and it will discuss to what extent traditional categories (which are usually based on descriptions of written language) are in fact relevant for the description of spoken syntax.

Chapter 9 widens the scope further by exploring how the use of syntactic constructions depends on the influence of textual and non-textual context. One aspect discussed in chapter 9 concerns the use of syntactic constructions to achieve particular textual and aesthetic effects, as in example (66).

(66) Ludo is conscientious. He bends closely to his work. He unscrews the plate and removes it from the door. *Behind the plate is a chiselled cavity. Inside the cavity is a polythene bag. Inside the bag are several smaller bags. Inside each of them is a single ounce of heroin.* (BNC-J13:3398-3404)

This piece of text is taken from the British National Corpus (BNC), which contains 100 million words of British English from the second half of the last century. Particularly striking in this sample are the last four sentences. They do not conform to the canonical word order of the English language, but are what is called 'inverted constructions', i.e. the subject swaps place with a constituent that usually occurs after the verb, in the cases above an obligatory adverbial. The effect this creates has been described as the 'camera-movement effect' (Dorgeloh 1997: 110), or the 'immediate-observer effect' (Kreyer 2006a: 202-207). It serves to create the illusion of immediacy on the part of the reader. In the above example, the succession of the four inversions creates a strong impression of experiencing the whole process of discovering the heroin. Such and similar exploitations of syntactic structures will be discussed in chapter 9.

Chapter 10 will deal with the relation of syntax and meaning. This may seem strange at first sight, because meaning is usually dealt with in a linguistic sub-discipline of semantics. Meaning is thought of as residing in words, and syntax may be considered as being concerned with words from a formal or functional perspective only and, accordingly, may be reduced to the study of the strings of formal and functional elements which are allowed in a language. However, what strings of word forms are allowed in a language to some extent also depends on the meaning of the individual words, as Chomsky's famous grammatical but meaningless example *colorless green ideas sleep furiously* makes clear. In addition, corpus linguistics has shown that aspects of meaning can have an influence on the choice of syntactic constructions. Finally, approaches in the field of construction grammar (see chapter 11 for details) have claimed that syntactic constructions have a meaning of their own, independent of the words that are used with them. Consider the verb *to drop*: it describes a particular action that is conducted by letting an object fall. More specifically, the verb *to drop* does not contain any meaning component which implies the transfer of an object from, say, one person to another. This, however, is exactly what we find in example (67).

(67) If he answers I'll drop you a note. (s1a-078:176)

The question is where this transfer meaning comes from, if it is neither part of the meaning of the verb *to drop*, nor part of the meaning of the other constituents. It seems reasonable, then, to assume that the transfer meaning is part of the meaning of the syntactic construction (in this case the ditransitive construction) in which the verb and the other constituents occur.

Chapter 11 will be concerned with an overview of some major approaches to syntactic description. Apart from the already mentioned construction grammar, a short sketch will be given of the standard model of generative-transformational grammar and X'-theory.

Chapters 1 to 11 explore syntax from the perspective of the linguist, i.e. it introduces concepts and theories that are useful in the description of a language as a closed system. By way of complementation, chapter 12 will look at syntax from the perspective of the psycholinguist. In particular, this chapter will describe and discuss experiments that aim to shed light on the psychological reality of syntactic units and on the processes that are going on in the head during sentence processing.

1.5 Further reading

Ouhalla (1996) provides a good overview of constituency tests.
Quirk et al. (1985: ch. 2) provide an excellent survey of English grammar and syntax.
Aarts & Aarts (1982) is a good overview of units of grammatical description and grammatical structures.

1.6 Study questions

1. How are paradigmatic and syntagmatic relations defined? Explain them with the help of the example *Peter is going to the zoo.*

2. For each of the constituents below name three constituents that stand in a paradigmatic relationship.
    [*The man*] [*will meet*] [*the woman*]
3. What is the aim of constituency tests?
4. Name the four constituency tests portrayed in this chapter and give an example each of how they work.
5. What are the two major descriptive dimensions that are used in syntactic description?
6. Which of the following concepts makes reference to formal and which makes reference to functional aspects?
    a) adverb phrase   b) noun   c) subject   d) complement   e) adverbial
7. Use constituency tests to show that the constituents in the sentence under 2. are constituents.
8. Draw a tree diagram or use bracketing to make explicit the syntactic structure of the following sentence.
    Peter stole the car from his friend.
9. Explain the relationship of categorisation and abstraction.

2 Words and Word Classes

2.1 The term 'word'

The concept 'word' seems to be simple and unproblematic given the fact that everybody is usually able to recognise words when he or she sees them. A useful first 'definition' of the term, for instance, would be 'a string of letters demarcated by spaces on both sides, or by a space on one side and a punctuation mark on the other'. And indeed, this definition would go a long way, since it can be applied to maybe 95 or even 99 per cent of all written words: This definition works with most of the words in the three previous sentences, but not with all. What do we do with a compound like *punctuation mark* above and the string *per cent*? In the second case we could argue that there is also a variant without in-between-spaces, *percent*, which would then point to the fact that *per cent* is one word and not two. Unfortunately, this does not work with *punctuation mark*. Even if it worked, we would still have to find a definition that can be applied to spoken language – usually there is no demarcation between individual words in connected speech.

An approach is needed that does not depend on information restricted to a particular medium. One suggestion is made by Bloomfield, who defines a word as "a minimum free form" (1933: 178), i.e. as the smallest meaningful element that can move about freely in a sentence. This way, the word is contrasted with the morpheme on the one side and the phrase (and larger units) on the other. A morpheme, the smallest meaningful unit, also has meaning but it cannot move freely in a sentence. Phrases, on the other hand, can move freely but are not minimal and, accordingly, could be defined as 'non-minimum free forms'. Again, while the definition of the term 'word' as a minimum free form may work with the string *per cent* (note that *cent*, here, is not the same as the unit of money), it fails with the string *punctuation mark*, since both, *punctuation* and *mark* are words, too (also see the discussion of *in front of* in section 1.1).

Even if we leave such problematic cases aside for now and take a word to be a string of letters demarcated by spaces and/or punctuation marks on both sides, the term 'word' remains ambiguous, as a look at example (1) makes clear.

(1) Peter gave Mary one flower, Sue two flowers and Jill three flowers.

The question "how many words are in this sentence?" is not trivial. Possible answers are: 12 words, 11 words, or 10 words. Obviously, we find 12 strings of letters that are demarcated by spaces and/or punctuation marks on both sides. Two of these are identical, namely the two occurrences of *flowers*; so we could argue that the above sentence contains 11 different words. Then of course one might say that *flower* and the two occurrences of *flowers* are essentially one word only. From this perspective the sentence under (1) contains 10 different words. On the whole, we end up with three different ways of understanding the term 'word'. Firstly, as the orthographic word form, i.e. a string of letters demarcated by spaces and/or punctuation marks on both sides. It is not possible to give a satisfactory definition of 'spoken word form' along similar lines, since we do not have clear demarcations in spoken language similar to spaces and punctuation marks in written language (see Robins [3]1980: 115 and Esser 2006: 68). It is probably easiest to simply understand the spoken word form as the spoken 'version' of the orthographic word form. Secondly, as grammatical word forms, to some extent marked by inflections. Thirdly, 'word' understood as a lexical unit in the sense of Cruse (1986: 78), i.e. "the union of a lexical form and a single sense", where 'lexical form' refers to the word forms (in the second sense of 'word') that instantiate this single sense. This definition becomes clearer if we take into consideration a fourth understanding of 'word', namely as a 'lexeme', as example (2) shows.

(2) Peter, in the flower of his youth, gave Mary one flower, Sue two flowers and Jill three flowers.

The first occurrence of *flower* in the sentence above has a different meaning than the other three occurrences, although the two meanings are related. Following Cruse (1986) we will talk of a lexeme FLOWER, which is instantiated by two lexical units, namely FLOWER$_1$ in the 'plant' sense and FLOWER$_2$ in the figurative sense. He understands a lexeme to be "a family of lexical units" (76), which nicely expresses the idea of related meanings (just like members of one family are related). By way of contrast consider the word *pupil*: here, we would have to speak of two lexemes, namely PUPIL$_1$ in the 'student' sense and PUPIL$_2$ in the 'part of the eye' sense, since the two do not appear to be related in meaning (although they are etymologically related). The distinctions discussed above are summarised in Table 2.1 below.

Table 2.1: The many senses of 'word'.

'Word' as ...	example
orthographic / spoken word form	*flower, flowers, flower's, flowers'* / flaʊə, flaʊəz
grammatical word form	flower_NN, flowers_NNS, flower's_NN$, flowers'_NNS$[2]
lexical unit	FLOWER$_1$ ('plant'), FLOWER$_2$ (fig.)
lexeme	PUPIL$_1$ ('student'), PUPIL$_2$ ('part of the eye')

These distinctions may seem like terminological hair-splitting, but they are relevant for syntactic description and will become relevant in the course of this book. Let it suffice for now to give two examples. One is discussed by Esser (2000), who shows how the two meanings of the lexeme TREE, i.e. 'plant' and 'drawing', exhibit strong tendencies with regard to their instantiation in word forms: "there is a strong association between the meaning 'drawing' and the singular form *tree*" (97). Consequently, realizations of TREE in the meaning of 'drawing', are not likely to occur with plural verbs simply because the plural word forms of this lexical unit are not used frequently. Similarly, FLOWER$_2$ will most likely occur in frames like '*the flower of* POSS N', such as *in the flower of her youth* or *before the flower of their might*. Numerous other examples are provided by the many cases of what corpus linguistics calls 'colligation', the association of a word form with particular syntactic structures. This term and the related concept of 'collocation', the associations of words forms with other word forms, are of course relevant for the study of syntax, i.e. the study of the arrangement of word forms in a linear sequence. Such issues will be discussed in more detail in chapter 10.

2.2 Word classes

2.2.1 Open and closed classes

Words (in the sense of lexemes) can be divided into two basic classes, i.e. those to which new words are or can be constantly added and those which remain stable. The first are referred to as open word classes, the second as closed word classes. Another set of corresponding terms, namely 'lexical words' and 'function words', highlights a different aspect: words from open word classes are often

---

[2] The tags are used to indicate the grammatical categories, i.e. 'singular noun' (NN), 'plural noun' (NNS), 'singular noun in genitive' (NN$), and 'plural noun in genitive' (NNS$).

treated as being the true carrier of the meaning of a sentence, whereas words from closed word classes are usually regarded as simply fulfilling a grammatical function. The pronoun *she*, for instance, does not have a lot of meaning apart from 'female' and 'singular'. It is used in a text to refer back to a full noun or a noun phrase, where the lexical words convey more meaning, such as *Mary, the beautiful girl, the woman living next door*, etc.

Within these two classes the following major word classes, often referred to as 'parts of speech', can be distinguished.

Table 2.2: Open (lexical) and closed (function) word classes (cf. Quirk et al. 1985: 67).

Open word classes	Closed word classes
noun – *car, book, friend*	preposition – *in, of, in spite of*
adjective – *beautiful, friendly, nice*	pronoun – *I, she, they*
main verb – *read, see, love*	determiner – *the, a, that, those*
adverb – *quite, nicely, happily*	conjunction – *and, but, although*
	modal verb – *can, may, will*
	primary verb – *be, have, do*

In between these two categories we may position a third class, namely that of numerals, e.g. *one, two, three, ...* In principle, it is open because any person can 'create' a number that is very likely to never have been used before (if that person just goes high enough). Obviously, however, this kind of creation is different from innovations such as the examples *muggle* and *google* discussed in section 1.4 above. Any 'new' number is predictable, whereas formations of the kind *muggle* and *google* often are not. So, the class of numbers is more restricted than other open word classes but still less restricted than the truly closed classes, to which new words can usually not be added.

2.2.2 Descriptive parameters – the example of the class 'noun'

Word classes can be described with regard to semantic, distributional and formal features, i.e. 1) what can be said about the meaning of a lexical unit?; 2) how does a lexical unit or its forms look?; and 3) where in a string of word forms does a word form occur (and what is its function therein)?

Semantic criteria probably are the most frequently used ones in pre-theoretical descriptions of word classes. The following definition of 'noun', taken from the 2003 edition of the *Longman Dictionary of Contemporary English* (LDOCE), is illustrative in this respect.

a word or group of words that represent a person (such as 'Michael', 'teacher' or 'police officer'), a place (such as 'France' or 'school'), a thing or activity (such as 'coffee' or 'football'), or a quality or idea (such as 'danger' or 'happiness'). [...] (LDOCE ^{4}2003: 'noun')

This kind of definition is often referred to as 'notional', i.e. they are based on rather vague and pretheoretical ideas (notions) about the characteristics of a particular word class and, therefore, are not entirely satisfying. The above definition, for instance, does not capture the whole range of bodily sensations or emotional states (although the LDOCE seems to list the latter under 'idea'). It becomes obvious that either the concepts used in the definitions are so general (as the concept 'idea' if it is supposed to encompass emotional states) that the whole definition becomes vague and unsatisfying, or, if we want to be more specific, we would end up with a list containing all the elements that fall under a given class, in this case the class 'noun'. However, as Aarts (1997) points out,

lists have no explanatory value [... and] lead to circular reasoning: why is a *car* a noun? Because it is on the list of nouns. Why is it on the list? Because it's a noun. This gets us nowhere. (Aarts 1997: 25)

With regard to the idea that nouns denote a thing, Huddleston and Pullum (2002: 30) comment that "we have no way of telling whether a word denotes (or is the name of) a thing unless we already know on independent, grammatical, grounds whether it is a noun". As an example they take the two sentences below:

(3) a) I was annoyed at their rejection of my proposals.
   b) I was annoyed that they rejected my proposals.

They argue that the sentences above

have essentially the same meaning, but *rejection* is a noun and *rejected* a verb. What enables us to tell that *rejection* belongs to the category of noun is not that *rejections* denotes a thing while *rejected* does not, but that they figure in quite different grammatical constructions. (Huddleston and Pullum 2002: 30).

In addition, notional definitions are bound to fail with categories that do not have clear semantics. For instance, we would be hard put to state meaning aspects that are shared by all or many prepositions. The only statement that holds for most prepositions is that they are used to 'link' noun phrases (e.g. *the car behind the house*) but this, obviously, is a distributional or functional criterion.

To sum up, semantic criteria are far from ideal when it comes to defining word classes. Even in those cases where semantic descriptions can be applied, additional reference to grammatical criteria, i.e. the form and the distribution (and function) of word classes, is usually indispensable.

Formal criteria concern the morphological features that are typical of word classes. This includes derivational as well as inflectional features. Some of the formal features relevant for nouns are summarised in Table 2.3 below.

Table 2.3: Derivational and inflectional morphemes common to nouns.

Morpheme	Examples
-hood	*neighbourhood, childhood*
-ness	*happiness, friendliness, softness*
-ment	*government, embodiment*
plural *-s*	*flowers, cats, peaches*
genitive singular *-'s*	*flower's, cat's, peach's*
genitive plural *-s'*	*flowers', cats', peaches'*

The endings *-hood* or *-ness*, for instance, are fairly reliable indicators of nouns. The suffix *-ment* is a similarly good indicator since this suffix attaches to verbs to create a noun. However, word forms like *vehement* or *ferment* show that this criterion is not always one hundred per cent reliable, and, of course, a large number of nouns do not show any noun-specific ending, e.g. *mouse, grass, pill*, etc.

Inflectional endings are not necessarily more reliable. Although, only nouns have plural and genitive endings these endings can be confused with homonymous strings of letters. A word ending in *-s* need not be a plural form, in many cases it might be a verb form with a present tense singular *-s*, as in *hears* or *assimilates*. Genitive markers can be thought of as being more reliable, although the genitive singular, *-'s*, might be confused with a contracted form *is*, as in *the man's an idiot*; in that case a wrong conclusion would lead to the correct result that *man* is a noun. Things get worse if we only have spoken data at our disposal. Due to homophony many contrasts that are expressed in written English vanish in the spoken medium: the spoken form flaʊəz, for instance, could instantiate the plural or both genitives of the noun FLOWER (and FLOUR, but we will ignore this here) and the 3rd person present tense singular form of the homonymous verb. Finally, many nouns have irregular plurals (e.g. *mice, fish, oxen* etc.) and the formal criterion of inflectional endings cannot be applied.

On the whole, formal criteria like derivational and inflectional endings are lacking in 'precision' as well as 'recall' (Ball 1994). That is, firstly, not all forms that are identified by these criteria are actually nouns and secondly, not all nouns can be identified with the help of derivational and inflectional endings. So, formal criteria might be useful to identify the word class in some cases, but in many cases they are too unreliable.

More reliable is the final criterion, the distribution and function of word forms. Many of the issues discussed with regard to inflectional endings, for instance, can be resolved if we take a look at the environment in which a given word form occurs.

(4) a) a flower
b) beautiful flower
c) his flowers
d) he flowers
e) they flower at home
f) their flower at home
g) her flower's beautiful
h) her flower's petals are beautiful
i) flowers are beautiful
j) he should get flowers

In (4a and b) the initial determiner *a* and the adjective *beautiful* make clear that *flower* in these cases must be a noun and not a verb. Similarly, the homonymy of the plural noun form and the 3rd person singular present tense verb form in (4c and d) is resolved by the preceding possessive determiner and personal pronoun, respectively. Note that a larger context for c) might change the whole picture. A sentence like *her business goes down but his flowers* would show that the form in question is actually a verb form. However, this does not invalidate the distributional criterion, since we are here dealing with the homonymy between the possessive determiner *his*, as in *I like his flowers*, and the possessive pronoun *his*, which in the above sentence denotes *his business*. This example shows that while the possessive determiner is a part of a noun phrase, the possessive pronoun stands for the whole noun phrase (see section 2.2.5 for a detailed discussion of this homonymy). Depending on which of the two is meant we have a different context, which provides different evidence as to the status of the word form. Examples e) and f) show that the context resolves the ambiguity between the singular noun form and the uninflected verb forms, and g) and h) show the distinction between the contracted form of *flower is* and the genitive form *flower's*. Finally, i) and j) show the form *flowers* in a position (and a function) that is occupied by nouns only, namely pre-verbally as the subject and post-verbally as the direct object. Information of this kind is also found in the definition that the LDOCE provides on the word 'noun'. Here is how the entry quoted above continues:

> […] Nouns can be used as the subject or object of a verb (as in 'The teacher arrived' or 'We like the teacher') or as the object of a preposition (as in 'good at football'). (LDOCE ^{4}2003: 'noun')

In summary, we have seen that different criteria can be applied to the description of word classes, namely semantic or notional, formal, and distributional (and functional) criteria. These three variables will serve as a descriptive framework for the analysis of the other open word classes. We have to keep in mind, however, that the first two are not always reliable (even though this will not always be made explicit in the following). In addition, we will see in section 2.2.4 that it is not always easy to assign a given word form to one word class or the other, as different criteria point in different directions

2.2.3 Main verbs

The LDOCE (^{4}2003) describes a (main) verb as

> a word or group of words that describes an action, experience, or state, such as 'come', 'see', and 'put on' (LDOCE ^{4}2003: 'verb')

As with all notional definitions, the above definition of 'verb' is not very precise. One problem, for instance, concerns the meaning of 'experience' and 'state': many would argue that states are described by nouns, such as *freedom, happiness, love*, and it could also be argued that all of these nouns describe an experience. We see that, at best, such a definition only gives a vague idea of the category 'verb'.

With regard to formal features we find that regular verbs typically have five distinct forms, whereas irregular verbs may have either more or less (see study question 5), as the following table taken from Quirk et al. (1985: 96) shows.

Table 2.4: The forms of some regular and irregular verbs (Quirk et al. 1985: 96)

	Regular verbs		Irregular verbs		
Base form	*call*	*want*	*speak*	*cut*	*win*
-*s* form	*calls*	*wants*	*speaks*	*cuts*	*wins*
-*ing* participle	*calling*	*wanting*	*speaking*	*cutting*	*winning*
Past form	*called*	*wanted*	*spoke*	*cut*	*won*
-*ed* participle	*called*	*wanted*	*spoken*	*cut*	*won*

An important distinction is that between finite and non-finite verb forms. The term 'finite' comes from Latin 'finitus' which means 'limited'. Finite verb forms are those that carry tense distinction and number concord. The -*s* form and the past tense form, the two kinds of finite verb forms, are limited in the sense that they are restricted to certain contexts. Verb forms with an -*s* can only occur after a third person singular subject in present tense environments, past tense forms only in past tense contexts.

(5) a) he *goes* home; *I/ you/ we/ you/ they *goes* home
    b) he *went* home yesterday; *he *went* home tomorrow

(5a) makes clear that present tense verb forms have to agree in number and person with the subject of a sentence. This is referred to as concord. The only other form that does show concord is the uninflected base form. Still it is less restricted than the *-s* form, as it can occur freely with all persons and numbers, except 3rd person singular:

(6) I/ you/ we/ you/ they *go* home; *He *go* home

This form is also relatively free with regard to tense: It is found in present tense environments but also in expressions that are used to make reference to future actions.

(7) Do you mind if I *go* to bed?, I *will go* home tomorrow, I *am going to go* home tomorrow.

Similarly, the two participle forms ending in *-ing* and *-ed* occur freely with subjects of different persons and numbers and with forms denoting past, present and future actions.

(8) a) I *am/* you *are/* he *is/* we *are/* you *are/* they *are going* home
    b) I *was/* you *were/* he *was/* we *were/* you *were/* they *were going* home
    c) I/ you/ he/ we/ you/ they *will be going* home.
    d) I *have/* you *have/* he *has/* we *have/* you *have/* they *have gone* home.
    e) I/ you/ he/ we/ you/ they *had gone* home.

The main feature as regards the distribution of main verbs is the fact that they are the final element in the verb phrase, which means, conversely, that they are often preceded by auxiliary verbs (verbs that are used to express grammatical categories like modality or aspect, such as the forms of *have, will, shall,* etc; see section 2.2.5).

(9) (he) will *go*   (he) should *go*
    (he) is *going*   (he) will be *going*
    (he) has *gone*   (he) should have *gone*
    (he) might have been *going*   ...

Also, main verbs are likely to occur before clause constituents like objects, adverbials or complements (see section 1.3), because these elements usually occur in post-verbal position. See the examples under (10) (the main verb is in italics, the relevant post-verbal constituent is underlined).

(10) a) I *enclose* <u>a cheque for £40</u>. (w1b-027:124)　　　SVO
　　　b) Just thirty-five would *be* <u>perfect</u>. (s1a-080:196)　　　SVC
　　　c) Nobody *was* <u>home</u>. (w2f-006:039)　　　SVA
　　　d) That *gives* <u>you</u> a great view of the road. (s2a-055:134)　　　SVOO
　　　e) He's *put* <u>his certificate</u> on his wall. (s1a-017:090)　　　SVOA
　　　f) I *find* <u>it</u> fascinating. (s1a-002:035)　　　SVOC

From the above data, another conclusion can be drawn. In four of the six cases above, the postverbal constituent is an object. These are usually realised by noun phrases, which leads to the conclusion that main verbs are often found immediately before noun phrases. Similarly, if the verbal part of a clause only consists of the main verb, the main verb usually occurs directly after the subject of the clause. Again, subjects are often realised by noun phrases. So we can conclude that in most cases main verbs are found either after auxiliary verbs (as in 10a, c and e) and before or after noun phrases (see 10b, d, and f).

2.2.4 Adjectives and adverbs

Adjectives are usually described as words that denote qualities, such as *beautiful, old, rich* and so on. Similarly to nouns, adjectives show a number of derivational and inflectional morphemes which in many cases betray their status, as the following table shows.

Table 2.5: Derivational and inflectional morphemes common to adjectives.

Morpheme	Examples
-ful	*successful, hateful, blissful*
-less	*soulless, merciless, loveless*
un-	*unhappy, unfriendly, uncomfortable*
comparative *-er*	*nicer, louder, colder*
superlative *-est*	*nicest, loudest, coldest*

These formal features, of course, are not completely reliable either. The prefix *un-*, for instance, frequently occurs in nouns, namely in those which are derived from adjectives with prefix *un-*, e.g. *unhappiness* or *unfriendliness*. The comparative ending *-er* is also problematic since it is homonymous with the suffix *-er* that derives nouns from verbs, such as *teacher, singer*, or *player*. In addition,

Words and Word Classes 39

the comparative and superlative are formed in the same way with adverbs, e.g. *soon - sooner - soonest*. So these suffixes are potentially ambiguous.

Adjectives show a number of telling distributional features. They occur either in attributive or in predicative function, as exemplified in (11).

(11) a) We had a *friendly* press conference. (s2b-025:120)
    b) The people are really *friendly*. (w1b-002:128)
    c) There is an *old* right of way that's been ploughed up. (s1b-037:070)
    d) If they are lead or iron they are *old*. (w2d-012:017)

In their attributive function adjectives serve to premodify a noun as in (11a and c). Adjectives in predicative function (in (11b and d)) fill the complement slot in an SVC sentence, which attributes a property (given in the complement) to the subject of the clause. Due to the first function, adjectives are frequently found between the determiner of the noun phrase (e.g. *a, his, that* in the example above) and the head noun of the noun phrase. Adjectives in predicative function usually occur after the verb in an SVC sentence. This is indeed a useful bit of information because the number of verbs that demand an SVC structure is fairly limited: these verbs form the class of what are called 'copulative' (from Latin *copulare*, 'to join') verbs. They do not have a 'real' meaning of their own, but mainly serve to link the subject of a clause with the complement that denotes the quality that we want to attribute to the subject. Such verbs are *be, seem, appear* (not in the 'arrive' or 'show up' sense) or *become*, etc. If the word following such verbs is not a determiner or a noun (recall that complements are often realised by noun phrases), we can be fairly sure that it is an adjective.

Two other pieces of distributional evidence for adjective-hood are given in (12) and (13) below.

(12) very interesting   extremely nice
    quite friendly   hardly painful
    completely blind   fully responsible

(13) more interesting   most interesting
    more beautiful   most beautiful
    more painful   most painful

The dataset in (12) makes reference to the structure of the adjective phrase. Without going into too much detail at this point (see chapter 5 for details), adjectives may be premodified by intensifying adverbs, as shown in the examples. That is, a word form occurring after an intensifying adverb is likely to be an adjective.

Finally, the English language provides two ways of grading adjectives, namely through inflectional morphology (i.e. *-er* and *-est*, see Table 2.5), also called synthetic grading, and through the use of *more* and *most* as in (13), also called analytic grading. The occurrence of *more* and *most*, therefore, often indicates that the word immediately following is an adjective. We have to be aware, though, that adverbs also may be graded analytically, e.g. *joyfully - more joyfully - most joyfully*. The feature of analytic grading, therefore, is potentially ambiguous between adjectives and adverbs.

The final open word class we want to discuss is that of **adverbs**. This class is notoriously difficult to define, as becomes clear from the following quote.

> Because of its great heterogeneity, the adverb class is the most nebulous and puzzling of the traditional word classes. Indeed, it is tempting to say simply that the adverb is an item that does not fit the definitions for other word classes. (Quirk et al. 1985: 438)

Nevertheless, some careful generalizations about this word class can be made. Firstly, some adverbs can be identified on the basis of their form, as Table 2.6 shows.

Table 2.6: Derivational morphemes common to adverbs.

Morpheme	Examples
-ly	*happily, successfully, loudly*
-wise	*lizardwise, fashionwise, strengthwise*
-wards	*homewards, upwards, northwards*

The adverbs ending in *-ly* are derived from adjectives, as can be seen in Table 2.6 above. Note, however, that some adjectives also end in *-ly*, e.g. *friendly*, *lonely*, or *lively*. With the suffix *-wise*, which derives adverbs from nouns, we can distinguish two meanings, a 'manner'/ 'dimension' and a 'viewpoint' meaning (Plag 2003: 98). *Lizardwise*, for instance, can be paraphrased as 'in the manner of a lizard' in the sentence *he is moving lizardwise*. *Fashionwise* can be interpreted as 'as far as fashion is concerned', in the sentence *London has a lot to offer, fashionwise*. Both uses of the suffix *-wise* have to be distinguished from adjective compounds with the adjective *wise*, such as *streetwise* or *clubwise*, which mean 'to be able to make one's way on the streets or in clubs', respectively. To make things worse, these adjectives are homonymous with the adverb, for which the two word forms would be paraphrased as 'as far as the street/clubs are concerned'. *-wards* is less ambiguous in this respect, but words like *awards* and *towards* show that not all words ending in this sequence of letters are adverbs.

Quirk et al. (1985: 439-441) distinguish two main functions of adverbs, namely as a modifier preceding adjectives or adverbs and as a clause element in the function of an adverbial. Adverbs as adjective premodifiers have already been discussed above (see the examples under (12)). They work similarly to premodification of adverbs, as shown under (14).

(14) a) I can get there *fairly* quickly. (s1a-003:109)
　　b) It went down *really* well. (s1a-005:237)
　　c) These forces can be known and expressed *only* indirectly. (w2a-002:027)

This, of course, also provides information as to the distribution of premodifiying adverbs: they occur most frequently immediately preceding an adjective or another adverb.

Reliable information on the distribution of adverbs in adverbial use is difficult to give, since these kinds of adverbials are fairly mobile and can occur in almost any place in the sentence. It, therefore, makes more sense to distinguish three functional classes of such adverbs, as listed in Quirk et al. (1985: 503), namely adverbs functioning as 'adjuncts', 'disjuncts' and 'conjuncts'. The terminology used by Biber et al. (1999: 549) is maybe more transparent. They distinguish between 'circumstantial', 'stance', and 'linking' adverbials, respectively. In the first case (Quirk et al.'s adjunct), the adverb provides information about the circumstances of the action described in the sentence, more specifically, details about time, manner and place.

(15) We've got to go *soon*. (s1a-039:161)
　　She stepped *hesitantly* across the small landing. (w2f-008:166)
　　The Ottomans are *here*. (s2a-059:024)

Adverbs functioning as stance adverbials (disjuncts) provide information on the speaker's or writer's view on the content of the clause, in particular regarding certainty or doubt about the content, attitude towards the content, and style in which the content is conveyed.

(16) I could *probably* manage to take you back to the station. (s1a-006:206)
　　~ 'I think it is probable that I manage to take you back to the station.'
　　Surprisingly, I managed to find my way to work. (w1b-002:129)
　　~ 'I am surprised that I managed to find my way to work.'
　　Frankly, those reasons are not good enough. (w2b-013:056)
　　~ 'Being frank, I have to say that those reasons are not good enough.'

Finally, linking adverbs (conjuncts) are used to connect clauses or sentences and even paragraphs. An example of the latter is the use of *finally* in the previous sentence; it links the present paragraph to the previous one. (17) below illustrates the use of linking adverbs between clauses and sentences.

(17) The early evidence suggests the strategy has worked but *nevertheless* Iraq's surviving aircraft will be more effective in daylight. (s2b-008:031)
I propose to score these transports and interfaces. The figures, *however*, are relative, intended simply as a guide. (w2b-040:059-060)

It should have become clear from the above discussion of open word classes that different criteria can be applied and that they are satisfactory to varying degrees. To conclude this section, we will take a look at cases where different criteria lead to conflicting analyses.

We would all agree that DANCE is a verb and that BISHOP is a noun, and we would all agree on the main notional and distributional features associated with these word classes. However, consider the examples below, discussed in Lyons (1981: 101-111).

(18) a) the girls are dancing
  b) the dancing girls ('the girls who are dancing')
  c) shoes for dancing
  d) dancing shoes

(19) a) the bishop's mitre ('the mitre of a particular bishop')
  b) the bishop's mitre ('the mitre of the kind that bishops wear')
  c) the episcopal mitre

While in (18a) *dancing* is obviously used as a verb, *dancing* in (18b) is used to characterise or describe the girls and it occurs in a position that is typically occupied by adjectives (cf. *the beautiful girls*). In (18c), *dancing* seems to be used as a noun similar to *tennis* in the phrase *shoes for tennis*. In (18d) *dancing* differs in its use from (18b), since the meaning of the phrase obviously is not 'the shoes that are dancing'. Rather, *dancing* seems to be used as a noun premodifier similar to *tennis* in the phrase *tennis shoes*. These examples show that a verb form can be used in functions and syntactic positions that are usually occupied by adjectives and nouns.

Similarly, the noun form *bishop's* occurs in two different functions in the examples under (19). In the first sentence the whole noun phrase *the bishop's* serves as a determiner, it is used to specify which mitre we are actually talking about. We call this a 'specifying genitive'. In the second sentence, however, *bishop's* is used to describe a subclass of mitres, namely those that bishops wear. This is called a 'classifying genitive'. Obviously, a genitive word form in this function is highly similar to the use of adjectives, as shown in example (19c).

These examples show that word forms from a given word class may be used in functions and positions usually reserved for other word classes. Applying formal criteria, we would have to say that *dancing* and *bishop's* in the above examples are verb and noun forms, respectively. With regard to their distribution we find that while some of these forms are used as we would expect them to be used, others are used like adjectives (and nouns in the case of *dancing*). How can this problem be resolved? Following Lyons (1981) it makes sense to reserve terms like 'verb' and 'noun' for what in section 2.1 has been called a lexical unit, i.e. the union of one single sense with a set of word forms that only differ with regard to inflectional endings: DANCE would then be a verb, and we would have to make the concession that one form of the verb DANCE, namely *dancing*, is sometimes used similarly to an adjective or similarly to a noun. In a similar vein, we would say that one form of the noun BISHOP, namely the genitive singular *bishop's*, can be used to premodify a noun, a function usually performed by adjectives. This way, we can keep up the traditional notions of word classes (or parts of speech) while at the same time doing justice to the use of word forms in syntactic positions commonly associated with word classes other than their own.

2.2.5 Closed word classes

Closed word classes are fairly stable in that new words are usually not added to them. Many of the classes are fairly small so that in these cases it is often enough to merely list the members. Recall from section 2.2.1 that words of closed word classes are also referred to as function words. Usually it does not make sense to describe these word classes in terms of their semantics or their form. As a consequence, the following description will focus on the function of these items. The six closed word classes are exemplified in (20) below.

(20) primary verb – *be, have, do*
    modal verb – *can, may, will*, ...
    preposition – *in, of, in spite of*, ...
    pronoun – *I, she, they*, ...
    determiner – *the, a, that, those*, ...
    conjunction – *and, but, although*, ...

Primary and **modal verbs**, in contrast to their lexical counterparts, fulfil a helping function, which is why they are usually referred to as 'auxiliary' verbs. A full description of these functions will be given in chapter 3. For now, a quick overview will suffice.

Both classes of verbs are used in negation (see (21)) and the formation of interrogative clauses (see (22)).

(21) It *might* not have anything to do with America. (s1a-093:145)
    But it *has* not been a very quiet game. (s2a-014:219)
    Clearly, this *is* not practical. (w2b-035:044)

(22) *Can* we dance for a bit actually? (s1a-001:025)
    Has he got a nice voice? (s1a-032:233)
    Now your parents *are* they alive and well? (s1a-051:305)

The primary verbs BE and HAVE, in addition, both contribute to the expression of progressive and perfect aspect, respectively (see (23)). Forms of the verb BE are also used in expressing passive voice, as (24) illustrates.

(23) I *am* graduating in June. (s1a-002:138)
    I*'ve* worked a little with mentally disabled. (s1a-002:017)

(24) She also knew she *was* being cheated. (w2f-020:121)

Modal verbs, as can be guessed from the name, help to express modality, e.g. shades of meaning concerning the likelihood of the action expressed by the verb or the degree to which the subject of the sentence is obliged or allowed to perform the action, as shown in (25) and (26), respectively.

(25) I thought Rebecca *might* think it was amusing. (s1a-022:153)
    They *will* need to be more technically aware. (w2a-011:053)

(26) The emphasis overall *must* be on integration. (w2a-011:003)
    They *may* be allowed into dance therapy. (s1a-001:112)

Further functions of auxiliary verbs will be discussed in more detail in chapter 3.
    The class of **prepositions** is not easy to describe: it is fairly large (Quirk et al. 1985: 665-671 list more than 100), and prepositions are used to convey a large number of different meanings, such as space, direction, manner, meaning, purpose, time, and so on. The most general claim that can be made about prepositions is that all of them express a relation between two objects. The second of these objects is denoted by the noun phrase following the preposition, often referred to as the 'prepositional object' or 'prepositional complement'. Together, the preposition and the prepositional object form what is called a 'prepositional phrase' (underlined in the following). In the examples under (27), these are related to the head of the noun phrase in which the preposition and its complement occur; they postmodify the head (in bold).

(27) **books** *at* the bedside (s1a-013:050)
    an **enclosure** *to* the left of a panel of judges (w2b-006:035)
    very few **people** *from* the estate (w2c-011:084)

In addition to the postmodifying function illustrated in (27), prepositional phrases can also be used in adverbial function. In that case, the preposition describes a relationship that obtains between the subject of the clause and the prepositional complement.

(28) the books are <u>at the bedside</u>
an enclosure is <u>to the left of a panel of judges</u>
very few people are <u>from the estate</u>

Pronouns, as the name says, stand for a noun or, to be more precise, a noun phrase. Therefore, they should be called pro-NPs rather than pro-nouns (cf. Aarts 1997: 29). *She* in (29), for instance, refers back to the whole NP *the lady in the wheelchair* and not just the noun *lady*.

(29) I wanted to say goodbye and thank you, to <u>the lady in the wheelchair</u> perhaps? *She* seems to be in charge. (w2f-018:153-154)

Table 2.6 lists the difference classes of pronouns together with examples.

Table 2.6: The English pronouns.

Pronoun class	Examples
personal	*I/me, you, she/her, he/him, it, we/us, they/them*
possessive	*mine, yours, hers, his, its, ours, theirs*
reflexive	*myself, yourself, herself, himself, itself, ourselves, themselves*
demonstrative	*this/these, that/those*
reciprocal	*each other, one another*
relative	*who, whom, whose, which, that*
interrogative	*who, whom, whose, which*
indefinite	*another, no-one, anyone, anybody, someone, somebody ...*

It is not always easy to see in what sense the pronoun stands for an NP. An example of this are relative pronouns as illustrated in (30) (also see study question 9).

(30) a) the <u>road</u> *which* carried Tom Jones from St. Albans (w2b-006:063)
   b) the <u>time</u> *that* I was given (s1a-001:032)

Relative clauses postmodify the head of the noun phrase in which they occur. The relative pronoun links up to this head, also called the 'antecedent', which means 'that which is preceding' (underlined in the examples above). At the same time, the relative pronoun fulfils a function in the relative clause. In (30a) *which* is the subject of the relative clause, in (30b) *that* is the direct object. The relative pronoun, thus, stands for the head (plus determiner) of the NP to which it belongs, as shown under (31).

(31) a) The road (*~which*) carried Tom Jones from St. Albans.
  b) I was given the time (*~that*).

Another frequent problem is that some of the pronouns are easily confused with a group of determiners of the English language, as we will see presently.

Determiners occur at the beginning of a noun phrase. Three kinds of determiners are distinguished, as can be seen in Table 2.7.

Table 2.7: The English determiners.

Determiner	Examples
Predeterminer	*half, all, both, twice*
Central determiner	*the, a/an, my, her, this, those, some ...*
Postdeterminer	*many, few, one, two, first, second, ...*

The names of the three classes are due to the position that determiners of one class take relative to determiners of other classes. The order given in (32) holds for all sequences of determiners, other orders are ungrammatical (see (33)).

(32) Predeterminer + central determiner + postdeterminer
  All   these   many   onerous tasks
  Half   those   Spanish coins
                          Some   books
  Both   problems
            The   first   feature
  Twice   his   weight

(33) * these all many onerous tasks
   * many all these onerous tasks
   * many these all onerous tasks
   * those half Spanish coins
   * first the feature
   * his twice weight

A subclass of central determiners, possessive and demonstrative determiners, is homonymous with most of the pronouns of the same name. Recall that pronouns stand for a noun phrase, whereas determiners are part of a noun phrase. Consider the examples under (34), where each first answer contains a pronoun and each second answer a determiner (note that the answers under (34c) would usually be accompanied by a pointing gesture).

(34) a) Can I borrow your car?   - Yes, you can have *mine*.
- Yes, you can have *my* car.
    b) Do you need his help?   - No, I don't need *his*, I need *yours*.
- No, I don't need *his* help, I need *your* help.
    c) Do you want this car?   - No, I want *that*. (~ car, bike, ...)
- No, I want *that* car/bike/....

While determiners fulfil a function within phrases, more specifically noun phrases, the final word class to be discussed here, **conjunctions**, works with all kinds of phrases and even clauses. Like prepositions, conjunctions are used to link elements. On a very basic level we can distinguish between coordinating and subordinating conjunctions. In the first case, the elements that are linked (the so-called 'conjoins'; underlined in the following examples) are of equal status and the relationship between them is symmetrical, as in the examples below.

(35) And it also makes you so aware of <u>your own ability</u> *and* <u>other people's abilities</u>. (s1a-002:027).
You either <u>study pure dance</u> *or* <u>you study dance therapy</u>. (s1a-001:105)
In both cases the point is <u>to employ contemporary materials and building techniques</u> *and* <u>to exhibit this employment in the design</u>. (w2a-005:111)
I'm <u>very surprised at their commitment</u> *and* <u>pleased</u>. (s1a-005:157)
She didn't want to view <u>a star which was a sludgy tea cloth</u>, *nor* <u>a biro message written on pine</u>. (w2f-020:146)

Subordinators, in contrast, link elements of unequal status, more specifically: a subordinate clause is 'inserted' into a clause on a higher level, the 'superordinate clause'. In most cases, the subordinate clause (underlined in the following examples) together with the subordinator functions as an adverbial in the superordinate clause.

(36) *After* <u>he married</u>, he told his wife not to open the metal box. (w2c-019:094)
I find it very hard to forgive *although* <u>I do</u>. (s1a-031:109)
While <u>this is an attractive theory</u> there is little or no contemporary evidence to support it. (w1a-001:029)

Subordinators are also used to introduce what is called nominal clauses, i.e. clauses that fulfil functions usually realised by noun phrases.
(37) *That* <u>Labour supporters and those on the left of Labour should believe this myth</u> is obvious. (s2b-035:093)
 I didn't know *whether* <u>you were Chinese or what you were</u>. (s1a-028:070)
 And she told me *that* <u>she was starting this class with Adam</u>. (s1a-002:005)

The first example shows a subject clause introduced by the subordinating conjunction *that* (which, by the way, must not be confused with the relative pronoun *that*). In the second example the subordinated clauses function as direct object, in the third as the indirect object of the clause. Note that all of the subordinated clauses could be substituted by an NP, e.g. *This fact is obvious* instead of *That Labour supporters and those on the left of Labour should believe this myth is obvious*.

The present chapter has given an overview of the commonly recognised word classes of the English language. This will be the basis for the discussion of the five different phrase types in the next three chapters.

2.3 Further reading

See Esser (2006: chs. 3.1 & 3.2) for a detailed discussion of the concept 'word'.
Fries (1952: ch. 5) is an excellent critical discussion of the traditional term 'part of speech'.
Huddleston and Pullum (2002: 28-33) provide an insightful discussion into the definition of word classes and other grammatical concepts.
Aarts (1997: ch. 3) provides a good discussion of notional, formal and distributional criteria for the identification of word classes, and a good overview of the major word classes of English.
Biber et al. (1999: ch. 2) provide interesting facts on the frequencies of word classes in different genres.

2.4 Study questions

1. What is a lexical unit and in which sense is it different from a lexeme? Give examples.
2. Name the three criteria that are used for the description of word classes and give examples.
3. What are open and what are closed word classes?
4. List the grammatical, the spoken and written word forms of the noun SHOW and the verb SHOW.

5. What is the highest number of grammatical word forms that a lexical unit of the English language has?
6. Think of three adjectives that do not show any of the formal features of adjectives listed in Table 2.5.
7. Apply the criteria introduced in this chapter to show that the form in italics is an adjective. Also discuss to what extent each criterion that you use is reliable or not.

   She is very *beautiful*
   This *sounds* unproblematic
   It is *easier* than it looks.
8. MARRY is usually regarded as a verb. Discuss this view taking into account the use of the word forms of MARRY.
9. In section 2.2.5 we analysed in what sense a relative pronoun stands for a noun phrase. In a similar fashion, illustrate that interrogative pronouns stand for noun phrases.

3 The Verb Phrase

The verb phrase is central to the study of syntax for several reasons: firstly, because the lexical verb in the verb phrase determines what other clause constituents are obligatory. The verb *give*, for example, demands somebody who gives, something that is given and somebody who is given that something, otherwise the sentence would be incorrect. This aspect will be discussed in more detail in chapter six. The second reason for the central status of the verb in syntax is that it actually occupies a central position in the declarative sentence, and the other clause constituents are grouped around the verb phrase. Thirdly, the finite verb phrase provides information regarding the event described in the sentence, such as the time of occurrence, completion or continuation of the event, likelihood or unlikelihood of the event, and so on. The first two sections of this chapter discuss the structure and the function of the finite verb phrase. The third section will then explore non-finite verb phrases.

3.1 The structure of the finite verb phrase

In section 1.3 we introduced the concept 'phrase' as a level of description between words on the one hand and clauses or sentences on the other. We also saw that phrases fulfil different functions in a sentence. The verb phrase denotes the action or the event described in the sentence. The verb phrase *has seen* in the sentence *the man has seen the car*, for instance, denotes the action itself, i.e. 'seeing', and also tells us that this action has happened at some point in the past and is of some relevance to the present. In this chapter we will take a closer look at the formal side of finite verb phrases.

Very simplified, we can define a verb phrase as a phrase which consists of verbal elements only, such as *goes, has lived, will be going, must have been sleeping*, etc. If the first element in the verb phrase is a finite verb, we speak of a finite verb phrase. Recall from section 2.2.3 that finite verbs are those that carry tense distinction and number concord. The finite verb phrase provides information on five important aspects of the event described in the sentence, which in first approximation, are shown in Table 3.1:

Table 3.1: Grammatical categories expressed in the finite verb phrase

Grammatical category	Aspect of the event described
tense	event occurred in the past vs. event occurs in the present
modality	likelihood / obligation of the event
perfect aspect	completion vs. lack of completion of the event
progressive aspect	continuation of the event
voice	active vs. passive; the subject as actor or undergoer of the event

The grammatical category **'tense'** might be confusing since in Table 3.1 it only relates to past and present. The point is that 'tense' is regarded "strictly as a category realized by verb inflection" (Quirk et al. 1985: 176). As a consequence, the English language only has two tenses, namely past and present (or non-past). The first is most clearly marked, namely through the *-ed* ending attached to the base (e.g. *reached, helped, hated*). The second is only marked in the 3rd personal singular through the *-s* suffix (e.g. *reaches, helps, hates*). Still, we all know that we can refer to events that occur in the future as well as events that occur before a given point in the past, and so on. This contradiction can be resolved if we follow Quirk et al.'s (1985: 175-177) distinction between three levels at which the notion of 'time' can be looked at. The first is the 'referential level'. It refers to time in relation to our understanding of and experience with the world around us. Here, we can distinguish at least three 'times', namely past, present and future. 'Present' in this sense, irrespective of the language one speaks, refers to the 'now' of our experience, and everything before this present moment is 'past', everything after this present moment is 'future', as shown in Figure 3.1.

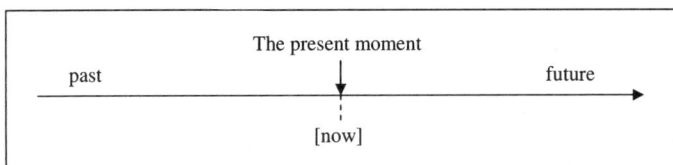

Figure 3.1: Past, present and future on a 'referential level' (Quirk et al. 1985: 175)

'Present' can also be understood on a 'semantic level' as "the most general and unmarked category" (176). In a sentence like *Albatrosses are large birds*, the statement may be applied to the past and the future as well. The sentence *Alba-*

trosses were large birds, in contrast, is less general and suggests that such birds may be extinct. From this perspective, 'present' can be understood as a semantic category that includes the time before and after the now. Consider Figure 3.2.

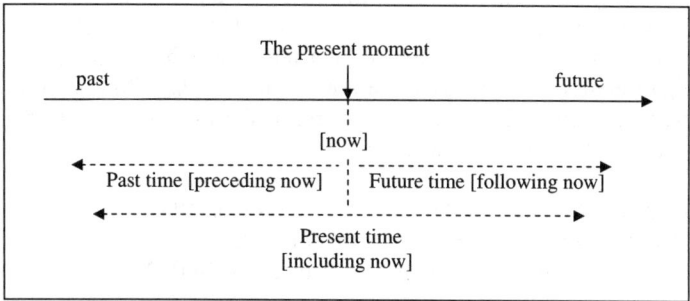

Figure 3.2: Present, past and future time on a 'semantic level' (cf. Quirk et al. 1985: 176).

The referential and the semantic level have to be distinguished from the 'grammatical' or 'structural level'. Referential and semantic conceptions of time are related to 'tense' in intricate ways. The meaning of the grammatical category past tense (on the semantic level) is that of past time, i.e. it refers to what was before the now (on the referential level). The meaning of the present tense, as we have seen, is inclusive in that it may encompass past and future time in addition to the now, so it may refer to the present moment and that which has been before and will come afterwards. Consider the examples below.

(1) a) There is something we *ate* in Turkey. (s1a-063:019)
    b) He knows Ben quite well because he *eats* there a lot. (s1a-055:094)
    c) Odysseus's and Silenius's description of how the Cyclops *kills* the sailors and how he *eats* them. (s1b-019:050)

The past tense form in (1a) makes reference to a particular period of time preceding the now, namely a stay in Turkey. It indicates that the person speaking does not eat this particular dish at present. (1b) does not only tell us that the person referred to as *he* eats at this particular place, but we also assume that he has done this before and will do so later. So, the present tense form *eats* refers to past, present and future time. (1c), in contrast, is usually interpreted as only making reference to the 'now' of Odysseus's and Silenius's description: the Cyclops has never before killed and eaten any of Odysseus's sailors and is not likely to do so in the future. The distinction between (1b) and (1c) is that between a habitual understanding of the present tense (in the sense of a recurring activity or on-going state) and an at-this-point-in-time interpretation.

From a structural perspective, then, the English language only has two tenses. This does not mean, however, that there are no ways of making reference to future time (on the semantic level) and the future (on the referential level). One way is through the use of the present tense, which will be given a future (time) interpretation in sentences like the one under (2a). Others are the use of modal auxiliaries (usually *will*) or of a form of BE plus *going to* to express future time, as in (2b and c), respectively.

(2) a) On Monday the removal men *arrive*. (s2a-020:114)
    b) I*'ll arrive* in Paris at ten forty. (s1a-074:019)
    c) He *was* not *going to leave* the Department. (w2b-012:019)

Note again, however, that the English language does not have a future tense, in the sense that it cannot make reference to future time through inflection in the finite verb form. From a grammatical or structural perspective, English only distinguishes between two tenses, namely past and non-past (or present).

The second grammatical category expressed in the finite verb phrase is that of **'modality'**. It is realised through the presence of a modal auxiliary in the verb phrase. Modality expresses shades of meaning concerning the likelihood of the event described in the sentence or the degree to which the subject of the sentence is obliged or allowed to perform the action denoted by the verb, as illustrated in examples (3a, b and c), respectively.

(3) a) There *will* be no disabled dancers in the class. (s1a-001:107)
       And you *may* be expected to study locally. (w2d-003:076)
       Plus it *might* rain or something. (s1a-006:048).
    b) We *should* get at least two quid each. (s1a-041:164)
       Any room where gas is used *must* be adequately supplied with air. (w2d-012:039)
    c) Readers *may* untie tape securing books. (w2d-006:051)
       You *can* be as personal as you like. (s1a-017:376)

In (3a), *will* expresses the highest degree of likelihood, i.e. the fact that no disabled dancers will be in the class is taken for granted. *May* expresses a lesser degree of likelihood, and with *might*, the event described is even less likely to happen. *Might* can be considered as the past tense form of *may*, but note that it does no refer to past time in (3a). This is another example that illustrates the necessity to keep tense and time apart conceptually. In (3b) *should* indicates a slighter de-

The Verb Phrase

gree of obligation than *must*, while in (3c) both *may* and *can* express permission, although the former is usually perceived to be more formal than the latter.

Aspect, similarly to tense, relates to distinctions of time expressed in the finite verb phrase. In particular, while tense points to differences regarding past and present, **'perfect aspect'** "in its broadest possible interpretation, [...] indicates anterior time: *ie* time preceding whatever time orientation is signalled by tense or by other elements of the sentence or its context" (Quirk et al. 1985: 190), consider the following figure.

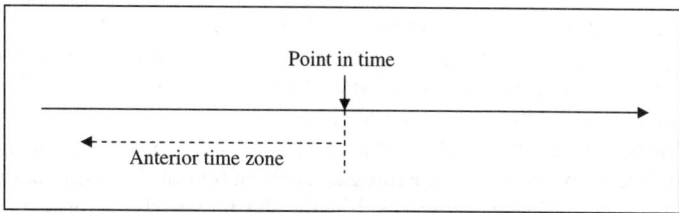

Figure 3.3: 'Perfect aspect' as an indicator of anterior time (cf. Quirk et al. 1985: 190)

This unspecified 'point in time' in Figure 3.3 can be located in the present, in the past or in the future. The perfect merely indicates that the verbal action took part before that point in time. Consider the examples under (4).

(4) a) I*'ve* already *mentioned* my first encounter with Harold. (s2a-041:088)
    b) Policies did change but [...] not so much as I *had feared*. (w2b-012:102)
    c) Within a short time the lowland forests *will have vanished* from the Philippines. (w2b-028:045)

In (4a) the point of time is that of speaking, in (4b) the fear was in the past, but before the change of the policies, which also occurred in the past, and in (4c) the point of time is within a short time from the point of speaking, i.e. it is in the future. As becomes clear from the above examples, perfect aspect is structurally realised by a form of HAVE and the past participle or *-en*[3] form of the main verb.

The present perfect is usually contrasted with the simple past in that it indicates a present relevance for the action that happened in the past, whereas simple past does not signal any such relevance. In (4a), for instance, the fact that the

---

[3] I here use *-en* to refer to the past participle verb form in order to distinguish it from the simple past form which is denoted by *-ed*.

first encounter with Harold has already been mentioned is important, as becomes clear if we take a look at how (4a) continues:

(5) I've already mentioned my first encounter with Harold. [...] Soon after that another example of his interest in his staff occurred. (s2a-041:089)

The fact that the speaker has already mentioned his or her first encounter with Harold is relevant for the present situation, since it enables the speaker to use this piece of information as a temporal reference point: the pronoun *that* in the second sentence refers back to the speaker's first encounter with Harold. The past perfect, in contrast, is used to express that the action occurred at some time before a given point of time in the past, as shown in example (4b): the point of time in the past is the moment when the policies actually changed. The fear of this change is situated before the actual change.

The **'progressive aspect'** also relates to the temporal dimension of the action denoted by the verb phrase but it expresses continuation of the action described in the rest of the verb phrase. More specifically, the progressive expresses duration but also makes clear that this duration is usually limited. Example (6) illustrates the distinction of duration vs. non-duration: the past progressive in (6a) makes clear that the event of spending was going on over an extended period of time, while the simple past in (6b) expresses that the £15 were spent at one moment in the past.

(6) a) Councils *were spending* twice as much money as there was in the pot. (w2c-009:023)
  b) I was then very bad and *spent* £15 on a ticket to go and see Elvis Costello on Monday night. (w1b-005:129)

The feature of limitation of duration distinguishes events of limited duration from habits, which are conceived of as unlimited. This is illustrated by the pair of examples under (7) below. (7b) shows that reading textbooks is a habit of the speaker which is likely to be permanent. In contrast, the event of reading the classics (in 7a) seem to be of a less permanent nature and is only happening at the moment of speaking (i.e. the *now* broadly conceived).

(7) a) I never read the classics or anything like that and now I'*m reading* them. (s1a-013:228)
  b) I told you I only *read* textbooks. (s1a-016:345)

Structurally, the progressive is realised through a form of BE and the *-ing* participle of the main verb, as is also shown in the examples above.

The fifth grammatical category expressed in the verb phrase is **'voice'**. It draws a distinction between events being construed as an action performed by the subject of the clause (8a, c) or something that the subject of the clause has to undergo (8b, d).

(8) a) Millions of people *watch* **Neighbours, The Bill and many others.**
b) **Neighbours, The Bill and many others** *are watched* by millions of people. (w2b-034:006)
c) The counter *represents* **ten separate clock periods.**
d) **Ten separate clock periods** *are represented* by the counter. (w2b-032:042)

As can be seen from the above, passive voice is realised by a form of BE followed by the *-en* participle of the main verb. In addition, passive voice changes the order of elements in the sentence: the subject of the active clause is moved to post-verbal position in a *by*-phrase. The object of the active clause moves to initial position and is the subject of the passive clause.

Often, passive clauses occur without a *by*-phrase, i.e. the doer of the action, the agent, is not made explicit. This is referred to as 'agent deletion'.

(9) a) Everything else has been stopped. (s1a-012:251)
b) A government inquiry was set up in 1934. (w2b-34:039)
c) They were all brought in there. (s1a-094:260)
d) The café was called Steps. (s1a-015:256)
e) The poet's life is described as 'dull and hoary'. (w1a-018:125)

A look at the examples under (9) also reveals that passive verb phrases occur with different sentence patterns, the only restriction being that the corresponding active sentence has a direct object. While the corresponding active sentences of examples (9a and b) only demand a subject (deleted in the passive version) and a direct object, (9c), for instance, demands a location to which *they* were brought, the verb *call* in (9d) demands a name, and the verb *describe* in (9e) demands a description. From a structural point of view, we can portray the relation between active and corresponding passive clause as follows.

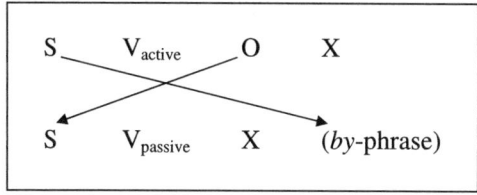

Figure 3.4: The correspondence of active and passive.

The fact that passive sentences move clause constituents to different positions in the clause can be exploited for text-structural purposes, as we will discuss in more detail in chapter 9.

So far we have looked at each of the grammatical categories and their realization in isolation. Table 3.2 sums up the observations made above.

Table 3.2: The structural realizations of the grammatical categories expressed in the finite verb phrase.

Grammatical category	Structural realization
tense	past tense form for past; unmarked form and 3rd person singular present tense -s for present
modality	modal auxiliary
perfect aspect	form of HAVE followed by -ed form of the main verb
progressive aspect	form of BE followed by -ing form of the main verb
voice	form of BE followed by -ed form of the main verb

Of course, more than one of the five categories can be realised at the same time in a given verb phrase. The question, then, is how the categories are combined and what combinations are possible. Take a look at the set of data below.

(10) a) We decided that we *would work* together. (s1a-001:048)
 b) She *had never used* it but she had kept it safe. (w2f-003:036)
 c) I *was working* in that role at the Mike Heafy Centre. (s1a-004:053)
 d) A large house *was demolished* on Westmoreland Hill. (s1a-007:126)

The examples under (10) illustrate the combination of past tense and each of the other grammatical categories expressed in the finite verb phrase, namely modality, perfect, progressive and passive (from top to bottom). As can be seen, the past tense ending is attached to the first verb form in the finite verb phrase. For instance, modality in (10a) is expressed by the string *will work*, which results in the past tense string *would work*, and so on. This is summed up in Table 3.3 below.

Table 3.3: *The structural realizations of past tense combined with each of the other grammatical categories.*

Grammatical category ...		Grammatical category ... + past
Modality:	will/shall/... + V	would/should ... + V
Perfect:	HAVE + V-en	had + V-en
Progressive:	HAVE + V-ing	was/were + V-ing
Passive:	BE + V-en	was/were + V-en

The data set under (11) shows the category modality combined with the other categories. (11a) is repeated for convenience only; it has already been used to illustrate the combination of past tense and modality.

(11) a) We decided that we *would work* together. (s1a-001:048)
    b) Mrs Thatcher *may have got* Philip Oppenheim's support. (s2b-003:068)
    c) And they *will be sitting* in the same places. (s2a-020:085)
    d) People who are nearer the camera *will be bleached out.* (s1a-009:24)

We see that the modal verb occurs first in all of the above verb phrases. The other categories are realised by an unmarked form of either HAVE or BE and the respective participles, i.e. the *-ing* participle for the progressive and the *-en* participle for the perfect and the passive. Consider the summary in Table 3.4.

Table 3.4: *The structural realizations of modality combined with each of the other grammatical categories.*

Grammatical category ...		Grammatical category ... + modality
Past tense:	V-ed	would/should ... + V
Perfect:	HAVE + V-en	will/shall/... have + V-en
Progressive:	HAVE + V-ing	will/shall/... be + V-ing
Passive:	BE + V-en	will/shall/... be + V-en

The examples under (12) illustrate the combination of perfect with the other categories (note that two examples are repeated from above).

(12) a) She *had never* used it but she had kept it safe. (w2f-003:036)
    b) Mrs Thatcher *may have got* Philip Oppenheim's support. (s2b-003:068)
    c) I*'ve been thinking* for years. (w1b-003:131)
    d) Everything else *has been stopped.* (s1a-012:251)

In these examples the strings that realise perfect, progressive and passive are merged (12c and d). The perfect is instantiated by a form of HAVE and the *-en* participle of the following verb, and the progressive is created by a form of BE and the *-ing* participle of the following verb. The combination of the two, as shown in (12c), is realised by a form of HAVE and the *-en* participle of the form of BE, i.e. *been*, which is then followed by the *-ing* participle. Perfect and passive is merged in a similar way: instead of the *-ing* participle, the *-en* participle of the main verb is used to express passive.

Table 3.5: The structural realizations of perfect combined with each of the other grammatical categories.

Grammatical category ...		Grammatical category ... + perfect
Past tense:	V-*ed*	*had* + V-*en*
modality:	*will/shall/...* + V	*will/shall/... have* + V-*en*
Progressive:	HAVE + V-*ing*	*have been* + V-*ing*
Passive:	BE + V-*en*	*have been* + V-*en*

The examples under (13) show the combination of progressive and the remaining categories. Again, three of the examples have already been used above.

(13) a) I *was working* in that role at the Mike Heafy Centre. (s1a-004:053)
　　 b) And they *will be sitting* in the same places. (s2a-020:085)
　　 c) I*'ve been thinking* for years. (w1b-003:131)
　　 d) The letters *are being sent* out tomorrow. (s1a-078:011)

(13d) is the only example that has not been discussed so far. As you can see, structurally, the combination of progressive and passive is similar to that of perfect and passive: the form of BE that is used is the *-ing* participle of BE, namely *being*, as shown in (13d). Table 3.6 sums up the insights concerning the combination of progressive and other grammatical categories.

Table 3.6: The structural realizations of progressive combined with each of the other grammatical categories.

Grammatical category ...		Grammatical category ... + progressive
Past tense:	V-*ed*	*was/were* + V-*ing*
Modality:	*will/shall/...* + V	*will/shall/... be* + V-*ing*
Perfect:	HAVE + V-*en*	HAVE *been* + V-*ing*
Passive:	BE + V-*en*	BE *being* + V-*en*

Finally, Table 3.7 lists all possible combinations of passive and the other grammatical categories. The same information can also be taken from Tables 3.3 to 3.6 but the relevant structures are summarised here for convenience.

Table 3.7: The structural realizations of passive combined with each of the other grammatical categories.

Grammatical category ...		Grammatical category ... + passive
Past tense:	V-*ed*	*was/were* + V-*en*
Modality:	*will/shall/*... + V	*will/shall/*... *be* + V-*en*
Perfect:	HAVE + V-*en*	HAVE *been* + V-*en*
Progressive:	BE + V-*ing*	BE *being* + V-*en*

From the combinations given in Tables 3.3 to 3.7 we can predict the realizations of more complex combinations. First of all, a closer look at these tables reveals the order in which the categories occur in the complex verb phrase. Note that the part of the finite verb phrase that expresses passive voice occurs last in all the structures in Table 3.7. Immediately preceding the passive structure is that bit of the finite verb phrase that signals progressive aspect, as becomes evident if we take a look at the bottom row of Table 3.6. Note also that the other structures in Table 3.6 all end with a form of BE and the -*ing* participle. That is, progressive occurs immediately before passive but after all other kinds of categories that are expressed in the finite verb phrase. From Table 3.5 it can be seen that perfect aspect marking is placed before both progressive and passive but follows modality and past tense marking. To express past tense without modality, *had* (the past tense form of HAVE) is used to signal perfect aspect. If modality is expressed, a modal verb precedes the unmarked form of HAVE. When expressing both modality and past tense, it is the modal verb that occurs in a past tense form, i.e. modality and past tense may occupy the same slot in the finite verb phrase. On the whole, then, the following can be said of the order of grammatical categories in the finite verb phrase.

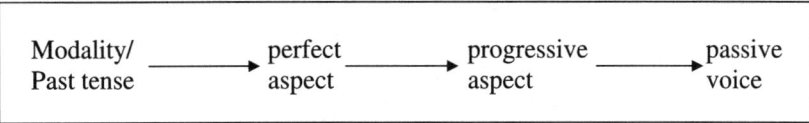

Figure 3.5: The order of grammatical categories in the finite verb phrase.

Considering the way each of these grammatical categories is structurally realised we arrive at the following example of the structure of a finite verb phrase, where all five categories are instantiated (the main verb is SEE).

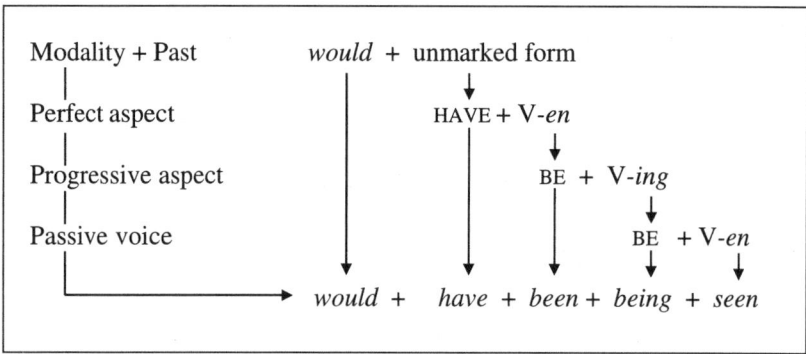

Figure 3.6: The fully expanded verb phrase.

The figure above also makes clear how less complex structures are created. If, for instance, we did not have perfect aspect, the marking for progressive aspect and passive voice would 'move up' one row and 'move left' one column in the above diagram. That is, the unmarked form following the modal *would*, is then *be*. Since there are no other changes, the resulting finite verb phrase is *would be being seen*. Below are some corpus examples of complex finite verb phrases where different grammatical categories are combined.

(14) a) **modality + past + perfect (+ HAVE)**
We *could have had* a cabin overnight. (s1a-021:097)
b) **modality + past + progressive (+ PUT)**
Farmers *should be putting* on less nitrogen, not more. (w2b-027:039)
c) **modality + perfect + progressive (+ CARRY)**
An aircraft which *may have been carrying* ground crews. (s2b-018:004)
d) **modality + perfect + passive (+ TRICK)**
He *may have been tricked* into carrying the bomb. (w2c-001:053)
e) **past + perfect + progressive (+ LOOK FORWARD)**
I *had been looking* forward to his visit. (w1b-002:084)
f) **past + progressive + passive (+ INTERVIEW)**
He was round his office while you *were being interviewed*. (s1a-017:091)
g) **modality + past + perfect + passive (+ REPORT)**
The event *should have been reported*. (s1b-031:045)

Verb phrases of a complexity of example (14g) or higher are usually very rare. The ICE-GB corpus, for instance, does not list any examples of 'modality+past+perfect+progressive' or 'modality+past+progressive+passive'. Still, we are able to state precisely how many structurally different realizations of the finite verb phrase are possible in English.

Note that each of the five grammatical categories are binary categories, i.e. either a category is realised or not. Let us assume someone wants to create a verb phrase. He or she would first need to decide whether the verb phrase should contain a modal or not. So, we have two possibilities here. From each of these, the next decision to be made is whether past tense should be realised: 2 times 2 yields 4 different possibilities, i.e. +modal/+past, +modal/-past, -modal/+past, and -modal/-past. Having chosen one of these four, the next decision concerns the realization of perfect aspect, resulting in a total of 8 different combinations. Taking progressive aspect into consideration yields a total of 16 combinations, which are multiplied by 2 if the choice passive or no passive is taken in account. On the whole we end up with $2 * 2 * 2 * 2 * 2 = 32$ possible structural realizations of the finite complex verb phrase in English[4] (see study questions 5 and 6).

3.2 The operator

In section 1.2 we saw that one basic distinction that can be made with regard to clause constituents is that between the subject and the predicate, i.e. that which the sentence makes a statement about and the statement itself; consider example (15), where the subject is in italics and the predicate is underlined.

(15) *This* would result in an overall reduction in development time.
(w2a-031:070)

A further distinction is made in the predicate, namely between what is called the 'operator' and the 'predication'. The operator is the first auxiliary in the predicate, i.e. *would* in the present example. Along these lines, the sentence under (15) can be given the structure shown in (16).

---

[4] More precisely, for most verbs we are dealing with 33 forms since we have two present tense forms, e.g. *see* and *sees*. The number of finite verb phrases with BE as a main verb is even larger (see study question 6).

(16)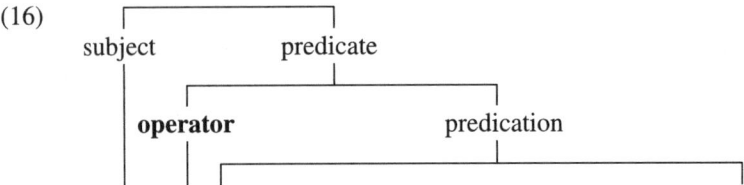

This would result in an overall reduction in development time.

The operator is given such a prominent position because it plays an important role in many sentence-level processes. Firstly, the operator swaps position with the subject of the sentence in the formation of *yes-no* questions and *wh*-questions, as shown in (17) and (18), respectively.

(17) This would result in an overall reduction in development time.

Would this result in an overall reduction in development time?

(18) The police have done something.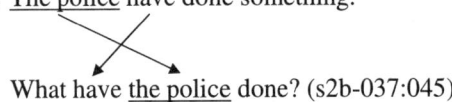

What have the police done? (s2b-037:045)

In addition, the operator plays a role in the formation of tag questions and in negation: it is the operator that is repeated in tag questions and it is the operator to which the negative particle is attached.

(19) This **would** result in an overall reduction in development time, **would**n't it?
(20) This **would**n't result in an overall reduction in development time.

Finally, being the first element in the finite verb phrase, the operator is the one that takes marking for tense and not any of the other verbal elements.

(21) This **would** result in an overall reduction in development time.
    *This will resulted in an overall reduction in development time.

The relevance of the operator for sentence-level processes becomes particularly evident if we consider the fact that in case a verb phrase does not contain any auxiliary the primary verb DO jumps in as a dummy operator for questions, tag questions and negation.

(22) The Romans first conquered Italy. (w2a-001:001)
   Did the Romans first conquer Italy?
   The Romans first conquered Italy, **did**n't they?
   The Romans **did**n't first conquer Italy.

This concludes our discussion of the finite verb phrase. The next section gives an overview of non-finite verb phrases.

3.3 The non-finite verb phrase

A non-finite verb phrase is defined by the absence of finite verb forms. Since finite verb forms always occur at the beginning of the verb phrase, we can say that a verb phrase that begins with a non-finite verb form is a non-finite verb phrase.

Non-finite verb forms are those that cannot show tense distinction or number concord. The English language knows three non-finite verb phrases, namely *to* infinitives, *-ing* participles and *-ed* participles, as illustrated in (23) to (25), respectively.

(23) a) He had refused *to increase* child benefits. (w2c-018:064)
   b) *To keep* a criminal in jail costs £300 a week. (w2c-007:065)
   c) They had a tendency *to cook* their coffee in sauce pans. (s1a-009:182)

(24) a) I remember *passing out* in Sainsbury's once. (s1a-040:322)
   b) But *creating* your own is a help. (s1a-59:230)
   c) There is a word *beginning* with D that would describe it. (s1a-018:193)
   d) *Being* one of the beautiful people he has high standards. (s1a-020:091)

(25) a) Internally *driven* I meant. (s1a-015:149)
   b) One service police locally *based*. (s2b-031:036)
   c) If *played* badly, it can have drastic consequences. (w2d-013:167)

As can be seen from the data above, all these non-finite verb phrases occur in non-finite clauses (underlined in the above examples), which show a variety of functions. For instance, the *to*-infinitive clause in (23a) is the direct object of the clause, in (23b) it functions as subject and in (23c) as a postmodifier within a noun phrase. Similar functions are exemplified for the *-ing* participle clause and the *-ed* participle clause. In addition, (24d) and (25c) show the use of this clause type as an adverbial. These functions of non-finite verb phrases (and clauses) will be discussed in more detail in the following chapters.

3.4 Further reading

Mindt (2000) is a corpus-based discussion of the English verb system with an innovative way of describing structural relations in verb phrases.

Biber et al. (1999: ch. 6) provide information on the frequencies of the realization of the five grammatical categories expressed in the verb phrase in different genres.

Esser (1992) discusses the complex finite verb phrase in detail.

3.5 Study questions

1. Explain the distinction between a finite and a non-finite verb phrase.
2. What are the five grammatical categories expressed in the finite verb phrase, and how are they realised structurally?
3. In what order do the five grammatical categories expressed in the finite verb phrase occur?
4. Explain why there are 32 structurally different kinds of finite verb phrases.
5. Fill in!

	Modal	Past	Perf.	Prog.	Passive
is being seen					
would have been seeing					
will be seeing					
	+	+	-	-	+
	+	-	+	-	-
	-	-	+	+	-

6. List all structural realizations of the finite verb phrase with the verbs SEE and BE.
7. In the sentence below mark the subject, predicate, operator and predication.
   He should not have eaten that apple.
8. What is the operator in the following sentence and why?
   My parents who live in Rome have come to see me.
9. What are the three kinds of non-finite verb phrases in English? Give examples.
10. Invent one example each of an *-ing* participle clause functioning as subject, direct object, indirect object and adverbial.

4 The Noun Phrase

4.1 The notion of 'head'

In the previous chapter we discussed the verb phrase. It was defined as a phrase that consists of verbal elements only. The noun phrase, however, cannot be defined as a phrase that consists only of noun phrases, since it contains words from a number of different word classes. Consider the examples below, where in addition to nouns we also find determiners, adjectives, adverbs, prepositions and verbs.

(1) a) your attitudes (s1a-002:048)
    b) other activities for the disabled (s1a-001:001)
    c) the problems associated with Edward's authority and status in the duchy of Aquitaine (w2a-010:084)
    d) a video of some of the work we'd done (s1a-001:119)
    e) the layout of buses (w2d-009:089)

Accordingly, we have to come up with another criterion to define the noun phrase. This criterion makes reference to the notion of 'head', namely: a noun phrase is a phrase which has a noun as its head. The problem, then, of course is to define 'head'. The head can informally be defined as the most important element of the phrase. This means if a phrase can be reduced to one of the words that it contains without leading to ungrammaticality, this word is the head of the phrase, as in the examples below (the noun phrase is in italics, the head in bold print).

(2) a) Have *your **attitudes*** changed towards disabled? (s1a-002:048)
    a') Have ***attitudes*** changed towards disabled?
    b) What did you see as missing from *other **activities** for the disabled*? (s1a-001:001)
    b') What did you see as missing from ***activities***?
    c) By 1290 *the **problems** associated with Edward's authority and status in the duchy of Aquitaine* were becoming more acute. (w2a-010:084)
    c') By 1290 ***problems*** were becoming more acute.

This criterion is not 100 per cent foolproof, as it does not work with the noun phrases under (1d and e). In these cases, the head has to be accompanied by the determiner; we cannot reduce the phrase to one of its elements and, accordingly, cannot say which of the elements below is the head.

(3) a) I showed *a **video** of some of the work we'd done* to some of my college students. (s1a-001:119)
    a') *I showed ***video*** to some of my college students.
    a") I showed *a **video*** to some of my college students.
  b) *The **layout** of buses* makes a quick getaway by trouble-makers difficult or even impossible. (w2d-009:089)
  b') ****Layout*** makes a quick getaway by trouble-makers difficult or even impossible.
  b") *The **layout*** makes a quick getaway by trouble-makers difficult or even impossible.

However, since the class of determiners is small and the determiners are known, it is still easy to identify the head of a noun phrase even if the phrase cannot be reduced to one element only.

An additional criterion is useful with those noun phrases that function as the subject of the clause. In these cases, the head of the noun phrase shows concord with the verb.

(4) a) *The **layout** of buses* makes a quick getaway by trouble-makers difficult or even impossible. (w2d-009:089)
  b) **The **layout** of buses* make a quick getaway by trouble-makers difficult or even impossible. (w2d-009:089)

The phrase in italics in example (4) contains two nouns, *layout* and *buses*. The verb form shows concord with the first of the two nouns, as the ungrammaticality of (4b) makes clear. It follows that *layout* is the head of the noun phrase.

The last criterion is of a semantic kind and draws on a concept introduced by Bloomfield (1933), namely 'endocentric construction'. The term 'endocentric' means having its centre within itself and refers to the fact that a construction consisting of two or more elements can be of the same kind as one or more of its constituents. An application of this concept is its use in the term 'endocentric compounds' (see, for instance, Marchand 1969). With endocentric compounds the whole compound describes a special kind of one of its component parts, e.g. a *steam boat* is a particular kind of boat and a *stone wall* is a particular kind of *wall*. A similar approach seems useful in determining the head of a noun phrase (and most other kinds of phrases, too). All of the five examples above are in line with the following formula: NOUN PHRASE is/are a special kind of HEAD.

(5) your attitudes   is/are a special kind of   attitudes
    other activities for the disabled   is/are a special kind of   activities
    the problems associated with Edward's
       authority and status in the duchy of
       Aquitaine   is/are a special kind of   problems
    a video of some of the work we'd done   is/are a special kind of   video
    the layout of buses   is/are a special kind of   layout

Note that this formula does not work with other nouns in the noun phrases.

(5') *a video of some of the work we'd done   is/are a special kind of   work
      *the layout of buses   is/are a special kind of   bus(es)

These semantic considerations point to an important functional difference of elements within noun phrases: while the head as the main element of the noun phrase denotes a general class of 'things', e.g. attitudes, activities, videos, and layouts, the elements preceding and following the head provide more detailed information on the nature of the head, they serve to 'modify' the head. The possible kinds of modification can be described in a systematic way, as will be shown in the next section.

4.2 The structure of the noun phrase

The head of the noun phrase conveniently divides a noun phrase into two parts (in addition to the head), namely that which precedes and that which follows the head; we will talk of 'pre-head' and 'post-head material' for now.

(6) | **pre-head material** | **head** | **post-head material** |
|---|---|---|
| your | attitudes | |
| other | activities | for the disabled |
| the | problems | associated with Edward's authority and status in the duchy of Aquitaine |
| a | video | of some of the work we'd done |
| the | layout | of buses |

Material in front of the head either functions as determiner or as premodification. That which follows the head always functions as postmodification. We will discuss each of these functions in turn.

4.2.1 The determiner

The function of the determiner is to establish a clear reference, i.e. it serves to relate the noun phrase to the extralinguistic world by establishing which part of the extralinguistic world is 'meant' by the noun phrase. This becomes apparent in contrasts like the ones below.

(7) a) a car - the car
 b) my car - your car - his car - her car - their car
 c) this car - that car
 d) some cars - many cars - most cars - all cars

(7a) shows the difference between indefinite and definite reference. The noun phrase *a car* does not refer to a specific car, while the noun phrase *the car* does. Compare the sentence *They throw a car out of a plane* (s1a-058:137), where the exact identity of the car is irrelevant, to the sentence *Do you know what the car is worth* (s1b-080:188), where the speaker talks about one specific car. The contrasts in (7b) identify what car we are actually talking about by making explicit who owns the car in question. The determiners in (7c) identify the car with regard to the location of the speaker, with *this car* referring to the car nearby and *that car* referring to the car further away. The determiners in (7d) draw distinctions as to the size of the set of cars referred to by the noun phrase, with an increase from left to right.

A noun phrase can contain up to three determiners, as you can see in the data below.

(8) a) all those other things (s1a-075:077)
 b) all your other letters (w1b-001:107)
 c) all its 113 bankers (w2c-013:068)
 d) the other side of the road (s1a-023:259)
 e) half the night (w2b-004:011)
 f) half an hour (s1a-007)
 g) another form of communication (s1b-003:154)
 h) all Daddy's books (s1a-025:324)
 i) once a week (w2b-022:093)
 j) twice the level of nineteen seventy-nine (s2b-035:029)
 k) her first reaction (s1a-010:249)
 l) those few begonias (s1a-007:022)
 m) her many public utterances on the subject (w2b-014:015)

These examples allow us to find out about different kinds of determiners, namely **pre-**, **central** and **post-determiners**. As the names suggest, these three classes are based on the position of the determiners relative to each other (see section 2.2.5). How can we establish which determiner belongs to which class? A combination of a close analysis of the (given) syntagmatic strings and of our paradigmatic knowledge about which elements could fill a slot in a given string yields the answer.

The most helpful are examples (8a to c) because here we have three determiners, which makes the first word a pre-determiner, the word form in the middle the central determiner and the final word form the post-determiner. So we find that *all* belongs to the class of predeterminers, since it occurs initially in all three cases. Example (8a) shows the demonstrative element *those* in medial position, we can therefore assume that the central-determiner position can generally be filled by demonstratives, i.e. *this, that, these, those.* (8b) is identical to (8a) apart from the medial element, namely *your* and *those*, respectively. Filling the same slot in an otherwise identical string we assume that *your* also functions as a central determiner. In addition we could have any of the following words in that slot: *my, her, his, its,* and *their* – the string *all my other letters*, for instance, is perfectly alright. Together with *your*, these words form the group of possessive determiners. With examples (8a and b) the word form *other* occurs as the post-determiner. Instead we could have elements such as *last, next, past* etc.: e.g., *all your last letters* or *all your next letters*. They form the group of 'general ordinals'. In (8c) we find the number *113*, and of course any other number larger than 1 could fill this slot. *113* is a member of a class called 'cardinals', and we see that cardinals can also work as post-determiners. How do we go on from here?

(8d) is indicative of *the* being either a central determiner or a pre-determiner because we find that it occurs in front of the post-determiner *other*. Decisive, here, is the fact that we can substitute *the* with any of the central determiners in examples (8a to c), i.e. *all the other things, all the other letters,* and *all the 113 bankers.* Accordingly, we assume that it functions as a central determiner. *The* belongs to the class of articles, which in addition to the definite article *the* also contains the indefinite article *a* and *an*. Further evidence that *a/an* functions as a central determiner can be seen in (8e and f), where *the* and *an* occur in identical contexts, i.e. *half + ___ + N*, and in (8g): the word *another* is a fused form consisting of *an* and *other*. Such a fusion points at frequent co-occurrence of the two constituent words, i.e. *an* has often occurred immediately preceding *other*, which is the position for the central determiner.

Another kind of central determiner is shown in (8h), namely the genitive noun phrase in *all Daddy's books*. The fact that *Daddy's* occurs after the pre-determiner *all* makes it a candidate either for central or post-determiner. Two pieces of evidence suggest that the former is the case: firstly, *Daddy's* can be substituted by the possessive determiner *his*, i.e. *all his books*. Since *his* belongs to the class of central determiners we would assign the same status to the genitive noun phrase. Secondly, we could insert the post-determiner *other* after the genitive yielding *all Daddy's other books*, another piece of evidence that points in the same direction.

As for pre-determiners, we have already seen that *all* figures prominently in the data under (8). Another class of pre-determiners is exemplified in (8i and j), namely the group of multipliers. Their status as predeterminers becomes apparent through the fact that both occur before the central determiners *a* and *the*.

In (8a and b) we saw the general ordinal *other* as a post-determiner and (8c) has shown the use of cardinals, i.e. one, two, three, etc., in that function. Other post-determiners are illustrated in (8k to m). Again, their status as post-determiners is evident from their position immediately following the central determiners *her* and *their*. (8k) illustrates the use of 'primary ordinals', a class that in addition to *first* contains words like *second*, *third*, *fourth*, etc. The last two examples show 'quantifiers' in post-determiner function. Other members of this class are *several, little, few* or *much*.

The aim of the discussion above was to introduce the three pre-head elements pre-, central and post-determiner, and to find out which classes of words can fulfil these functions. The following excursion is basically an exercise in linguistic argumentation, where we take a closer look at some problematic cases and see how the application of linguistic concepts and methods deal with them. Consider the set of examples under (9) below.

(9) a)   many a   tale (w2d-017:031)
    b)   such a   structure (w2a-032:103)
    c)   all his many critics (BNC-FBP:1216)
    d)   three such   blocks of literature (w2a-014:020)

Examples (9a and b) suggest that *many* and *such* are pre-determiners, as they occur in front of the central determiner *a*. However, in (9c and d) the two words occur either in post-determiner position after the central determiner *his* or after a cardinal, which functions as post-determiner, respectively.

To account for the first four examples, it makes sense to conclude that both *many* and *such* can occur either as pre-determiner or as post-determiner. In the first case, as indicated by (9a and b), they are always immediately followed by the indefinite article *a*. In post-determiner function, there are no such restrictions. However, a possible point of criticism against the analysis of *such* as post-determiner in (9d) might be that this slot is already filled with the cardinal *three*. As a consequence, we would have to come up with a fourth category of determiners, maybe called 'post-post-determiner', with *such* being one member of that category. An alternative way to account for (9d) would be to allow for post-determiners to be combinable. That this second analysis is preferable becomes apparent if we take a look at additional data provided in (10).

(10) a) some other bells (s1a-029:271)
   b) two other things (s1a-005:097)
   c) the other two gang members (w2b-009:124)
   d) the first ten minutes of the opera (s1b-044:005)
   e) the last two tax years (w2d-004:025)
   f) the last few centuries (s2b-035:125)
   g) the next few days (s1a-039:144)
   h) a few other Conservative MPs (w2e-004:019)

The data under (10) show that the general ordinal *other* can occur with quantifiers, as in (10a), and with cardinals, as in (10b and c). Example (10d) shows the ordinal *first* together with the cardinal *ten*, while examples (10e to g) illustrate the use of a general ordinal with a cardinal or a quantifier. Finally, (10h) shows that quantifiers may precede general ordinals. If we stuck to the assumption that a noun phrase can only have one post-determiner and that, accordingly, determiners following this post-determiner would have to be analysed as post-post-determiners, we would run into severe difficulties with the set of data above: the cardinal *two*, for instance, would then occur in post-determiner as well as post-post-determiner position, as would the general ordinal *other* and the quantifier *few*. That is, we would end up with two categories, 'post-determiner' and 'post-post-determiner', which are highly similar with regard to the members that they contain. The information value in the category labels would thus be very close to zero, i.e. such categories would be rather pointless. Instead, we dispense with a fourth category and admit that more than one post-determiner may co-occur in a noun phrase. In summary, we have seen that *such* and *many* may function both as pre- and as post-determiner, and we have found out that post-determiners may be combined in a noun phrase.

The focus of the above discussion was on linguistic argumentation rather than on an exhaustive listing of all pre-, central and post-determiners of the English language. As a consequence, not all of the English determiners have been mentioned or illustrated above. The following table, based on Greenbaum (1996: 213-216), is supposed to give at least a fairly comprehensive overview of the most common determiners.

Table 4.1: The determiners of English (cf. Greenbaum 1996: 213-216).

Pre-determiner	Central determiner	Post-determiner
all, both, half multipliers: *once, twice, double* *many (a)* *such (a)* *what (a)*	Articles: *the, a(n)* possessives: *my, your,* ... demonstratives: *this, that, these, those* genitive NP, e.g. *Peter's* indefinites: *some, any, either, no, neither* interrogatives: *which, what, whose*	cardinals: *one, two, three,* ... (primary) ordinals: *first, second, third,* ... general ordinals: *other, another, last, next* quantifiers: *many, much, several, few, little*

4.2.2 Premodification

The premodification of the noun phrase can be defined very easily as those elements that come between the final determiner and the head of the noun phrase. Premodification can be of different formal kinds. Biber et al. (1999: 588) list the following four structural types of premodification as most important: premodification by adjective phrase, *-ed*-participle, *-ing*-participle, and noun phrase. We will discuss each type in turn.

Adjective phrases, according to Biber et al. (1999: 589) are the most frequent kind of premodifications in the English noun phrase. This is also supported by a look in the ICE-GB, which shows that 33,389 out of 43,510 instances of noun-phrase premodification are adjective phrases. Some examples are given below.

(11) a) the main   perception (s1a-001:012)
    b) your initial   reaction (s1a-001:045)
    c) a very nice   group (s1a-002:110)
    d) the political and military   ramifications (s2b-015:026)
    e) cultural, political and/or economic   aspects (w2a-012:017)
    f) the very real and crucial psychological dimension (w2a-017:010)

Cases of premodification by a single adjective as in (11a and b) are the most frequent kind: of the 33,389 instances of adjective phrases as noun-phrase premodifiers, ICE-GB lists 31,149 cases with just one adjective. Still, the other examples show that more complex kinds of adjective phrases also occur, involving premodification of the adjective head by adverbs, as in (11c), and co-ordinated adjective phrases, as in (11d to f).

In case an adjective phrase contains more than one adjective, the order of the adjectives is restricted to a certain extent. An exact description of this order is difficult to provide, since different sources make different suggestions. The most comprehensive one seems to be given in Quirk et al. (1985: 1337-1341), on which the following account is based. The authors distinguish four zones which they term 'precentral', 'central', 'postcentral' and 'prehead'. In precentral position we mostly find peripheral adjectives, i.e. adjectives that only show some of the features typically associated with adjectives, namely occurrence in attributive and predicative position, gradability and premodification by *very* (Quirk et al. 1985: 402-404; see also sections 2.2.4 and 7.2 for details). Typical adjectives in that position are intensifying adjectives, i.e. those adjectives that have a heightening or a lowering effect on the noun they modify (see Quirk et al. 1985: 429), such as *sheer* in *sheer arrogance* or *definite* in *a definite loss*.

The central position is reserved for those adjectives that are most adjectival in the sense that they fulfil all of the four criteria, e.g. *tall, green, old, flat, attractive, sleepy* etc. Within this class there are further restrictions. Firstly, there seems to be a tendency for non-derived adjectives (e.g. *tall* and *green*) to occur before deverbal adjectives (e.g. *attractive* and *repulsive*) which, again, occur before denominal adjectives (e.g. *sleepy* and *hilly*). Secondly, among the non-derived adjectives, those that are of an emotive or evaluative kind (e.g. *lovely, nice, wonderful*) tend to precede adjectives that describe size, length and height, which precede other non-derived adjectives.

In the post-central zone we find participles like *retired* or *watching* (see section 2.2.4 and below for a discussion of participles and adjectives) and colour adjectives, e.g. *red* or *green*.

Finally, adjectives in prehead position are those that denote nationality, provenance or style such as *American, English* and *French*, and denominal adjectives that express meanings like 'consisting of', 'involving' or 'relating to'. Examples of the latter would be *wooden, experimental* or *commercial*. Figure 4.1 below sums up the order of adjectives in noun-phrase premodification.

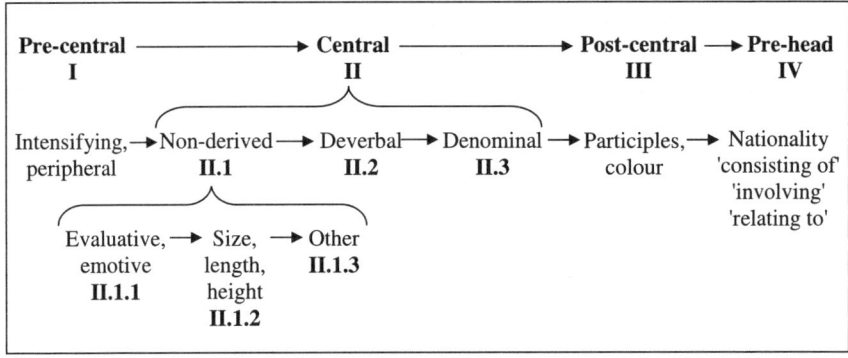

Figure 4.1: The order of adjectives in noun-phrase premodification.

The examples in Table 4.2 below show that a slot may be filled more than once.

Table 4.2: Some examples of sequences of adjectives in premodification.

Sequence	Det.	Adjectives	Head (Source)
III_IV	a	retired French	polisher (BNC-K97:7441)
II.1.2_II.1.3_IV		tall green German	bottles (BNC-ED9:3540)
II.1.1_II.1.2_III		funny little whickering	noises (BNC-AT4:1675)
II.1.3_ II.1.3_ II.1.3		circular flat round	shells (s1a-009:302)
I_II.3		certain cognitive	states (BNC-ECV:1320)
I_I_II.3		certain general statutory	restrictions (BNC-FBC:1150)
II.1.1_II.1.1_IV	the	efficient marvellous commercial	enterprise (s1b-005:123)

It is important to note that the sequence shown in Figure 4.1 is not absolute but shows prevalent tendencies. Other orders may occur and need not be ungrammatical or clumsy. The noun phrase *the old isolated arrogant notion* (s2a-040:042), for instance, shows the sequence 'II.1.3_III_II.1.3'. Also, it is sometimes hard to tell if we are dealing with a proper name or a 'divergent' sequence of adjectives, as in the example *the old Irish black horses* (s2a-011:085).

Related to adjectival premodification is that of premodification by *-ed-* **and** *-ing-***participles**, since these are often treated as adjectives (see section 2.2.4 and below). ICE-GB lists 3,401 of the first and 2,038 tokens of the latter. Again, we see different degrees of complexity, ranging from simple to premodified and coordinated participles.

(12) a) the measured separation (w2a-033:082)
   b) linearly polarized light (w2a-025:035)
   c) distinctively rounded and unrounded vowels (s2a-030:124)
   d) an overwhelming motive (s2b-016:139)
   e) the only remaining problem (w2e-008:041)
   f) this really sort of like dirty sounding voice (s1a-055:095)

A word of caution is in order here, concerning the distinction between premodification by adjective phrases and by participles and their respective frequencies. Since participles are forms of verbs, we would have to conclude that almost 5,500 nouns in ICE-GB are premodified by a verb form. However, maybe this number is too large. The compilers of the ICE-GB (from which the frequency data is drawn), make a form-based distinction between 'general', '-ed participle' and '-ing participle' adjectives. This strong commitment to form, however, occasionally leads to counterintuitive classifications. The word forms *interesting* and *boring*, for instance, are counted as adjectives of the -*ing*-participle kind, although their verbal nature seems to be disputable at best. This becomes apparent if we take a look at dictionaries. The LDOCE, for instance, simply lists such and similar forms, e.g. *remaining* and *overwhelming*, as adjectives. A consequence of the classifications in ICE-GB is that the relative frequency of premodification by participles is fairly high compared to that by nouns, namely 3,401 and 2,038 as opposed to 241 tokens. In contrast, the *Longman Grammar of Spoken and Written English* by Biber et al. (1999) claims that nouns are the second-most frequent premodifiers whereas "the other premodifier categories [i.e. -*ing*- and -*ed*-participles] are relatively uncommon in comparison with adjectives and nouns" (589). The moral of this aside is that numbers derived from an analysis even of modern corpora (i.e. the ICE-GB and the Longman Spoken and Written English Corpus) have to be taken with care. Much depends on the annotation that has been put into the corpora – and this can lead to drastic differences in the results, as we have seen above.

The final kind of noun-phrase premodification to be discussed here is that by another **noun phrase**. Again, different degrees of complexity are found.

(13) a) a Bridgend couple (w2c-017:021)
   b) the peasant girl (s1a-018:081)
   c) art performances (s1b-022:043)
   d) language acquisition (s1b-003:046)
   e) Health and safety arrangements (s2b-041:043)
   f) Labour and Liberal Democrat councillors (w2c-009:010)
   g) United Nations Environment Program (w2a-030:038)
   h) Tissue and cell culture technology (s2b-046:009)
   i) European Community agriculture and trade ministers (s2b-007:033)

As the first four examples show, it is not always easy to tell whether we are actually dealing with premodification by a noun or a compound noun (see Novak 1996: ch. 3). There seems to be a cline from clear cases of noun premodification as in (13a) to clear cases of compound nouns as in (13d). Examples (13e to i) are more complex and some of them will be dealt with in more detail below.

With regard to position, noun premodifiers share the pre-head slot with the adjectives that occur in that position. Usually nouns are closest to the head of the noun phrase. That is, adjectives will occur before the noun premodifier, as the examples under (14) show:

(14)   a friendly Bridgend couple   *a Bridgend friendly couple
           the American peasant girl   *the peasant American girl
           exquisite art performances   *art exquisite performances

A special case of noun-phrase premodification that merits mention is that of premodification by a noun-phrase in the genitive case, as shown in example 15.

(15)   Our local boys' school (s1a-012:230)

In particular, it is not trivial to distinguish a case like that in (15) above from that shown in (16).

(16)   Our lovely friend's bike.

In the first case the genitive noun phrase serves as a premodifier of the head noun, i.e. it is a school for boys, not a school that is owned by the boys. The string *boys' school* describes a subclass of schools. This is an example of the 'classifying genitive' (see section 2.2.4), as opposed to the 'specifying genitive' in (16). Here, the string *friend's bike* does not denote a subclass of bikes but it points at one specific bike, i.e. the genitive determines the reference of the head noun. It follows from this that while a classifying genitive serves as a premodifier, the specifying genitive serves as a determiner (see also section 4.2.1). This has important consequences for the structures that we would ascribe to the two examples.

(15')   [Our[local[boys' school]]]
(16')   [[Our[lovely friend]'s] bike]

In the first case, the genitive *boys'* forms a constituent with the head *school* and both are premodified by the adjective *local* and determined by the determiner *our*: it is not just *some local school* but *our local school*. In the second case, in contrast, the head noun *bike* is not premodified but only has a determiner, namely *our lovely friend's*, which has a somewhat complex structure. Being a noun phrase, the string itself can be described along the lines laid out above. The head of the determiner noun phrase is *friend*, and it is premodified by the adjective *lovely* and determined by the possessive determiner *our*: it is not just *some friend* or *their friend* but *our friend*. Further evidence for the status of *our lovely friend's* as determiner can be seen if we insert the premodifying adjective *expensive* in (15) and (16).

(15") Our expensive local boys' school.
(16") Our lovely friend's expensive bike.

In (15") the adjective *expensive* is inserted before the genitive *boys'* whereas in (16") is occurs after the genitive. This points to the premodifier status of the genitive in the first and the determiner status of the genitive in the second case.

So far, we have only discussed the major kinds of premodification. The discussion of our examples (15) and (16), however, has shown that the internal structures of the premodifiers is important as well. We will turn to this aspect now by taking a closer look at a number of examples, some of which have already been shown above and will be repeated here for convenience.

(17) a) Health and safety arrangements (s2b-041:043)
    b) cultural, political and/or economic aspects (w2a-012:017)
    c) the very real and crucial psychological dimension (w2a-017:010)
    d) distinctively rounded and unrounded vowels (s2a-030:124)
    e) a three tier gilt and scarlet plush auditorium (s1a-044:002)

The internal structure of such more complex kinds of premodification can conveniently be determined with the help of paraphrases that 'translate' the premodification into a postmodification. (17a), for instance, can be described as 'arrangements concerning health and safety'. The two noun premodifiers, as coordinated elements, equally premodify the head of the noun phrase. In that it is similar to example (17b), which denotes 'aspects of a cultural, political and/or economical nature'. These similarities also show in the structural descriptions given below:

(17a') [[Health and safety] arrangements]
    ~ 'arrangements concerning health and safety'
(17b') [[cultural, political and/or economic] aspects]
    ~ 'aspects of a cultural, political and/or economical nature'

With (17c and d) the paraphrases are of a different kind. The noun phrase in (17c) could be described as 'a dimension of a psychological kind that is very real and crucial'. It is similar in that respect to (17d), where the following paraphrase would fit: 'vowels that are rounded and unrounded in a distinctive fashion'. In contrast to the paraphrases in (17a and b), the latter two contain two postmodifying structures, one subordinate to the other. This hints at a hierarchical organisation which is also expressed in the structural descriptions of the two examples.

(17c') [the [[[very real] and crucial] [psychological dimension]]]
  ~ 'a dimension of a psychological kind that is very real and crucial'
(17d') [[distinctively [rounded and unrounded]] vowels]
  'vowels that are rounded and unrounded in a distinctive fashion'

A yet more intricate structure is given in example (17e), as the following structure and paraphrase make clear.

(17e') [a [[three tier] [[gilt and [scarlet plush]] auditorium]]]
  ~ 'an auditorium with three tiers which is held in gilt and in plush that is scarlet'.

Of course, complexity does not end here. The noun *plush*, for instance, could be further pre- or postmodified. Like any other phrase, the noun phrase is "indefinitely complex" (Quirk et al. 1985: 1238), as will also become apparent in the following discussion of postmodification in noun phrases.

4.2.3 Postmodification

Postmodification in noun phrases is more frequent than premodification; ICE-GB lists 65,420 tokens, as opposed to 43,510 instances of noun-phrase premodification. We will here discuss the most important and versatile kinds of postmodification, namely by prepositional phrase, by finite clause (more specifically, relative and appositive clause) and by non-finite clauses (i.e. *–ed-* and *-ing-*participle clause and infinitive clause). Biber et al. (1999: 606) report that **prepositional phrases** "are by far the most common type of postmodification in all registers [i.e. conversations, fiction, news and academic writing]", a finding that is supported by the ICE-GB data, where we find 41,296 instances of premodification by prepositional phrases, i.e. 63%.

(18) a)   a natural part **of** art (s1a-001:081)
     b)   your initial reaction **towards** each other (s1a-001:045)
     c)   patients **from** the Spinal Unit (s1a-003:058)
     d)   the few lines **before** the above quote (w1a-018:012)

e)	the driving force	**behind** the new interest **in** hearing voices (s2b-038:046)
f)	contact	**with** other people **out of** the chair (s1a-003:086)
g)	a room	**in** a house **of** young women **in** want **of** nocturnal company (w1b-015:021)
h)	similar raids	**on** crack gangs **across** estates **in** west and south London **in** May (w2c-011:081)

The data under (18) show that postmodification by prepositional phrases can become fairly complex. This is due to the fact that prepositional phrases can be stacked easily, because each prepositional phrase consists of a preposition plus noun phrase, the head noun of which can again be postmodified by a prepositional phrase. This is what has happened in (18g'), the structure of which is given below (note that some details have been omitted):

(18g')

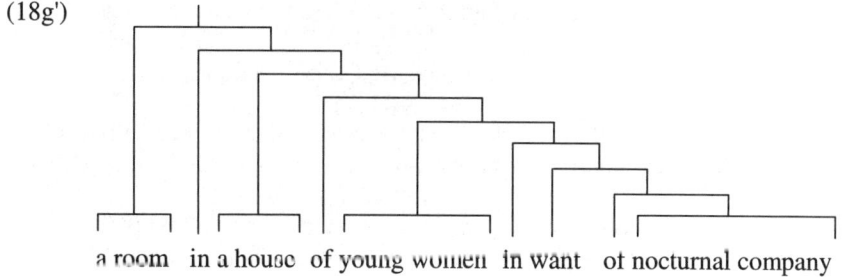

This is an instance of what is usually called 'right-branching' (see, for instance, Quirk et al., 1985: 1039). A look at the diagram above makes clear why this term is used: as can be seen, the syntactic tree grows continuously to the right if we start from the root on top. This particular kind of structure is usually easy to process; even larger structures of this kind would still be possible to process. Note, however, that a sequence of prepositional phrases as postmodifiers does not automatically lead to simple right-branching structure, as the structure of example (18h) shows (again, details have been omitted).

(18h')

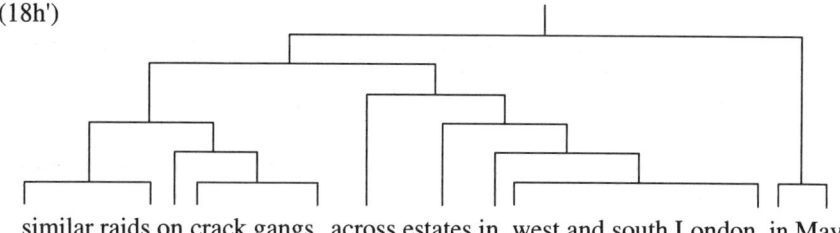

In this example we have a huge amount of left-branching. Starting from the top, we see that the major part of the structure is on the left of the first node, and we also find considerable amounts of structure on the left of the second node. Such structures are more difficult to process since it is not easy to keep track of all the interrelations between the individual phrases that occur. This becomes most apparent with the final prepositional phrase, *in May*. Having reached the string *in May* it might be difficult for many language users to immediately tell what this prepositional phrase actually modifies (although the fact that semantically it can only refer to the raids is of some help).

Postmodification by **finite clauses** is of two major kinds, namely relative clauses and appositive clauses. **Relative clauses** are exemplified below.

(19) a)   those people   **who** heard Michael Whittaker's talk a week or so ago (s2a-051:034)
  b)   the sub   **that** sank the trawler (s2b-003:005)
  c)   an age   **when** they might want to take things easy (s2b-024:106)
  d)   a residential home   **where** she used to be a parlour maid (s2b-024:113)
  e)   the things   **which** satisfy us as we get older (w1b-001:193)
  f)   the other countries   **whose** farmers are far poorer than those in France and Germany (s1b-053:114)
  g)   Susan Fox   **whom** I mentioned earlier (s2a-069:060)
  h)   this stupid girl   **(zero)** he falls in love with (s1a-006:112)

As the examples show, the relative clause contains a clause-initial relative pronoun (in bold under (19)), which even may be realised by *(zero)*, as in (19h). This pronoun refers back to the head of the noun phrase which the relative clause postmodifies: *who* in (19a), for instance, relates to the head *people*, *that* in (19b) to the head *sub*, and so on. The head is called the 'antecedent' of the relative pronoun, a Latin term which can be translated as 'that which is preceding'.

Within the relative clause itself, the relative pronoun can fulfil various functions as clause constituent. In (19a, b, and e), for instance, the relative pronoun functions as the subject of the relative clause.

(19) a')   **who** (~those people) heard Michael Whittaker's talk a week or so ago
  b')   **that** (~the sub) sank the trawler
  e')   **which** (~the things) satisfy us as we get older

The relative pronouns *whom* and *(zero)* in (19g and h) function as direct objects of the relative clause, whereas *when* and *where* in (19c and d) are the adverbials.

(19) g') I mentioned earlier **whom** (~ Susan Fox)
  h') He falls in love with **(zero)** (~ this stupid girl)
  c') They might want to take things easy **when** (~ [at] an age)
  d') She used to be a parlour maid **where** (~ [at] a residential home)

Finally, the relative pronoun *whose* in (19f) does not function as a clause constituent but as the determiner of the noun phrase that follows it, i.e. *farmers*.

(19) f') **whose** (~ the other countries') farmers are far poorer than those in France and Germany

A distinction is usually made between restrictive and non-restrictive relative clauses. Quirk et al. (1985: 1239) define the first as follows: "The modification is restrictive when the reference of the head is a member of a class which can be identified only through the modification that has been supplied". Whether this is the case, of course, always depends on the given context and can often not be determined on the basis of a single clause or sentence. A look at the context, for instance, shows that in (19a) *those people* is a class of which *those people who heard Michael Whittaker's talk a week or so ago* is a sub-class. This sub-class can only be identified through the postmodifying relative clause. Similarly, the relative clause in (19b) denotes a particular submarine, namely the one *that sank the trawler*. In contrast to that, with non-restrictive modification "the referent of a noun phrase [...] is] viewed as unique or as a member of a class that has been independently identified" (1239). An example is given in (19g): the proper name *Susan Fox* uniquely identifies the referent of the noun phrase, namely the person with that name. The relative clause, in that case, only provides additional information on the referent. In writing, restrictive and non-restrictive clauses are differentiated in that a comma is placed before the latter – one of the rare 'real' rules of punctuation in English. The reason that we do not have a comma in (19g) is due to the fact that this example was transcribed from speech without any punctuation being added.

Appositive clauses are either introduced by *that* or a *wh*-word.

(20) a) the assumption **that** ownership is absolute or it's not ownership (s3b-046:086)
  b) the problem **that** either he had to make a clean sweep [...] or he would have to consider the feasibility of selling the business (s2a-070:073)
  c) the conviction **that** the only hope for salvation is to have been 'born again'. (w2a-012:049)
  d) the issue **whether** there had been a breach of the Code (BNC-FBK:892)

e) the question **how** far aggression of fears of aggression [...] provided Rome with motives (w2a-001:027)
f) the question **where** power resides and **how** it is exercised (BNC-EVP:1329)
g) the question **which** organization is best fitted to undertake a particular project (BNC-EEH:121)

Note that in *that*-appositive clauses, the *that* is not a relative pronoun and it does not have a function in the appositive clause. But it functions as a conjunction in the superordinate structure, where it cannot be left out: **the assumption ownership is absolute or it's not ownership* is ungrammatical unless we make use of metatextual comments to indicate the status of the appositive clause, e.g. *the assumption 'ownership is absolute or it's not ownership' is false*. Where appositive clauses have *wh*-words, the appositive clause itself is similar to a question, and the *wh*-word represents the bit of information that is asked for.

Although appositive clauses may seem similar to relative clauses, the two should not be confused. The initial elements of appositive clauses can never be omitted, whereas zero realisation of relative pronouns is possible if the relative pronoun functions as the object of the relative clause (see example (19h)). Another difference becomes apparent from a comparison of the head nouns in the examples under (19) and those under (20). While relative clauses allow for any kind of antecedent, the head nouns with appositive clause are much more restricted semantically. In all of the above examples the head nouns denote abstract concepts which can serve as empty 'shells' for statements, questions, etc., i.e. they work as a container for the proposition expressed in the appositive clause. The final and most characteristic and distinctive feature of appositive clauses is the fact that the appositive clause is identical in reference to the head noun that it postmodifies, i.e. it stands in a paraphrasing relation to the head: the appositive clause **is** the assumption in (20a), the problem in (20b), the conviction in (20c), and so on. Because of that it is possible to insert a form of BE between the head and the appositive clause, as is shown below for two of the above examples. Note, in contrast, that this is not possible with relative clauses as example (21) shows.

(20) a') the assumption is **that** ownership is absolute or it's not ownership
    b') the problem is **that** either he had to make a clean sweep [...] or he would have to consider the feasibility of selling the business

(21) the problem **that** clinicians have in caring for newborn infants (s2a-046:109)
    *the problem is **that** clinicians have in caring for newborn infants

In addition to postmodification by finite clauses, the English language also knows postmodification by **non-finite clauses**, i.e. postmodifying clauses that are introduced by a non-finite verb form. Recall from section 2.2.3 that non-finite verbs are those that do not carry tense distinction and number concord. Accordingly, a non-finite clause is a clause of which the verbal element is non-finite. In English we have three of these, namely *–ed*-participles, *-ing*-participles and infinitives. It follows that we can distinguish three kinds of non-finite clauses.

Examples of **–*ed*-participle and –*ing*-participle clauses** are given below.

(22) a) something **called** Tai Chi (s1a-004:072)
 b) the short sword **used** by Roman gladiators (w2c-010:009)
 c) a poll **published** yesterday in Dublin (w2e-004:091)
 d) a table **loaded** with presents (w2f-019:097)
 e) tourists **blocking** the pavement, **staring** heavenwards with their mouths open (w1b-009:109)
 f) researchers **looking into** this aspect of plants (w2b-030:105)
 g) a UN resolution **sanctioning** the use of force (w2e-004:051)

Quirk et al. (1985: 1263-1264) point out that both *-ed* and *-ing* clause can be related to relative clauses in which the relative pronoun is the (syntactic) subject of the relative clause. The noun phrase *something called Tai Chi*, for instance, corresponds to relative clauses of the following kind.

(22) a') something **which** is called Tai Chi
 something **which** was called Tai Chi
 something **which** has been called Tai Chi
 something ...

Similarly, the noun phrase *tourists blocking the pavement* relates to the following relative clauses.

(22) e') tourists **who** are blocking the pavement
 tourists **who** were blocking the pavement
 tourists **who** have been blocking the pavement
 tourists ...

However, as Quirk et al. (1985: 1263) point out, "*-ing* forms in postmodifying clauses should not be seen as abbreviated progressive forms in relative clauses". This becomes apparent with stative verbs, which cannot have a progressive form in the finite verb phrase. They occur as *-ing* forms in *-ing* clauses but not in any of the corresponding relative clauses. Consider example (23)

(23) so many Dutch people **wanting** to come here (s1a-021:217)
so many Dutch people **who** want to come here
so many Dutch people **who** wanted to come here
so many Dutch people ...
*so many Dutch people **who** are wanting to come here

In contrast to *-ed* and *-ing* clauses, the **infinitive clause** corresponds to relative clauses in which the relative pronoun functions as subject, object and adverbial; consider (24a, b, and c), respectively.

(24) a) a limousine **to take** him to the aeroplane (s1a-010:254)
 a') a limousine **that** takes him to the aeroplane
 b) the question **to ask** now is how did this happen? (BNC-BMF:711)
 b') the question **which** you should ask now is how did this happen?
 c) the time **to go** on external training courses (BNC-CBV:1292)
 c') the time **at which** you go on external training courses

A closer look at examples (22) to (24) reveals that non-finite clauses are less explicit postmodifiers than finite clauses. This shows in the fact that one non-finite postmodifying clause has several corresponding relative clauses. The reason for that lies in the tense, mood, aspect and voice distinctions that can be made in the finite verb phrase but not in the non-finite one. Postmodification by prepositional phrases is even less explicit since, not containing a verb, it does not provide the information that the verb form in the non-finite clause provides. Take a look at example (25).

(25) a) the pale, sullen girl **who stood** over by the teatrolley (BNC-ACB:2653)
 a') the pale, sullen girl **standing** over by the teatrolley
 b) the pale, sullen girl **over by the teatrolley**

The relative clause in (25a) provides information on the verbal action, the fact that the action happened in the past and the location, while (25b) is unspecific about the time of the action, and (25c) only informs us about the location. With regard to explicitness in postmodification we, thus, find a cline from relative clauses over non-finite clauses to prepositional phrases, with maximum, medium, and minimum informativity, respectively.

To conclude this chapter on the English noun phrase, Figure 4.2 below lists all its elements in their usual order (from top to bottom). Note that bidirectional arrows indicate that the elements in front and at the end are interchangeable as far as sequence is concerned.

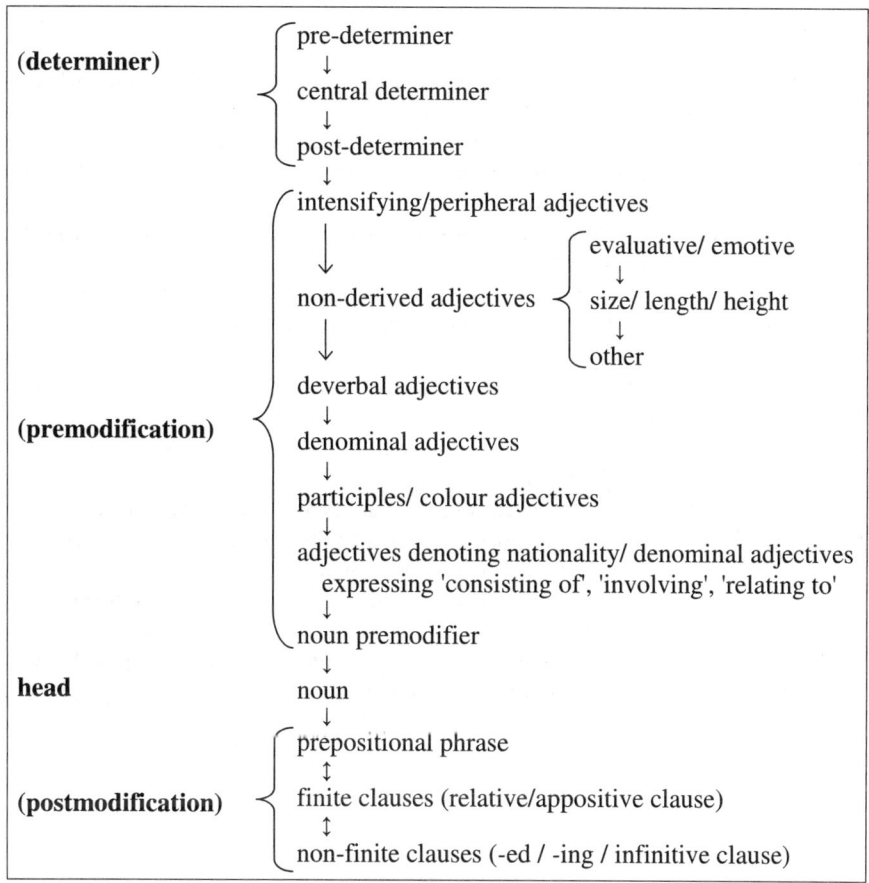

Figure 4.2: The elements of the English noun phrase in their usual order.

4.3 Further reading

Biber et al. (1999: 589 and 606) provide more detailed information on the frequencies of types of pre- and postmodification in different registers.

See Quirk et al. (1985: 1292-1296) for minor types of post-modification that have not been discussed in this chapter.

Aarts & Aarts (1982: ch. 3.2) provides a concise overview of the structure of the noun phrase.

4.4 Study questions

1. What is the head of the subject noun phrase in the clause *The beauty of eagles is stunning*? Apply the criteria discussed in the text.
2. Name the four basic slots in the structure of the noun phrase.
3. How many determiner-slots can be distinguished in the noun phrase? Give an illustrative example.
4. In which order would the premodifiers *Spanish, brown, beautiful, wood, long* occur in the frame *These _____ houses*?
5. In the phrase *that old woman's cat*, is the woman old or is the cat old? Use your knowledge of determiners and premodifiers to substantiate your analysis.
6. Give a structural analysis (either in terms of bracketing or a tree diagram) of the following noun phrase.
   The interest from the disabled people in the community who want to join in (s1a-033:086)
7. Explain the differences between relative clauses and appositive clauses.
8. In the phrase below, is the postmodifier a relative clause or an appositive clause? Give reasons to substantiate your claims.
   The conviction that the only hope for salvation is to have been 'born again'. (w2a-012:049)
9. Name the six types of postmodification presented in this chapter and give illustrative examples of each of them. What can you say about their explicitness?

5 Adjective, Adverb and Prepositional Phrase

The two previous chapters dealt with the most important phrases of the English language, the verb and the noun phrase. This chapter will give a short overview of the three remaining phrases, namely adjective, adverb and prepositional phrase.

5.1 The adjective phrase

Like the noun phrase, the adjective phrase can be defined with regard to its head, i.e. an adjective phrase is a phrase the head of which is an adjective. The adjective phrase is similar to the noun phrase in that it contains premodifiers and postmodifiers. It differs from the noun phrase in that it does not contain determiners. The basic structure of the adjective phrase, accordingly is 'premodification - head - postmodification', consider the examples under (1) (the head is in bold print):

(1) a) more   **traditional**   (w1a-012:043)
    b) almost   **impossible**   (w2b-016:067)
    c) hugely   **unprofitable**   (w2b-016:048)
    d) very   **restricted**   (s1a-001:104)
    e) far more **simple**   (s2a-034:050)
    f)   **bigger**   than that (s1a-001:054)
    g)   **aware**   of how they can work with the disabled student (s1a-001:110)
    h)   **uninterested**   in conquering and controlling Fiji (w1a-012:010)
    i)   **unlikely**   to appreciate the irony of their situation (w2e-008:002)
    j) much   **cheaper**   than anybody else (s1a-010:036)
    k) very   **surprised**   at their commitment (s1a-005:157)
    l) quite   **happy**   to send their daughter to a boys' school (s1a-012:223)
    m) far too   **late**   for tinkering with the environment (w2b-013:004)

As can be seen, adjectives (in addition to occurring on their own) can be premodified, postmodified or both. Aarts and Aarts (1982: 67) point to two special classes of adjectives. The first are adjectives that never occur with a modifier.

Examples are *latter* in *the latter view* (w2a-006:081) or *former* in *the former chief of defence staff* (s2a-019:022). Such adjectives only occur as noun-phrase premodifiers, i.e. in attributive but never in predicative function (see section 2.2.4). The second class are adjectives that cannot occur without modification, more specifically without postmodifier. Examples are adjectives like *fond* as in *quite fond of him* (s1a-049:025) or *averse* as in *averse to securing the dispatch* (w2b-015:068).

As regards **adjective premodifiers**, this function is fulfilled by **adverb phrases** only. As the examples in (1a to e) show we are mostly dealing with simple adverb phrases that just consist of a head, although longer 2-word adverb phrases are also possible.

The main **adjective postmodifiers** are prepositional phrases, finite clauses and non-finite clauses. Examples of **prepositional phrases** as postmodifiers are given below.

(2) a) involved in the Mike Heafy project (s1a-002:001)
    b) important for someone (s1a-003:019)
    c) visible through the skin (w2d-017:072)
    d) clean of the sawdust (w2d-017:075)
    e) important to the Turkish and Cypriotic communities, where it employs thousands of people (w2e-002:080)
    f) full of tales about a surge of popular enthusiasm for Halloween at its expense (w2e-003:061)

In addition to prepositional phrases, there are different kinds of **finite clauses** as adjective postmodifiers, namely postmodification by *that*-clause (3a and b) or by *wh*-clause (3c to g).

(3) a) conscious that your society is older than my department by some forty years (s2b-045:005)
    b) surprised you didn't all make it a group effort and all go and look at all your graphs and in that way save all doing hundreds of points (s1a-008:090)
    c) (not yet) known where the jobs will be cut (s2b-015:085)
    d) doubtful whether any of these large parrots live within its boundary (w2b-028:084)
    e) (not) sure how funding would be applied (s1a-035:094)
    f) (not) sure who he was talking to (BNC-CG3:1151)
    g) uncertain where he was ultimately headed (BNC-ECK:200)
    aware what's going on in your field nationally (BNC-KRP:949)

Adjective, Adverb and Prepositional Phrase

In some cases, the conjunction *that* can be omitted. This is what has happened in (3b). Here, we could also have *surprised that you didn't* .... Examples (3c to h) show that all kinds of *wh*-words can be used to introduce postmodifying finite clauses. A special kind of finite clause occurs after comparative adjectives.

(4) a) taller than his brother was at that age (BNC-H0Y:1060)
    b) younger than Beatrix was (BNC-G0N:1264)
    c) (more) dangerous than we realize (BNC-FSK:683)

Here, the postmodifying clause is introduced by the conjunction *than*. In some cases, the clause can be reduced by leaving the verb out, as in the examples below.

(4) a') taller than his brother (BNC-ALX:480)
    b') younger than Bridget (BNC-HTR:1013)

However, in these cases it is not clear whether we are actually dealing with a reduced clause or the structure '*than* + NP'. Especially since some comparative clauses cannot be reduced (without a substantial change of meaning), as the one in (4c).

(4) c') *(more) dangerous than we

The only type of **non-finite clause** in postmodification is the *to*-infinitive **clause**.

(5) a) able to use some French (s1a-014:113)
    b) desperate to stop him getting there (s2b-043:060)
    c) reluctant to get overexposed (w2c-013:012)
    d) uncertain what to do (s1b-040:009)
    e) (not) sure where to find your nearest Careers Office (BNC-CHB:2432)
    f) uncertain who to mate with (BNC-HTT:347)
    g) easier for Adam to concentrate (s1a-004:020)
    h) hard for us to understand (s2b-029:015)
    i) (too) familiar for her to believe that she wouldn't always have the spectacle to behold (w2f-010:070)

(5a to c) instantiate the variant of the bare *to*-infinitive clause. In (5d to f) the infinitive clause is introduced by a *wh*-word. In (5g to i) we see that the infinitive clause is introduced by the conjunction *for*. This is because the clause itself contains an overt subject, i.e. in (5g) it is Adam who concentrates on something, in (5h) it is we that understand something, and in (5i) a female person (*she*) believes or does not believe that something is likely to happen.

The examples in (1j to m) have already shown that pre- and postmodification can occur together in an adjective phrase (which shouldn't be a surprise for you). From such cases we have to distinguish instances of **discontinuous modification**, where part of the modifier occurs before the head and part after the head. Some of these are discussed below (see Aarts and Aarts 1982: 121-122 for a more detailed overview).

The first is the type '*so* + **adjective** + *that*-**clause**'.

(6) a) so huge that you can only tackle them [problems] by narrowing down the scope (s1b-007:246)
    b) so weak they cannot even brush flies away from their faces (w2c-002:049)

Again, we see that the conjunction can be omitted: (6a) would be perfect without *that*, just as (6b) would be with *that*. At first sight it is not clear why examples like the ones above warrant a category on their own. After all, could we not just treat these as instances of a premodification by *so* with additional postmodification by a *that*-clause, as we would the following examples?

(7) a) so upset that they weren't allowed to do what the Aaronites could do (s1b-001:023)
    b) so confident she'd got him (s1a-020:122)

The same analysis would not work with the examples under (6). This becomes apparent if we take a closer look at the semantics of the phrases. The adjective head and the *that*-clause stand in a causal relation. With the examples under (6) the head provides the reason for what happens in the clause, i.e. because the problems were so huge they can only be tackled by narrowing down the scope, etc. This causal relationship is reversed in the examples under (7). In (7a), for instance, the clause provides the reason for the feeling denoted in the adjectival head, i.e. they are upset because they were not allowed to do what the Aaronites could do. Of course it is not always easy to tell which is the cause and which is the consequence: in (7b), for instance, the person's confidence might be a result of her having got him or she might be more confident now that she has got him, although the first analysis seems more likely given the surrounding context (which is not shown here).

Similar questions arise with the second type of discontinuous modification, namely the pattern '*too* + **adjective** + *to*-**infinitive clause**', as exemplified in (8).

(8) a) too late to enrol this year (w1b-022:166)
    b) too complex to be stated in simple non-esoteric language (w2a-017:050)
    c) too immense for us to try and cope with the other amount of information we have to cover (s2a-052:044)

Again, the question is whether these are not simple cases of premodification by *too* plus postmodification by a *to*-infinitive clause. And again, the answer is 'no', as an analysis of the semantic relations involved makes clear. In all of the instances above, the adjectival head denotes the reason for the content expressed in the following clause. In (8a) it is impossible to enrol this year because it is too late, in (8b) something cannot be stated in simple non-esoteric language because it is too complex, and so on. In the examples below (modified versions of (5b and c), a different relationship holds.

(9) a) too desperate to stop him getting there
    b) too reluctant to get overexposed

In (9a) the person's desperation to stop him getting there has reached a level that is too strong. Similarly, in (9b) the reluctance to get overexposed is too strong. In both cases, there is no causal relationship involved whatsoever. In these examples, the semantics also become apparent from a structural description, which would look as follows.

(9) a') [too [desperate [to stop him getting there]]]
    b') [too [reluctant [to get overexposed]]]

In the examples under (4) we have seen the use of postmodification with comparative adjectives. These are used to express that something has more or less of the quality denoted by the adjective. If we want to express that two entities show a given quality to a similar extent, the structure **'as + adjective + *as* + comparative clause or noun phrase'** is used. Consider the examples below.

(10) a) as horrified (by it) as Professor Standfast had been (w2f-006:226)
     b) as inclined as his mother (to see a foreign hand at work) (w2b-011:083)

To conclude this discussion, Figure 5.1 sums up the structure of the adjective phrase.

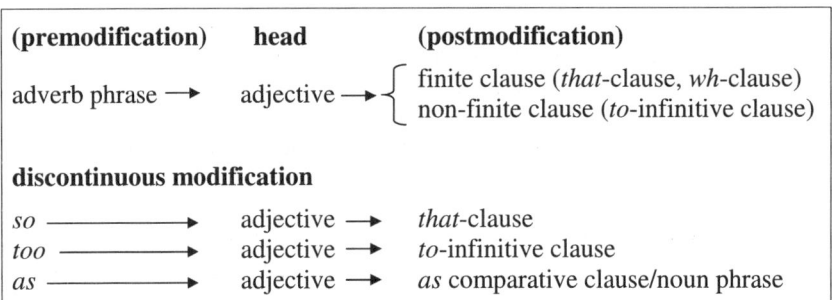

Figure 5.1: The structure of the adjective phrase.

5.2 The adverb phrase

Adverb phrases are structurally similar to adjective phrase in consisting of premodifier, head (realised by an adverb) and postmodifier, although they are more restricted with regard to the structural realisation of the individual functions.

Premodification in adverb phrases is usually realised by **intensifying adverb phrases**, which generally consist of one intensifying adverb only, as can be seen below.

(11) a) fairly quickly (s1a-003:109)
 b) very rarely (s1a-002:064)
 c) purely linguistically (w1b-006:113)
 d) extremely hard (w1b-001:004)

With regard to **postmodification**, adverb phrases are similar to adjective phrases. Just like comparative adjectives, comparative adverbs can be postmodified by a **finite clause** or by a **noun phrase introduced by *than***, see examples (12a to c) and (12d to f), respectively.

(12) a) (they train) harder than we play (BNC-A80:249)
 b) (he went on his rounds) earlier than he should have done (BNC-ACB:2029)
 c) (he [...] arrived) later than he intended (BNC-APM:2894)
 d) (nation usually speaks) louder than ideology (BNC-AHN:779)
 e) (nobody fought) harder than Jimmy (BNC-A0V:730)
 f) (profits rise) faster than a certain rate (BNC-A69:489)

In some cases, postmodification by noun phrase could be regarded as postmodification by a reduced finite clause, as shown in (12d' and e').

(12) d') (nation usually speaks) louder than ideology does
     e') (nobody fought) harder than Jimmy did

A similar version of (12f) is also possible, as is seen in (12f').

(12) f') (profits rise) faster than a certain rate does

Note, however, that the original in (12f) allows two possible readings. One is made explicit in (12f'): profits as well as a certain rate rise and the profits rise faster. The other (and maybe more likely) interpretation is that the rate is understood as a measure of the rise of the profits, similar to a speed limit in a phrase like *he drove faster than 50 km/h*. In the end, context has to decide whether this analysis is plausible.

Note also that often it is not possible to reduce the non-finite clause to a noun phrase, as examples (12a to c) make clear. In these cases, the result either is a change of meaning (as in (12a')) or a meaningless clause, as in (12b' and c').

(12) a') (they train) harder than we
     b') (he went on his rounds) earlier than he
     c') (he […] arrived) later than he

Adverb phrases show the same types of discontinuous modification as adjective phrases. The first type is '*so* + **adverb** + *that*-**clause**'.

(13) a) (you must never diet) so quickly that you lose the muscle tissue (BNC-AD0:428)
     b) (they do it) so rarely that it is good for them (BNC-CFK:23)
     c) (they concentrate) so hard that they don't recognise that they are drifting away (BNC-A0H:1102)

The second pattern is '*too* + **adverb** + *to*-**infinitive clause**'.

(14) a) (it happened) too fast to feel much (BNC-A3A:163)
     b) (it had fallen) too slowly to break (BNC-CDB:1894)
     c) (He'd been working) too hard to spend time with women (BNC-BP1:158)

In contrast to the first two patterns of discontinuous modification in the adjective phrase, we do not have any potential ambiguity here, as adverbs do not allow postmodification by *that*- or *to*-infinitive clause. As far as semantics is concerned we can, again, posit a causal relationship between the non-finite clause and the rest of the sentence. In (14a) it was impossible to feel much because something happened so fast, just as in (14b) something did not break because it had fallen too slowly. Note, however, that such structures may be ambiguous. (14c), for instance, can be understood as an instance of the discontinuous modification pattern ('he could not spend time with women because he had been working too hard'), but it can also be understood as a clause containing an adverbial, which becomes apparent if we paraphrase it like this: 'he had been working too hard at trying to get a woman, which is why he failed'.

Another problem is the distinction of instances of the above discontinuous modification pattern and what is called 'catenative verbs'. The term stems from Latin *catina* meaning 'chain'. So, catenative verbs are verbs that occur or create chains of verbs. Examples of such chains are *I happened to be the only Junior left in the Chambers* (w2f-011:023) or *he wanted to serve the Government* (s2b-006:096). Such verbs can lead to confusion, as the examples below show.

(15) a) a lawyer [...] may not try too hard to reconcile husband and wife.
 (BNC-ABH:775)
 b) But if manufacturers were to try too hard to come up with new ideas we'd be constantly faced with designs to rival Gibson's semi-mythical Moderne and Burns' Flyte in the grossness stakes.
 (BNC-C9H:1193)

The above examples do not show instances of discontinuous modification but catenatives, namely *try to reconcile* and *try to come up with*. In both cases, we have an adverb phrase immediately following the verb form of *try*. This phrase functions as an adverbial and describes the manner in which the person/s tries/try, i.e. too hard. It is inserted between the two verbs in the catenative structure. That is, the following *to*-infinitive is not part of a non-finite clause modifying the adverb but part of the catenative structure. This is obvious with (15a), where a paraphrase of the kind discussed with examples under (14) does not work: *'he could not reconcile husband and wife because the lawyer may not try too hard'. With (15b) we have a case of ambiguity between both analyses. A paraphrase like 'they won't come up with new ideas because the manufactures try too hard' is possible, but it is unlikely considering the surrounding context. Another piece of evidence that suggests that we are dealing with catenatives is the fact that in both cases it is possible to move the adverb phrase towards the end of the clause (although it may lead to other kinds of ambiguity or sound clumsy).

(15) a') a lawyer [...] may not try ___ to reconcile husband and wife <u>too hard</u>.
    b') But if manufacturers were to try ___ to come up with new ideas <u>too hard</u> [...]

The final type of discontinuous modification to be discussed here is the pattern **'*as* + adverb + *as* comparative clause or noun phrase'**.

(16) a) (He yelled the name) as loudly as he could (BNC-ACW:1742)
    b) (they often vanish) as swiftly as they arise. (BNC-CRK:610)
    c) (he screamed) as loudly as his horse. (BNC-CMP:44)
    d) (his men have done) just as badly as the old guard. (BNC-ABF:2640)

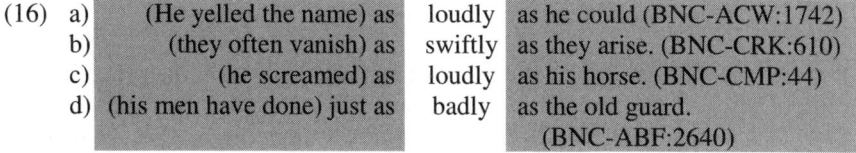

Figure 5.2 sums up the structure of the adverb phrase.

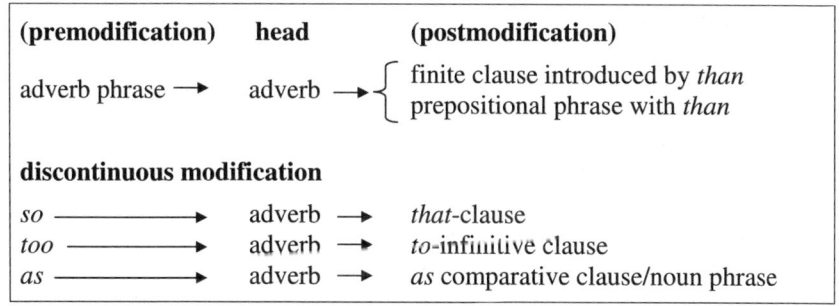

Figure 5.2: The structure of the adverb phrase.

5.3 The prepositional phrase

The phrases we have discussed so far, i.e. verb, noun, adjective and adverb phrase all can be reduced to one element only, namely their head. This is what is called an **endocentric phrase**, which means having the centre in itself. Take a look at the following examples.

(17) a) Within a short time the lowland forests *will have vanished* from the Philippines. (w2b-028:045)
    a') Within a short time the lowland forests ~~will have~~ vanished from the Philippines.
    b) By 1290 *the problems associated with Edward's authority and status in the duchy of Aquitaine* were becoming more acute. (w2a-010:084)

b')By 1290 ~~the~~ problems ~~associated with Edward's authority and status in the duchy of Aquitaine~~ were becoming more acute.
c) The Levites were *so upset that they weren't allowed to do what the Aaronites could do.* (s1b-001:023)
c')The Levites were ~~so~~ upset ~~that they weren't allowed to do what the Aaronites could do~~.
d) He'd been working *too hard to spend time with women.* (BNC-BP1:158)
d')He'd been working ~~too~~ hard ~~to spend time with women~~.

Prepositional phrases are different in that respect. They form the group of **exocentric phrases**; literally (and maybe somewhat misleadingly), phrases that have their centre outside themselves. Practically, this means that all prepositional phrases consist of exactly two functional elements, namely a head, which is always realised by a preposition (bold in the following examples), and a prepositional complement usually realised by a noun phrase (underlined in the following examples). And it is not possible to replace the whole phrase by any one of its two members.

(18) **for** <u>a while</u> (s1a-001:022)
      with <u>somebody who is in a wheelchair</u> (s1a-001:060)
      of <u>the places</u> (s1a-028:264)
      into <u>dance therapy</u> (s1a-001:112)
      in <u>economic conditions</u> (w2c-013:083)
      on <u>the Australian market</u> (w2c-013:072)
      at <u>the operating level</u> (w2c-013:081)
      around <u>the world</u> (w1b-002:016)

Although prepositions generally consist of one word only, the English language also has complex prepositions (recall the discussion of *in front of* in section 1.1). Some examples are given below.

(19) **in front of** <u>Mason</u> (s2a-009:030)
      in terms of <u>the way that you have to dance</u> (s1a-002:123)
      instead of <u>fertilizing the land</u> (w2b-027:015)
      in lieu of <u>the money</u> (s1b-063-102)

It is true that noun phrases are the most frequent realisations of the prepositional complement, but the following two elements also occur with some frequency, namely *wh*-clause and *-ing*-participle clause.

(20) **aware of** how they can work with the disabled student (s1a-001:110)
      from what I have said (s2a-065:056)
      through trying things out (s1a-001:062)
      towards earning extra pension (w2d-002:053)

The most frequent kind of premodification in prepositional phrases is that by an adverb phrase (usually consisting of a single adverb only), as shown below.

(21) a) 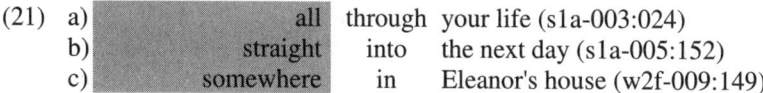 through your life (s1a-003:024)
     b) into the next day (s1a-005:152)
     c) in Eleanor's house (w2f-009:149)

Figure 5.3 sums up the (fairly simple) structure of the prepositional phrase.

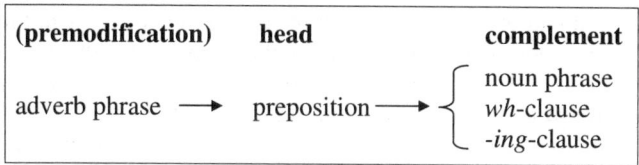

Figure 5.3: The structure of the prepositional phrase.

5.4 Three sample analyses

So far we have only discussed the structure of phrases in isolation and we have not yet looked in detail at how phrases of different kinds interact to form larger phrases. This section explores this aspect, focusing on the hierarchical relations that phrases enter into. We start with a fairly simple phrase as our first example (see also the discussion of this phrase in section 4.2.2).

(22) The very real and crucial psychological dimension. (w2a-017:010)

The head of this phrase is the noun *dimension*, i.e. we are dealing with a noun phrase. This noun phrase has the definite article *the* as determiner, more specifically as central determiner. Since there are no other determiners the string *very real and crucial psychological* must be the premodification of the head. The question, of course, is that as to the internal structure of the premodifier and its relation to the head. At first sight one might think that we are dealing with two coordinated adjective phrases, namely *very real* and *crucial psychological*. This would then lead to a structure as shown below.

(22')   [The [[very real] and [crucial psychological] dimension]]

A look at the internal structure of the two supposedly coordinated adjective phrases, however, makes clear that this cannot be. The first adjective phrase is in line with the description given in Figure 5.1, since it consists of an adverb premodifier and an adjectival head. The second, however, is problematic: we have seen that adjectives can only be premodified by adverbs but not by adjectives, i.e. the string *crucial psychological* cannot be an adjective phrase, and, accordingly, we have to rethink our first analysis. More specifically, we have to assign new functions to *crucial* and *psychological*. Since *psychological* is an adjective, it can serve as a premodifier of the noun phrase head *dimension*, i.e. we are talking about a *psychological dimension*. The question now is how the adjective phrases *very real* and *crucial* fit into this picture. Basically, there are two alternatives. Firstly, *very real*, *crucial* and *psychological* serve as modifiers of the head *dimension*. This means we have a 'flat' structure, with the three adjective phrases in coordination. This analysis, however, is not likely as in that case we would have the coordinator *and* between the second and the third adjective phrase, i.e. *the very real, crucial and psychological dimension*. As a consequence, the second alternative is the only plausible one, namely that we have a coordination of the two adjective phrases *very real* and *crucial*, and together these premodify the noun phrase *psychological dimension*. The structure of this phrase is depicted in Figure 5.4 below.

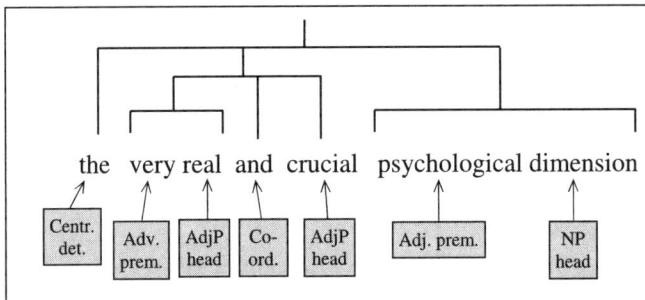

Figure 5.4: The structure of the noun phrase <u>the very real and crucial psychological dimension.</u>

As another example consider the slightly more complex noun phrase under (23).

(23)   The driving force behind the new interest in hearing voices. (s2b-038:46)

The head of this noun phrase is the noun *force*. *The* is a central determiner and *driving* is an *-ing*-participle premodifying the head *force*. In the postmodifying string we have two prepositional phrases, namely *behind the new interest* and *in hearing voices*. Again, the question is how do these relate to each other and how do they relate to the head. Obviously, the first prepositional phrase postmodifies the head, i.e. we are talking about the force that is behind the new interest. The second prepositional phrase *in hearing voices* cannot be a postmodifier to the head only, since a string like *the force in hearing voices* does not make much sense. Consequently, we treat it as a postmodifier to the noun *interest* that is part of the preceding prepositional phrase, i.e. *the interest in hearing voices*. So, we see that the head noun *force* is postmodified by one prepositional phrase only. It consists of the preposition *behind* and the prepositional complement *the new interest in hearing voices*. The prepositional complement has a somewhat intricate structure, being a noun phrase with the central determiner *the*, an adjective premodifier *new*, the head *interest* and a postmodifying prepositional phrase *in hearing voices*. This last prepositional phrase can be analysed as consisting of the preposition *in* and an *-ing*-clause as prepositional complement. All in all the structure of example (23) looks like this.

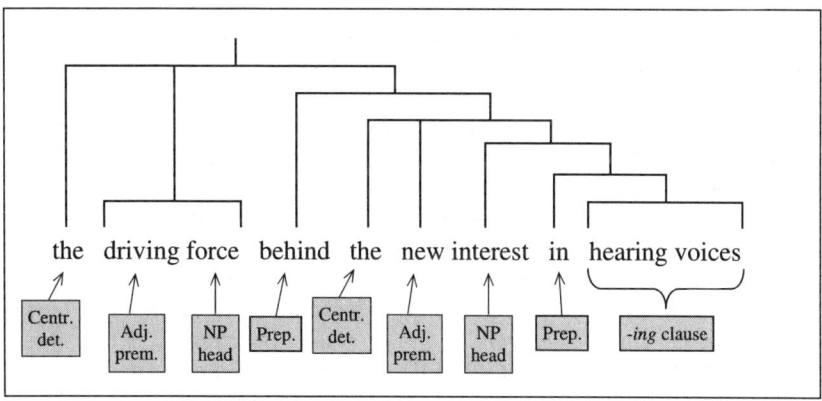

Figure 5.5: The structure of the noun phrase <u>the driving force behind the new interest in hearing voices</u>.

This analysis deserves some further discussion. Both *force* and *interest* are premodified by an adjective (or an *-ing*-participle) and postmodified by a prepositional phrase. Notice, however, that the premodifying adjective occurs at different positions in the tree. The adjective premodifier *driving* forms a constituent with *force*, which is then further postmodified by the prepositional phrase *behind the new interest in hearing voices*. In contrast, the analysis above assumes that *interest* forms a constituent with the prepositional phrase *in hearing voice*, which is then further premodified by the adjective *new*. That is, although the ingredients are identical, we have two different structural analyses, namely '[[Adj N] PP]' versus '[Adj [N PP]]'. Semantic considerations make this distinction plausible. In the first analysis we are not talking about a force behind the new interest in hearing voices that is driving something, but about the force that drives this particular new interest. That is, it is a particular driving force that stands behind the new interest. This is what is expressed in the analysis above. Another way to justify this analysis would be to consider *driving force* as a compound noun, in which case the problem would not have arisen in the first place. In contrast, in the second analysis we are talking about the interest in hearing voices and we say that this particular kind of interest is new, i.e. *new* premodifies the whole NP *interest in hearing voices*.

As a final example we will discuss the following noun phrase, which is adapted from an actual example from the ICE-GB corpus.

(24) All these many interests from the most severely disabled people in the community who want to join in. (adapted from s1a-033:086)

The head of this noun phrase is *interest*. The phrase does not contain any premodifiers but three determiners, namely the predeterminer *all*, the central determiner *these* and the postdeterminer *many*. Again, the head is postmodified by a prepositional phrase with a fairly complex internal structure. The prepositional complement is a noun phrase with the head *people*. This head is preceded by the determiner *the* and premodified by the adjective phrase *most severely disabled*, which, in turn, consists of the head *disabled* and the premodifying adverb phrase *most severely*. The head of the noun phrase, *people*, is postmodified by the string *in the community who want to join in*. This string consists of two potential noun-phrase-head postmodifiers, namely the prepositional phrase *in the community* and the relative clause *who want to join in*. Again, the question is how these relate to each other and to the head of the noun phrase. From a semantic point of view, it does not seem reasonable to interpret the relative clause as a postmodifier of the noun *community* in the prepositional phrase *in the community*. Rather, it modifies the whole string *the most severely disabled people in the community*, i.e. it is this particular group of people who want to join in. The structure of this noun phrase is given in Figure 5.6.

Adjective, Adverb and Prepositional Phrase 103

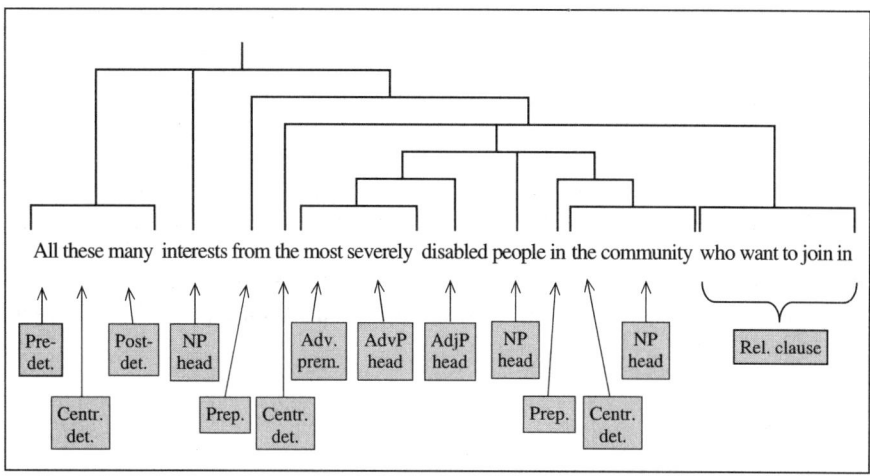

Figure 5.6 The structure of the noun phrase <u>all these many interests from the most severely disabled people in the community who want to join in</u>.

A note is in order here concerning the relative positions of the modifiers of the noun *people* in that phrase. The above analysis does not show any kind of subordination. Instead, both adjective premodifier and prepositional phrase postmodifier are seen as modifiers on the same level of structure. This can be expressed through the following paraphrase as 'the people that are most severely disabled and that live in the community', i.e. both modifying strings modify the head noun itself. In the above case, however, alternative analyses would also be possible. We could paraphrase the relevant noun phrase as 'the people that are most severely disabled who live in the community', i.e. there is a group of most severely disabled people and we are talking about a subgroup of them, namely those that live in the community, not those that live somewhere else. This analysis would be accounted for by the following structure:

(24')   [the [[most severely disabled] people] in the community]

That is, the adjective phrase together with the head noun is postmodified by the prepositional phrase. An alternative analysis has the head noun and its postmodification premodified by the adjective phrase as shown below:

(24")   [the [most severely disabled [people [in the community]]]]

This analysis would have the paraphrase 'the people that live in the community who are most severely disabled'; we have a group of people, namely those that live in the community, and we are interested in a subgroup of these, namely those that are most severely disabled. Which of the three analyses is the 'correct' one cannot be said – the string is ambiguous and different structures can be ascribed to it. Note, however, that the different structures do not have any influence on the semantic interpretation. From a set-theoretical point of view all three interpretations lead to the same result, namely there is a group of people which at the same time is most severely disabled and lives in the community. Nevertheless, this example should be taken as evidence that it lies in the nature of language data to be ambiguous and that multiple analyses are possible and often cannot be ignored.

5.5 Further reading

Aarts & Aarts (1982: chs. 3, 5 and 6.2) as well as Greenbaum (1996: 288-304) provide an overview of the structure of the phrases discussed in this section.

Quirk et al. (1985: 1296-1300 and 1342-1349) discuss in some detail problems that arise with the structural description of multiple modification in phrases.

5.6 Study questions

1. What are endocentric and exocentric phrases and which kind of phrase belongs to which class? Give examples.
2. Name the main postmodifiers of adjectives and give examples.
3. What are the three kinds of discontinuous modification in the adjective phrase? Give examples.
4. What are the two kinds of postmodification that we find in the adverb phrase? Give one example each.
5. What are the two obligatory elements in a prepositional phrase? What are possible realisations of the second constituent? Give examples.
6. Give illustrative examples of prepositional phrases with premodifying adverb phrases and premodifying noun phrases.
7. Is the string *too complex to be stated in simple non-esoteric language* a case of an adjective phrase with pre- and postmodification or a case of discontinuous modification? Substantiate your answer with the help of semantic arguments.
8. Give a structural analysis of the following phrase: *his many terribly stupid utterances on this important subject which were difficult to understand*

6 Clauses and Sentences

In the second chapter we looked at words as the basic building blocks of syntactic structures. In chapters 3 to 5, then, we explored how words of different word classes fulfil functions on the phrase level, namely as head, determiner, premodifier, or postmodifier. That is, we saw how an assemblage of words creates a structural unit on the next higher level, namely the level of phrases. In addition, we have seen in section 5.4 how phrases can also have functions within other phrases. In the present chapter we will see how phrases form the next higher structural unit, namely clauses or simple sentences. And just as phrases can be embedded in other phrases, so can clauses be embedded in other clauses; in that case we speak of a 'complex sentence', e.g. *That syntax is boring is not true*, where the subject of the whole clause is a clause itself, i.e. *that syntax is boring*. If more than one clause is co-ordinated, we speak of 'compound sentences', e.g. *Syntax is not boring but it is demanding*. Figure 6.1 below shows how the structural units interact on different levels of linguistic description. The simple arrows mean 'form' whereas the rectangular arrows mean 'are embedded in'.

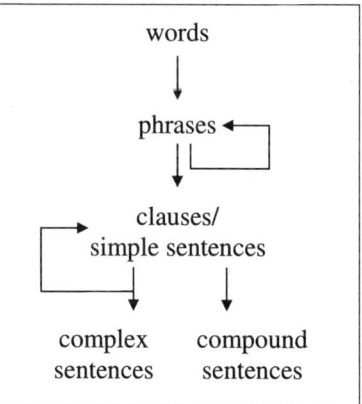

Figure 6.1: The interaction of linguistic units on different levels of description.

Note that there is a difference between the rectangular arrows on the phrase level and on the clause level. In the first case, we are dealing with two phenomena. Phrases are put together to form clauses (the straight arrow), as in the clause *[[The study of syntax] is [very interesting]]*, and one phrase can be embedded in another phrase (the rectangular arrow), as in the phrase *[the study [of [English syntax]]]*. In the second case, we are dealing with one phenomenon only: it is by embedding one clause into another clause that we form complex sentences, as in *[[That syntax is boring] is not true]*. That is why the rectangular arrow and the straight arrow are merged.

6.1 The clause elements

In the previous chapters we talked about the functional slots in phrases. For example, the noun phrase consists of determiners, premodifiers, a head, and postmodifiers. In a similar way, each type of clause can be described with regard to the functional elements that it contains. These are referred to as 'clause elements'.

6.1.1 Verb

The most important and most central constituent is the verb, V for short. Note, that here we are not talking about the word class 'verb' but about a functional constituent of the clause. Admittedly, this constituent is always realised by a verb phrase, and therefore consists of verbs only; but still, it is important to keep in mind that we are dealing with concepts on different levels of description, and these levels have to be kept apart. The V constituent denotes the action that is described in the clause. It is the most central of the clause constituents for the following three reasons: firstly, it is the only constituent that can be found in virtually all clauses. Secondly, it usually occurs in medial position in the clause, i.e. it is central in that other constituents occur to the left and the right. Thirdly, the V constituent determines what other constituents are needed to make the clause grammatically correct. We will discuss these aspects in more detail in section 6.2 below, for now we will just look at some examples; the V constituent is in bold print.

(1) That's the challenge. (sa1-001:042)
Chalutsky **fought** unsuccessfully for a resolution. (s2b-042:072)
But some ships **come** occasionally from as far afield as Hull. (s2b-42:030)
People **would get** full counselling before starting the process. (w2c-018:082)
I **do remember** Betty vaguely. (w2f-020:210)
More time **should have been given** to sanctions. (s2b-018:093)
Look! (s1a-010:184)

6.1.2 Subject

The second most important constituent in the clause is the subject (S). With the exception of imperative clauses, as the last example under (1), usually all clauses need to have a subject. There are various characteristics that are typical of subjects, and we will discuss each of them in turn.

The first is the **'agent'** criterion. Consider the examples below.

(2) a) **The House** will acknowledge the extraordinary change in central and eastern Europe. (s1b-054:014)
   b) **A person seeking admission as an Occasional student** should obtain a form of application from the Assistant Registrar of the School. (w2d-007:110)
   c) **Matching the speed of your bike to the differing pace of the instructor** will show you how to handle your bike in slow-moving traffic. (s2a-054:118)
   d) **To list and describe them all** would take too much space here and would be confusing. (w2a-037:055)

In all of these four cases, the string in bold print denotes the doer of the action described in the rest of the clause. In (2a), for instance, *The House* acknowledges something, and in (2b) a particular kind of person has to do something, and so on. The 'agent' criterion, thus, makes reference to the semantic role that a phrase has. However, it does not work with all kinds of subjects, as the examples below show.

(3) a) **She** smells I mean like really nice. (s1a-085:025)
   b) **This** tastes lovely. (s1a-022:309)
   c) **The flight pattern** consisted of a series of straight and level runs. (w2a-029:045)

The verbs in (3a to c) are called 'stative' verbs, i.e. they describe states in which the subject of the clause is, such as the state of smelling nice, of tasting lovely, or of consisting of something. Obviously, with such stative verbs we cannot really speak of an action that is going on, and it is difficult to regard the subject as an agent in that case. In addition, sometimes the agent is not the subject of the clause, as the following passive clause shows.

(4) a) Their comments were described by Harry Fletcher. (w2c-001:074)

In (4a) we have two possible candidates for the subject, namely *their comments* and *Harry Fletcher*. The doer of the action obviously is the person called Harry

Fletcher; he is the one that describes the comments, i.e. he is the agent. Other criteria (see below for details), however, clearly identify the first noun phrase as the subject. A solution to this problem is provided by the distinction of 'syntactic subject' versus 'psychological subject'. While the agent criterion (and the following 'aboutness' criterion) makes reference to the second interpretation of the term 'subject', formal and distributional criteria (to be discussed below) focus on an understanding of 'subject' as a syntactic phenomenon. To sum up, we have seen that although many subjects encode the semantic role 'agent', we also find clauses which do not have this semantic role. Furthermore, in some cases, the semantic role 'agent' does not always coincide with the syntactic subject.

The next criterion, **'aboutness'**, is also of a semantic kind but on a more general level. It draws on a distinction introduced by Aristotle between the subject of the sentence and its predicate: the subject is who or what the sentence is about, and the predicate is what we say about the subject. If you take a look at the examples under (2) and (3) again, you will find that each of the sentences is about the subject in that either it describes what the subject does or it describes a feature of the subject. Again, the aboutness criterion does not manage to characterise all subjects that we find in authentic language data, as the examples below show.

(5) a) **There** is no evidence for what went on in the great majority of parishes. (w2a-006:051)
   b) **There** is drugs in the book. (s1b-024:123)
   c) **It** seems to me that that was the nub of the problem. (s2a-065:060)

The first two sentences are examples of what is called 'existential *there*'. These sentences merely state the existence of the entity or entities referred to after the verb, i.e. a particular kind of evidence and drugs. It is important to note that the word *there* in these cases does not refer to a location. This becomes most apparent in example (5b), where another location is given by the prepositional phrase *in the book*. The point is that *there* does not refer to anything which the clause could be about. That is, the aboutness criterion fails in these two cases. Similarly, in (5c) the pronoun *it* does not stand for another noun phrase, it is an example of 'non-referential *it*', i.e. *it* does not refer to something and, accordingly, the whole sentence cannot be about the subject *it*.

In some cases it is difficult to tell what the clause is supposed to be about.

(6) a) Last night **I** was ready to tip beer over one of them. (w1b-005:144)
   b) Hardbacks **I** wouldn't lend to anyone. (s1a-013:087)

With these cases it could be argued that the clause is not about the subject *I* but about the constituent that occurs before the subject, i.e. about *last night* and what happened then and about *hardbacks* and the value that they have for somebody.

Fortunately, there is a whole set of formal and distributional criteria that characterise the subject of the clause. The first is that the subject usually is a **noun phrase**: in ICE-GB we find 108,391 instances of subjects, the vast majority of which, namely 107,502, are realised by noun phrases. Note, however, that impressive though these figures may look, we have to be aware of the fact that other functional constituents, for instance the direct object, are also often realised by noun phrases. If a constituent is a noun phrase we cannot automatically conclude that this constituent is the subject. Rather, if a constituent is not a noun phrase then we can be fairly safe to conclude that this constituent is not the subject of the clause. But of course, we also find that subjects may be realised by other units, for instance clauses, as in examples (2c and d), where the subject is realised by what is called a nominal clause (see section 6.4 for details).

More reliable is the second distributional criterion: usually the subject is the **first noun phrase** in the sentence. This is true for most of the examples discussed under (2) and (3), but counterexamples can also be found, as can be seen below.

(7) a) Every day **she** goes out at six. (s1a-019:193)
    b) Last night **I** was ready to tip beer over one of them. (w1b-005:144)
    c) Next door, **Hugo Dichter** paces up and down his room. (w2f-016:093)
    d) Hardbacks **I** wouldn't lend to anyone. (s1a-013:087)

Criterion number three holds for any subject. It states that the subject determines the form of the verb as regards number, i.e. we have **'number concord'** between subject and verb: if the subject is singular, then the form of the finite verb in the verb phrase has to be singular, too. If the subject is plural, we have a plural form of the verb. This criterion was applied in our discussion of example (5b) above, *there is drugs in the book*. Because the finite verb has a singular form, *drugs* cannot be the subject. Unfortunately, this criterion is only helpful to some extent, as a clear singular marking, with most verbs, only shows in their third person present tense form. None of the other verb forms show a distinction between singular or plural. With examples like the following the 'number concord' criterion does not work, as all verb forms are in simple past.

(8) a) I heard that story as well. (s1a-065:020)
    b) They bought a piece to go in their window. (s1a-007:052)

If we put the above examples in present tense, number concord would be sufficient to identify the subject.

(8) a') I hear that story as well.
　　b') They buy a piece to go in their window.

The concord criterion does work in (8a'), where the form *hear* would not work if the noun phrase *that story* was the subject. That is, only *I* can be the subject. Similarly, the verb form *buy* in (8b') would not go with the noun phrase *a piece*. So, *they* must be the subject. To sum up, the subject always shows concord with the verb. As a criterion to identify the subject, however, this feature is not always helpful since number is rarely marked in the finite verb.

More helpful is the fact that the subject of the clause is that constituent which is substituted by a pronoun in **tag questions**. This criterion, for instance, helps to decide the cases under (7) where the first noun phrase in the clause was not the subject, here repeated for as (9) convenience.

(9) a) 　Every day she goes out at six. (s1a-019:193)
　　a') 　Every day she goes out at six, doesn't **she**?
　　b) 　Last night I was ready to tip beer over one of them. (w1b-005:144)
　　b') 　Last night I was ready to tip beer over one of them, wasn't **I**?
　　c) 　Next door, Hugo Dichter paces up and down his room. (w2f-016:093)
　　c') 　Next door, Hugo Dichter paces up and down his room, doesn't **he**?
　　d) 　Hardbacks I wouldn't lend to anyone. (s1a-013:087)
　　d') 　Hardbacks I wouldn't lend to anyone, would **I**?

Problems with this criterion would only arise in the (rare) cases when the pronoun could refer to more than one of the noun phrases, as in the following example.

(10) a) 　They gave us the most explicit instructions. (w1b-012:091)
　　 a') 　They gave us the most explicit instructions, didn't **they**?

In the above case, the pronoun *they* in the tag question is co-referential with a plural noun or a plural pronoun. A 'mechanical' application of the tag-question criterion would yield two possible subjects, namely *they* and *the most explicit instructions*, since both of these express plurality (we will ignore the pronoun *us*, since it is not in the nominative case, which we have with subjects).

Such problematic cases can be decided by the final criterion, namely the fact that in **yes-no questions** the subject swaps the position with the operator, i.e. the first auxiliary in the verb phrase (see section 3.2). If we want to find out whether a constituent in a declarative clause is the subject, we merely have to transform the declarative into a *yes-no* question and see which constituent apart from the operator moves. If the underlying clause does not have an auxiliary, the dummy operator *do* will be used to form the question (see section 3.2), and the subject would usually immediately follow the initial form of *do*. This diagnostic, for instance, would correctly identify the subjects in all the examples discussed so far. A selection is given below.

(11) a) Every day she goes out at six. (s1a-019:193)
 a') Does **she** go out at six every day?
 b) Hardbacks I wouldn't lend to anyone. (s1a-013:087)
 b') Would **I** lend hardbacks to anyone?
 c) I heard that story as well.
 c') Did **I** hear that story as well?
 d) They gave us the most explicit instructions.
 d') Did **they** give us the most explicit instructions?

As can be seen from the data above, the '*yes-no* question' criterion even works with the problematic case (10a), here shown under (11d and d'). The features that are characteristic of subjects are listed in Table 6.1. Note that they are characteristic to different degrees: the first four features need not hold with all subjects, while the last three do.

Table 6.1: Characteristic features of subjects.

The subject of a clause ...
is the agent
is what the clause is about
is a noun phrase
is the first noun phrase
is in number concord with the verb
is repeated as a pronoun in tag-questions
occurs after the operator in *yes-no* questions

6.1.3 Direct and indirect object

The English language has two kinds of objects, namely a direct object and an indirect object. One way to distinguish between the two is to take a look at the semantic roles in those cases where both objects are realised, as in the examples below; the direct object is in bold print, while the indirect object is underlined.

(12) a) Iraq's given the UN **figures of civilian casualties**. (s2b-018:013)
  b) I brought you **a present**. (w2f-002:220)
  c) **Nonsense**, she told herself. (w2f-020:024)

While the subject is described as the doer of the action (the agent), the direct object is often characterised as the undergoer of the action; it "refers to an entity that is affected by the action denoted in the clause" (Quirk et al. 1985: 727), a semantic role described as 'patient'. For instance somebody does something with *the figures of civilian casualties* in (12a), with *the present* in (12b) and the utterance *Nonsense* in (12c): they are given, brought and told, respectively. The indirect object, in contrast, usually refers to the entity that 'benefits' from the action, it is the goal of the action or the 'recipient'. In (12a) *the UN* is given that which is referred to in the direct object, in (12b) somebody (*I*) does something (bringing a present) to somebody else (*you*). And the woman or girl in (12c) does something to *herself*, namely telling herself that something is nonsense.

Similarly to the subject, direct and indirect objects are usually realised by noun phrases (see the examples under (12)), although direct objects are fairly frequently realised by clauses.

(13) a) He was refusing **to take necessary tough action to restore order**. (s2b-040:068)
  b) The jury was told **the event went off well and there was no trouble until it was winding up shortly before 3 am**. (w2c-011:014)
  c) You said **they weren't together**. (w2f-006:237)

As the examples under (12) and (13) show, objects usually occur immediately after the main verb in clauses with active voice, but objects may also be fronted as in (12c) (see section 6.3 for details on fronting). If we have both direct and indirect object, the indirect object usually precedes the direct object, as in (12a and b). In passive sentences, objects swap position with the subject of the corresponding active clause, as the modified versions of example (12a) under (14) show. Note that both direct and indirect object may be moved.

(14) a) Iraq's given the UN **figures of civilian casualties**. (s2b-018:013)
  ~ **Figures of civilian casualties** have been given the UN by Iraq.
  ~ The UN has been given **figures of civilian casualties** by Iraq.

Finally, indirect objects realised by a noun phrase correspond to locative adverbials (see section 6.1.5 for details) realised by a prepositional phrase, which usually occur directly after the direct object.

(15) a) Iraq's given the UN **figures of civilian casualties**. (s2b-018:013)
Iraq's given **figures of civilian casualties** to the UN.
b) I brought you **a present**. (w2f-002:220)
I brought **a present** to you.

Table 6.2 provides a summary of the above discussion.

Table 6.2: Characteristic features of direct and indirect objects.

Direct object	Indirect object
'Patient' of the action	'Recipient' of the action
Mostly realised by noun phrases but also by clauses	Mostly realised by noun phrases but corresponds to adverbial realised by a prepositional phrase introduced by *to*
Immediately follows the verb or the indirect object	Between verb and direct object (unless realised by a prepositional phrase introduced by *to*)
Can swap position with subject in a passive clause	Can swap position with subject in a passive clause

6.1.4 Complement

Complements are used to describe or identify the clause constituent to which they relate, which either is the subject or the object. Accordingly, we can distinguish **subject complements** and **object complements**. Consider examples (16a to d) and (16e to g), respectively.

(16) a) I was **lucky**. (s1a-001:090)
 b) It's **very simple**. (s2a-064:055)
 c) These are **the costs the grey parties never talk about when they allow the system to go on**. (w2b-013:097)
 d) All he's been saying today is **I'm not a member of the Security Council**. (s2b-010:084)
 e) I find it **fascinating**. (s1a-002:035)
 f) It made it **very difficult**. (s1a-072:223)
 g) Tacitus calls northern Britain **Caledonia**. (w1a-009:103)
 h) I call them **wild flowers**. (s1a-036:205)

In the first four examples the complement describes or characterises the subject of the clause. In (16a) it is the speaker, *I*, who was *lucky*, in (16b) the referent denoted by the pronoun *it* is described as *very simple* and so on. In the last four examples the complement relates to the direct object of the clause. For instance, in (16e and f) an object referred to by the pronoun *it* is characterised as *fascinating* and *very difficult*, respectively; in (16g) the direct object *northern Britain* is identified as *Caledonia*, and in (16h) the entities denoted by *them* are described as *wild flowers*.

As can be seen from the above examples, complements show a wider range of formal realisations than subjects and objects, the most frequent one being the adjective phrase. With regard to position, we find that subject complements usually occur immediately after the main verb, whereas object complements usually immediately follow the direct object, to which they relate. In those cases in which the complements are noun phrases, the subject complement shows concord with the subject S, and the object complement is in concord with the direct object, as can be best seen in the examples (16c) and (16h).

A final note is in order here concerning the distinction between a subject complement and a direct object. What is the difference between the two postverbal constituents shown in (17a) and (17b)?

(17) a) He was a very popular person. (s1a-003:053)
   b) He meets a very popular person.

Apart from the verb, both sentences are identical with regard to the word forms used. However, the two instantiate different structures since the final noun phrase *a very popular person* realises a subject complement in sentence (a) and a direct object in sentence (b). This distinction is grounded in the referential identity or non-identity of subject and subject complement or subject and direct object. In (16a) the pronoun *he* and the noun phrase *a very popular person* refer to the same entity, whereas in (16b) the pronoun and the noun phrase do not refer to the same person. Only when we have referential identity do we have a subject complement.

Table 6.3 below sums up characteristic features of the subject and object complements.

Table 6.3: Characteristic features of subject complements and object complements.

Subject complement	Object complement
Describes, characterises and/or identifies the subject	Describes, characterises and/or identifies the object
Wide range of formal realisations	Wide range of formal realisations
Immediately follows the verb	Immediately follows the direct object
If a noun phrase, in concord with the subject	If a noun phrase, in concord with the direct object

6.1.5 Adverbial

Adverbials are special in that in many respects they are more varied than the other constituents discussed so far. Adverbials show different functions, they fulfil different semantic roles, they are realised in a number of different ways, they can occur in different positions in the clause, we can have more than one adverbial in a clause, and many adverbials in contrast to the other clause constituents are optional and not obligatory (cf. Biber et al. 1999: 762-763).

As regards the function, we distinguished three main functions in section 2.2.4, i.e. 'adjunct', 'disjunct' and 'conjuncts' in the terminology of Quirk et al. (1985) or 'circumstantial', 'stance', and 'linking' adverbials in the terminology of Biber et al. (1999), to which we will stick here.

Circumstantial adverbials are most similar to the other clause constituents discussed so far, because just like the other constituents they fulfil a function within the clause by adding information about the event or the state described in the clause. A distinction has to be drawn between those adverbials that are demanded by the verb, i.e. obligatory adverbials, and those that are not, i.e. optional adverbials. Consider the examples under (18) and (19), respectively.

(18) a) I'm sitting **in the garden of Bob & Tom's house**. (w1b-013:003)
 b) One is used to send a dummy Boolean parameter **to the Channel**. (w2a-038:107)
 c) These images came mainly **from points, novels, articles, cartoons, postcards, films and posters**. (w2a-009:023)

(19) a) They played with the Gilmore girls **in the garden**. (w2f-007:096)
 b) **Yesterday** we went on one cable car up to the mountain. (w1b-009:017)
 c) So Chris Louis son of John Louis leads **after the first lap**. (s2a-012:073)

With the examples under (18), the adverbial (in bold print) cannot be left out without resulting in ungrammaticality of the clause, whereas the deletion of the adverbials in (19) does not have an influence on grammatical correctness.

(18') a) *I'm sitting …
  b) *One is used to send a dummy Boolean parameter …
  c) *These images came mainly …

(19') a) They played with the Gilmore girls …
  b) … we went on one cable car up to the mountain
  c) So Chris Louis son of John Louis leads …

In these cases, grammaticality or ungrammaticality depends on the kind of information that the verb demands. The verb *sit*, for instance, usually demands somebody or something that sits and a location where this somebody or something sits. Because of that the adverbial *in the garden of Bob & Tom's house* in example (18a) is obligatory. If this bit of information is missing and we are not in a context like *I'm not standing, I'm sitting* you are inclined to ask *where are you sitting?* The same holds for (18b and c). If something is sent we need to know the destination, and if something comes we need to know the source it comes from. The verb *play*, in contrast to *sit*, does not need information about the location in which people play. This information is of an additional nature only and not essential, which is why the adverbial *in the garden* can be left out in (19a) without leading to ungrammaticality. Similarly, it is not necessary for the verbs *go* and *lead* to provide information on the exact time of the verbal action.

The circumstantial adverbials in the above examples are used to express location and time, i.e. they answer questions as to the when and where of the verbal action. Other semantic aspects expressed by adverbials are the manner of, the extent of, and the reason for the verbal action, as shown below.

(20) a) Her face **suddenly** registered embarrassment. (w2f-007:133)
  b) **All too frequently** manoeuvring tests at model scale are scheduled late in the test programme. (w2a-039:061)
  c) I think the question is bigger than that **because it's from both sides**. (s1a-001:054)

The examples under (19) and (20) also illustrate the wide range of formal realisations of adverbials, encompassing prepositional phrases, noun phrases, adverb phrases and even clauses.

Note also that most of the adverbials in the above examples are fairly mobile, as the following variations of the examples under (20) show.

(20) a') **Suddenly** her face ... registered embarrassment.
   a") Her face ... registered embarrassment **suddenly**.
   b') ... manoeuvring tests at model scale **all too frequently** are scheduled late in the test programme.
   b") ... manoeuvring tests at model scale are scheduled late **all too frequently** in the test programme.
   b''') ... manoeuvring tests at model scale are scheduled late in the test programme **all too frequently**.
   c') I think, **because it's from both sides**, the question is bigger than that ....
   c") I think the question, **because it's from both sides**, is bigger than that ....

With regard to the example (20c) it might be tempting to also put the adverbial clause in initial position as shown below.

(20) c''') **Because it's from both sides** I think the question is bigger than that ....

Note, however, that in that case we change the meaning of the clause. In examples (20c, c', and c"), the adverbial clause is usually understood as providing a reason for the claim that *the question is bigger than that*. By placing the adverbial clause in initial position in (20c'''), the adverbial is more likely to be understood as providing a reason for the speaker's thought and his or her act of thinking. This phenomenon is discussed under the term 'scope', which refers to "the semantic 'influence' which [...] words [, phrases or clauses] have on neighbouring parts of a sentence" (Quirk et al. 1985: 85). If the adverbial clause is placed at the beginning of the sentence, its scope includes all the rest of the sentence, whereas in the other cases the scope merely includes the statement *the question is bigger than that*. This leads us to the discussion of the second functional class of adverbials, namely disjuncts or stance adverbials.

Stance adverbials are different from most circumstantial adverbials as they are not integrated in the structure of the clause. Rather, they should be regarded as comments by the speaker on the clause itself, either regarding the content of the clause or the style in which the content is phrased. The first class falls into two subcategories, namely **'epistemic'** and **'attitude stance adverbials'**. The former makes a comment as to the truth value of the proposition that is expressed in the clause, providing information as to certainty, reality, or sources (Biber et al. 1999: 764). Examples are given below.

(21) a) **Without doubt**, this was the most powerful Corvette so far produced. (w2b-037:168)
   b) **Supposedly** at the other end there's this big pay-off. (s1a-079:102)
   c) The nice thing about the epidermis **from my point of view** is that it is basically made up of one cell type. (s2a-046:067)

Attitude stance adverbials, as the term implies, provide information on the speaker's attitude towards the content of the clause.

(22) a) But **unfortunately** both Saturday and Sunday it was really foggy. (s1a-036:159)
   b) But **most importantly perhaps** the monarchy is also used to conserve and protect an elaborate system of established privilege and power. (s2b-032:072)

While the first two kinds of stance adverbials are concerned with the content of the clause, **style stance adverbials** are used by the speaker to make a comment on the style in which the proposition is expressed.

(23) a) So I don't think they have behaved well at any stage **frankly**. (s2b-013:065)
   b) **To be honest** on that kind of car it's not really worth it. (s1b-074:395)

In the above examples the utterances are fairly blunt and harsh. The style adverbials are used to signal to the hearer that the speaker is aware of this, thus mitigating possible negative effects on the interlocutors' relationship.

Note, however, that these adverbials, just like epistemic stance adverbials, are optional as far as the verb is concerned; if they were deleted the resulting sentence would still be grammatical.

(21) a')..., this was the most powerful Corvette so far produced.
   b') ... at the other end there's this big pay-off.
(22) a') But ... both Saturday and Sunday it was really foggy.
   b') But ... the monarchy is also used to conserve and protect an elaborate system of established privilege and power.
(23) a') So I don't think they have behaved well at any stage ....
   b') ... on that kind of car it's not really worth it.

Also similarly to epistemic adverbials, attitude and style stance adverbials are fairly flexible with regard to their position in the clause. Note also that all stance adverbials can be realised by different formal elements.

While circumstantial adverbials are usually fully integrated into the clause and stance adverbials usually have scope over the entire clause in which they occur, the third class of adverbials, namely conjuncts or **linking adverbials**, can be regarded as the least integrated kind of adverbials. They have a connective function, i.e. they occur between clauses and serve to express the relationship in which these two clauses stand. These relationships can be of different kinds, such as addition, result or concession.

(24) a) There will also be a steep vertical gradient as BOD is progressively removed. **In addition** there will be an increase in wastewater alkanality resulting from dissolved CO, and a high oxygen concentration as the oxygen introduced by the draught tubes is not removed by oxidation. **Consequently**, the lower reaches often harbour a large population of autotrophic nitrifying bacteria. (w2a-021:029-031).
b) [...] the rush pen was not held vertically in the typical Chinese fashion but at an angle. The grip was not unlike that most commonly adopted by modern European writers using the thumb and the first and second fingers. The action **however** we should describe more as painting than scripting. (s2a-048:083)

Like stance adverbials, linking adverbials are always optional and could, in principle, be left out. In contrast to stance adverbials, however, linking adverbials are usually tied to clause-initial position, although sometimes they may occur after the subject (as in (24b)) or the main verb. In addition, linking adverbials are much more reduced as regards the formal realisation, which is restricted to prepositional phrases and adverbs. Table 6.4 sums up the major findings concerning adverbials.

Table 6.4: Characteristic features of adverbials.

Circumstantial adverbials	Stance adverbials	Linking adverbials
express location, time, manner, extent, reason	express speaker's attitude towards truth of proposition or style and content of the utterance	express logical relationships between clauses, sentences, and paragraphs.
distinction between optional and obligatory adverbials	optional	optional
if optional, fairly mobile	mobile	usually restricted to clause-initial position
wide range of formal variation	wide range of formal variation	formally restricted

6.2 The structure of the clause

Having discussed the basic building blocks of the clause, we can now have a closer look at the structure of the English clause (or the simple sentence). Clause structure is described with regard to the obligatory, i.e. the necessary, constituents in the clause. Which constituents are obligatory depends on the main verb of the clause. Following Quirk et al. (1985: 53), we can distinguish three main types of verbs, namely 'intransitive', 'copular' and 'transitive' verbs, depending on the number and kinds of constituents that they demand. Some of these may lead to more than one clause structure, so that we end up with seven different clause patterns. Each of the three types and its resulting clause patterns is exemplified below.

(25) **Intransitive** – SV
  a) [The word deletion]$_S$ [will not occur]$_V$. (s2a-030:133)
  Copular – SVCs, SVAs
  b) That$_S$ was$_V$ [an interesting period]$_{Cs}$. (s1a-001:049)
  c) I$_S$ ['m sitting]$_V$ [in the garden of Bob & Tom's house]$_{As}$. (w1b-013:003)
  Transitive – SVOd, SVOiOd, SVOdCo, SVOdAo
  d) You$_S$ ['ve missed]$_V$ [the most obvious one]$_{Od}$. (s1b-007:052)
  e) [The enzymes]$_S$ give$_V$ you$_{Oi}$ [a particular form of this]$_{Od}$. (s2a-034:022)
  f) I$_S$ find$_V$ it$_{Od}$ fascinating$_{Co}$. (s1a-002:035)
  g) I$_S$ put$_V$ [my leg]$_{Od}$ [onto the top shelf]$_{Ao}$. (s1b-066:030)

The first type of verb is that which, apart from the subject, does not need any further constituents. It is called an **'intransitive'** verb and is exemplified in example (25a) above. The second group of verbs are those that in addition to the subject either need a subject complement (Cs) or a subject-related adverbial (As), as shown in examples (25b) and (25c), respectively. These are called **'copular'** verbs. The term stems from Latin *copulare*, which means 'to join' or 'to connect'. Copular verbs, thus, can be understood as a link between the subject of the clause and the piece of information about the subject that the clause provides, e.g. a characteristic feature or its location. The largest group of verbs (exemplified in 25d to g) are those that demand a direct object (Od). They are called **'transitive'** verbs, a label derived from the Latin verb *transire*, which could be translated as 'to cross' to 'pass over'. This term may strike one as odd, but it makes sense if we imagine that a transitive verb describes the 'transition' of an action from a subject (as actor) to an object (which is acted upon). Intransitive and copular clauses do not have any passive versions (in a sense, copular clauses are also intransitive – the nomenclature is not fully consistent in this respect). In addition, three types of transitive verbs can be distinguished, namely **'monotransitive'**, **'ditransitive'**, and **'complex transitive'** ones. Monotransitive verbs are those that only need a direct object, whereas ditransitive verbs demand a direct as well as an indirect object. Complex transitive verbs, in addition to the direct object, either need an object complement or an object-related adverbial.

Note that copular clauses and complex transitive clauses are similar to a certain extent. In both cases the complement or the adverbial provide information on another constituent of the clause, namely on the subject and the direct object, respectively. This can be illustrated if we change the clauses in (25f and g) to copular clauses with the object as subject.

(25) f) I_S find$_V$ it$_{Od}$ fascinating$_{Co}$.
    f') It$_S$ is$_V$ fascinating$_{Cs}$.
    g) I_S put$_V$ [my leg]$_{Od}$ [onto the top shelf]$_{Ao}$.
    g') [My leg]$_S$ is$_V$ [on(to) the top shelf]$_{As}$.

A list of the verb types, the seven corresponding clause patterns and illustrative examples are given below.

Table 6.5: Types of verbs and their clause patterns.

Verb type	Clause pattern	Example
Intransitive	S V	*The word deletion will not occur*
Copular	S V Cs	*That was an interesting period*
	S V As	*I'm sitting in the garden of Tom's house*
Transitive (Mono-)	S V O	*You've missed the most obvious one*
(Di-)	S V Oi Od	*The enzymes give you a particular form*
(Complex-)	S V Od Co	*I find it fascinating*
	S V Od Ao	*I put my leg onto the top shelf*

With regard to the practical analysis of clause structure you can proceed in two (complementary) directions. Either you identify the main verb and determine which constituents the verb demands, which will, then, yield the clause types. Or you determine the constituents of the clause and identify those that are not necessary for the clause to be grammatical. The obligatory constituents that remain will tell you which type of clause you are dealing with, which will then tell you what kind of verb the main verb is. In trying to spot the optional constituents it is helpful to keep in mind that only adverbials are potential candidates. Furthermore, obligatory adverbials usually denote a location: adverbials that describe a point in time, a reason or a manner, for instance, are very likely to be optional. A sample analysis of the following clauses will illustrate the identification of clause patterns and verb types.

(26)   I gave Mr. Sainsbury a letter before we went away. (s1b-061:168)

With regard to (26) we find the main verb is GIVE. This verb demands three bits of information: a giver, a receiver or 'givee', and a given. The giver in the above example is the person referred to by the pronoun *I*; this is the subject of the clause (S). The receiver is *Mr. Sainsbury*, the indirect object of the clause. The given is *a letter*, the direct object. If any of these bits of information are left out the sentence is not grammatical. The circumstantial adverbial *before we went away*, however, is optional. It can be left out without loss of grammaticality.

(26') * ~~I~~ gave Mr. Sainsbury a letter before we went away.
       * I gave ~~Mr. Sainsbury~~ a letter before we went away.
       * I gave Mr. Sainsbury ~~a letter~~ before we went away.
       I gave Mr. Sainsbury a letter ~~before we went away~~.

The clause, thus, is a ditransitive clause with the structure SVOiOd. If we want to include the optional adverbial in the description, we put it in brackets, i.e. SVOiOd(A).

A final aspect deserves mention with regard to obligatoriness and optionality (and verb and clause types). In some cases is not easy to say whether a constituent is in fact obligatory or optional. The example that we discussed in passing above was the verb SIT. While in the clause *I'm sitting in the garden* the verb is likely to be classified as copular, it would maybe not be classified that way in the clause *He was not standing, he was sitting*, where it appears to be intransitive. A similar problem arises with the two examples below.

(27) a) Are we going to be eating at your parents'? (s1a-099:107)
     b) I ended up just eating sort of lumps of chicken and things. (s1a-011:249)

Although superficially similar, it makes sense to distinguish the cases of SIT and EAT. It is reasonable to assume that the location in the 'sitting' example is implicitly understood – if you sit you have to sit somewhere (see Aarts 1997: 16-17 for a similar discussion). Accordingly, we would talk of a copular verb SIT in this case, even though the obligatory postverbal constituent is not made explicit. With EAT, however, it seems preferable to think of two different verbs, one being intransitive and one being monotransitive, This analysis has to be favoured in the light of the fact that in the first case, EAT can be replaced by the monotransitive verb DINE, whereas in the second we cannot.

(27) a') Are we going to be dining at your parents'.
 b') *I ended up just dining sort of lumps of chicken and things.

This example already hints at the interaction of syntax (here: clause patterns) and semantics (here: verb meaning) to be discussed in more detail in chapter 10.

6.3 Non-canonical order and secondary clause patterns

The structures discussed in the previous section are usually described as the major clause patterns. These major clause patterns can be realised in a 'canonical' or a 'non-canonical' fashion. This distinction refers to the order of elements in the clause. The canonical order is the one shown in Table 6.5, i.e. the subject occurs in initial position, the verb follows the subject, and so on. With non-canonical realisations this usual order is changed to a certain extent. Some examples together with their canonical counterparts are given below.

(28) a) **SVC → CSV**
 Oh that'd be great.
 Oh great that'd be. (s1a-042:132)
 b) **SVOiOd → OiSVOd**
 I ask everybody that cooks how they make pastry.
 Everybody that cooks I ask how they make pastry. (s1a-057:131)
 c) **SVOd → OdSV**
 She did not consider her duty to her husband, fighting on foreign field for his and her freedom, at all.
 Her duty to her husband, fighting on foreign field for his and her freedom, she did not consider at all. (w2f-005:027)
 d) **SVOdCo → CoSVOd**
 I thought him distinctly brilliant.
 Distinctly brilliant I thought him. (s1a-094:312)
 e) **SVOdAo → AoSVOd**
 You've got the axons of the ganglion cells on the innermost surface of the retina.
 On the innermost surface of the retina you've got the axons of the ganglion cells. (s1b-015:114)
 f) **SVC → CVS**
 The continuous logging of the forests is equally important in terms of forest depletion.
 Equally important in terms of forest depletion is the continuous logging of the forests. (w1a-013:071)

g) **SVA → AVS**
Some delightful votive paintings are <u>on the walls of the church</u>.
<u>On the walls of the church</u> are some delightful votive paintings. (s2b-027:126)

Among the above examples we can distinguish two large groups. (28a) to (28e) are examples of what is called '**fronting**', i.e. a constituent that usually occurs after the verb is put into initial position without changing the relative order of the other constituents. As can be seen, any post-verbal constituent can undergo fronting. Examples (28f and g) illustrate what is usually referred to as '**full-verb inversion**'. In that case, the verb remains in its central position and the subject swaps place with a post-verbal constituent. This phenomenon is usually restricted to copular clauses.

It is important to note that non-canonical word order does not change the underlying clause type: an SVOd clause, for instance, is an SVOd clause, regardless of the position of the direct object. This becomes apparent immediately if we recall that the clause types depend on the main verb of the clause. To stick with the above example, transitive verbs require a subject and a direct object, i.e. they lead to transitive clauses, which on an abstract level can be described by the structure SVOd. In their concrete instantiations, this structure can either be realised in the canonical order (SVOd), or the direct object can be fronted (OdSV). Although we have two different realisations, on the abstract level we are still dealing with a transitive clause and the clause pattern SVOd. So, we are dealing with two levels of abstraction (see section 1.3): on a low degree of abstraction we could treat SVOd and OdSV as two different structures. These are essentially identical if we ignore the order of constituents and merely focus on which constituents are obligatory. The same is true for the other examples above. Still, the different realisations fulfil different functions, as will be shown in detail in chapter 9.

In addition to the major clause patterns (and their canonical and non-canonical realisations) the English language also has a couple of secondary clause patterns. These are based on the major clause patterns but introduce additional elements into the clause, which is why they are grouped in a separate class.

A fairly common structure is the **passive clause**, which we glanced at in sections 3.1, 6.1.2 and 6.2. With the most frequent kinds of passive clauses the direct or the indirect object in a transitive clause is put into initial position while the subject occurs in a *by*-phrase at the end of the clause or is omitted. Consider example (14a) again, here repeated as (29).

(29) Iraq's given <u>the UN</u> **figures of civilian casualties**. (s2b-018:013)
~ **Figures of civilian casualties** have been given <u>the UN</u> (by Iraq).
~ <u>The UN</u> has been given **figures of civilian casualties** (by Iraq).

The relation of a transitive clause and its corresponding passive clause is summarised in Figure 6.2, which is a more elaborate version of Figure 6.4 in section 3.1 above.

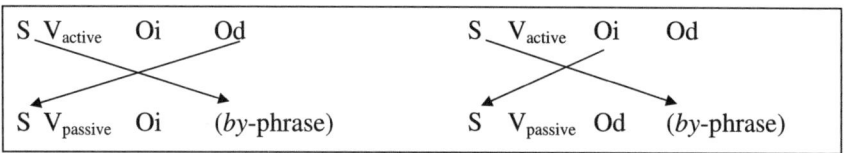

Figure 6.2: The relation of active and passive sentences.

Another secondary clause type we have already looked at is the **existential-*there* sentence**.

(30) a) There is a conservatory modelled on Kew Gardens. (w1b-012:066)
  b) There is a significant decrease in administration costs. (w2c-016:028)

Existential-*there* sentences usually occur with verbs of the existence or appearance, i.e. they can be related to a simple intransitive SV structure or a copular SVAs structure. One might argue that we are actually dealing with an inverted SVAs clause, with *there* functioning as an adverbial denoting a location. With the clause in isolation and without the context it is usually impossible to decide on the correct analysis. However, it is important to keep in mind that existential-*there* (i.e. not the locational *there*) does not refer to a location. This becomes apparent if other locative expressions also occur in the same clause.

(30) a') There is a conservatory modelled on Kew Gardens in Golden Gate Park.
  ~ 'A conservatory modelled on Kew Gardens is/can be found in Golden Gate Park.'
  a") There is a conservatory modelled on Kew Gardens here.
  ~ 'A conservatory modelled on Kew Gardens is/can be found here.'

The two examples above also make clear what motivates the use of existential-*there* sentences: the subject noun phrase of the canonical sentences begins with an indefinite article, which shows that the entity denoted by the noun phrase has not been part of the previous discourse, i.e. it is new to the reader. New information usually occurs at the end of the clause and not at the beginning. Existential-*there* sentences, therefore, are a means of putting new information where the reader or hearer would usually expect it – at the end of the clause. We will discuss such aspects in more detail in chapter 9.

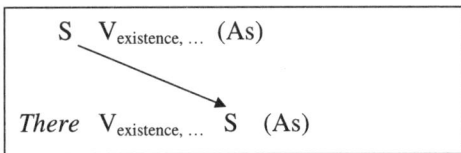

Figure 6.3: The relation of existential-there sentences and their corresponding canonical clause patterns.

Clauses with *it*-**extraposition** are similar to existential-*there* clauses in that they, too, serve to put the subject of a copular clause in a position towards the end of the clause (the subject is 'extraposed'), as can be seen in the following examples.

(31) a) It seems amazing now that somebody I remember as so conventional should have been so ahead of her time in female rights. (s1b-041:150)
  a') That somebody I remember as so conventional should have been so ahead of her time in female rights seems amazing now.
  b) It is simply too stupid and too dangerous to continue playing the national identity dynamic game in domestic politics. (w2a-017:046)
  b') To continue playing the national identity dynamic game in domestic politics is simply too stupid and too dangerous.
  c) It is therefore relevant that quite a large range of variation has been observed, perhaps two-fold, in the rates of protein turnover of different individuals. (w2a-024:023)
  c') That quite a large range of variation has been observed, perhaps two-fold, in the rates of protein turnover of different individuals is therefore relevant.

In contrast to existential-*there* sentences the motivation for this phenomenon is not so much related to the position of new information in the clause but to complexity and processability. With *it*-extraposition the subject of the underlying clause also is a clause and, therefore, long and complex. The English language, however, has a tendency to place elements that are complex and difficult to process towards the end of the clause. In complying with this general tendency, *it*-extraposition facilitates the comprehension of the clause, as can be seen if you compare the *it*-extraposed examples with their non-extraposed counterparts under (31). Again, the influence of aspects of processability will be discussed in more detail in chapter 9. Figure 6.4 describes the relation between *it*-extraposition and the underlying non-extraposed sentence.

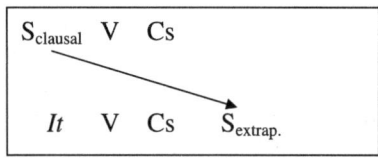

Figure 6.4: The relation of it-extraposition and its corresponding canonical clause pattern.

We will conclude this discussion with a short description of **cleft sentences**. The name is due to the fact that in this construction the underlying sentence is cut (or cleaved/cleft) into two sentences, the first of which contains a specially focused element. Cleft sentences are of two kinds: *it*-cleft and *wh*-cleft sentences. The following examples illustrate the ***it*-cleft**.

(32) a) It is the species composition of this layer which determines the treatment efficiency. (w2a-021:009)
   a') The species composition of this layer determines the treatment efficiency.
   b) It's exercise you need, not rest. (w2f-013:119)
   b') You need exercise, not rest.
   c) It was to the Corkscrew that I directed my steps. (w2f-009:136)
   c') I directed by steps to the Corkscrew.
   d) It is during this phase of distal axon growth that the Tinel sign is most useful. (w2a-026:142)
   d') The Tinel sign is most useful during this phase of distal axon growth.
   e) Maybe it was because I found much academic study of the law almost wilfully obscure and introverted that I felt for the common bloke whose benefit it was all supposed to be. (s2a-039:034)
   e') I felt for the common bloke whose benefit it was all supposed to be because I found much academic study of the law almost wilfully obscure and introverted.

As can be seen from the above examples, the *it*-cleft sentence consists of an initial dummy subject *it*, and a form of BE followed by the specially focused element. These constituents form the first clause in the cleft sentence. The remaining elements form the second clause. This second clause is attached to the focused element and is similar to a relative clause in being introduced by *who/which*, *that* or *zero*. The order of the remaining elements is identical to the order they had in the underlying clause. The function of *it*-clefts is to emphasise the element that occurs in final position of the first clause, e.g. the subject *the species composition of this layer* in (32a) or the direct object *exercise* in (32b), and so on. As you can see, cleft sentences are fairly versatile means of emphasis because in addition to subjects and objects (32b), they also highlight different kinds of adverbials (32c to e). We will discuss possible reasons for the use of cleft sentences in more detail below. Figure 6.5 provides a diagrammatic description of *it*-cleft sentences on the basis of the example of SVOA clauses. Note, however, that cleft sentences can also be used with other clause patterns (see study question 7).

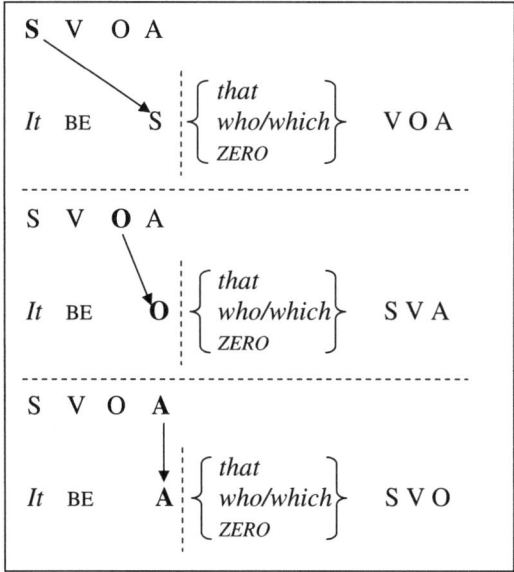

Figure 6.5: The three main types of it-cleft sentences.

The second kind of cleft sentence, the **wh-cleft**, is exemplified below.

(33) a) What I need is a personal intro to him. (s1a-027:22)
 a') I need a personal intro to him.

b) What's been useful is <u>Bob's contact with the union</u>. (s1b-078:226)
b') <u>Bob's contact with the union</u> has been useful.
c) What is now important is <u>to get on with life</u>. (w1b-008:118)
c') <u>To get on with life</u> is now important.

The structure of the canonical underlying sentence usually is SVO (as in the first example) or SVC (as in the other three examples). The *wh*-cleft itself can be described as an SVC sentence, with the subject, a *wh*-clause (which has given the construction its name), usually introduced by *what*. In contrast to *it*-clefts, the focused element is not part of the first clause in the construction but occurs in final position, which, again, complies with the tendency to put new and important information towards the end of the clause. However, there must be yet another function, as the construction does not lead to a change of elements in the case of (33a). This, most likely, lies in drawing attention to the sentence itself, which then can be exploited for various text-structuring purposes, as will be discussed in more detail in chapter 9.

In addition, we also find what Biber et al. (1999: 960) call 'reversed *wh*-clefts': in all of the above examples you could invert the construction, as is shown below (see Esser 1984: 100-103 for a more general discussion of the movability of elements in *wh*-clefts).

(33) a") A personal intro to him is what I need.
 b") Bob's contact with the union is what's been useful.
 c") To get on with life is what is now important.

As a consequence, the focused element now occurs in initial position. One function of reversed *wh*-clefts, in contrast to the regular *wh*-cleft, thus seems to be to establish a smooth transition from one sentence to another by putting the focused element in front position (in case the focused element contains given information and, therefore, can provide a link to the previous discourse). This time we change the order of elements in (33a") but not in (33b") and (33c"). The last two examples, therefore, must be motivated by other functions, which will be explored in chapter 9. Figure 6.6 provides a structural description of the two kinds of *wh*-clefts.

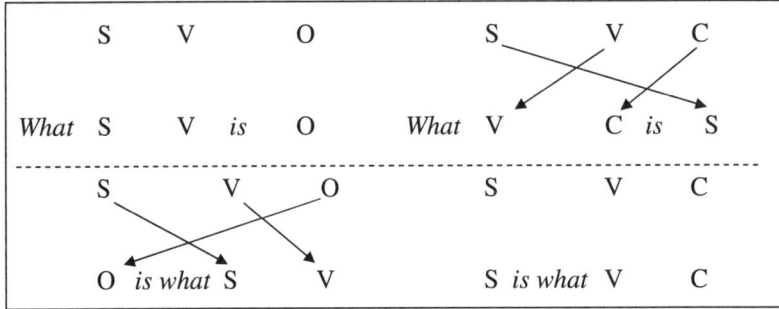

Figure 6.6: The structure of wh-clefts (top) and reversed wh-clefts (bottom).

6.4 Complex and compound sentences

So far we have mainly focused on clauses in which the constituents were realised by phrases. But we saw in the introduction to this chapter that clause constituents may also be realised by clauses. Examples of this are the *wh*-clefts and the non-extraposed counterparts of *it*-extrapositions. We will now take a more systematic look at clauses as realisations of clause constituents.

In section 6.2 we identified five basic clause elements, namely verb, subject, (indirect and direct) object, complement and adverbial. With the exception of the verb (and the indirect object), each of these can be realised by clauses, as the following examples show.

(34) a) [Whether he speaks or not]$_S$ remains to be seen. (s2a-008:175)
b) We decided [that we would work together]$_{Od}$. (s1a-001:048)
c) My earliest memory of the theatre is [going to the Hippodrome in Ipswich]$_{Cs}$. (s1b-023:036)
d) The tackle by Galiamin was adjudged by the referee [to be a foul]$_{Co}$. (s1a-001:098)
e) [When you start working in a new class like that]$_A$ everybody is ignorant. (s1a-002:090)

All of the above sentences illustrate what is called a '**complex sentence**', i.e. a clause which contains one or more constituents that is realised by a clause itself: in (34a) the subject is a clause, in (34b) the direct object, and so on. The 'containing' clause is called the 'main clause' or the 'superordinate clause'. The clause that realises a constituent of the superordinate clause is called a 'subordinate clause' or 'dependent clause'. In (34a), for instance, the whole clause is the main or superordinate clause, and the clause *Whether he speaks or not* is the subordinate clause.

Subordinate clauses can be divided into 'nominal clauses', 'adverbial clauses' and 'relative clauses'. The first class encompasses all uses of subordinate clauses as subjects, objects and complements. These functions are usually instantiated by noun phrases, hence the term 'nominal clause'. Examples are given in (34a) to (34d) above. These examples also show the four formal realisations, namely from top to bottom: *wh*-clause, *that*-clause, *to*-infinitive clause, and participle clause. Note that each formal type can fulfil each of the functions, i.e. a subject, for instance, may also be realised by a *that*-clause, participle clause, or *to*-infinitive clause.

Adverbial clauses are those that function as circumstantial adverbials, providing information on time, place, manner, etc. (34e) is an example of a temporal adverbial clause. In many cases adverbial clauses are introduced by subordinators, little words that mark the clause as subordinated and also indicate what kind of circumstantial information the adverbial clause provides. In example (34e) the subordinator is *when* and it points at circumstantial information regarding time. Other subordinators indicate locational, conditional, causal or concessional relations; consider (35a) to (35d), respectively.

(35) a) [**Where** I was] they made no move to advance. (s2b-014:086)
 b) [**If** you give and take when there's that close bodily contact] it's great. (s1a-003:146)
 c) It was a freedom [**because** everybody there wanted to talk about the life of the mind in one form or another]. (s1b-046:144)
 d) [**Although** the Queen technically in law has the right to withhold] convention says that she doesn't. (s1b-011:069)

A distinction must be drawn between nominal and adverbial clauses on the one and relative clauses on the other hand. All three kinds of clauses are grouped together as subordinate or dependent clauses, because they do not occur independently but are integrated into a superordinate structure. With nominal and adverbial clauses, this superordinate structure is a clause, and the dependent clauses fulfil a function on the level of the clause, i.e. as subject, object, complement, or adverbial. Relative clauses, in contrast, do not function within the clause but within a noun phrase, namely as one kind of postmodification of the noun phrase head. They are thus fundamentally different from nominal and adverbial clauses and should not be confused.

Compound sentences, in comparison to complex sentences, are fairly simple from a structural perspective. While with complex sentences two or more clauses stand in a relationship of super- and subordination, clauses that form compound sentences are in a co-ordination relationship, i.e. both clauses are situated on the same level of hierarchy and no clause depends on the other. Coordination is usually made explicit by co-ordinators, here in bold print.

(36) a) [You don't know what to expect] **and** [I think we're all in the same situation]. (s1a-002:087)
b) [I can't remember exactly when it was,] **but** [it was after the Gulf war began]. (w1b-015:076)
c) [I may be staying around to the end of the week] **or** [I may go back tomorrow]. (s1a-098:048

6.5 Two sample analyses

To conclude this chapter, this section provides a detailed sample analysis of two sentences taken from the ICE-GB corpus. The first (slightly adapted) is given below.

(37) Yesterday, I told them how Thomas had enjoyed *Trumpets in Grumpet Land*, which is one of their books. (s1a-018:137)

We first want to find out what the structure of the whole clause is. As can be seen, the main verb is a form of TELL, which is a ditransitive verb, i.e. we are dealing with the clause structure SVOiOd. More specifically, this means that the adverbial *Yesterday* is not demanded by the verb, which makes it an optional adverbial. Subject and indirect object are *I* and *them*, respectively. The direct object, i.e. that which is told, is a nominal clause of the *wh*-type: *how Thomas had enjoyed Trumpets in Grumpet Land, which is one of their books*. The structure of the superordinate clause is as follows (the brackets around the indexed A indicate the optionality of the adverbial):

(37') Yesterday$_{(A)}$, I$_S$ told$_S$ them$_{Oi}$ [how Thomas had enjoyed *Trumpets in Grumpet Land*, which is one of their books]$_{Od}$.

The subordinate nominal clause, introduced by the subordinator *how*, is an SVOd clause with the main verb ENJOY. The noun phrase *Thomas* is the subject, *had enjoyed* is the verb, and the noun phrase *Trumpets in Grumpet Land, which is one of their books* is the direct object.

(37'') Thomas$_S$ [had enjoyed]$_V$ [*Trumpets in Grumpet Land*, which is one of their books]$_{Od}$.

Note that the subordinate clause that is part of the direct object is a relative clause. It does not have any function within the sentence that is analysed in (37"). It merely serves to postmodify the head *Trumpets in Grumpet Land*. Still, it can be analysed with regard to the clause patterns. The relative clause is of the SVCs type, with the relative pronoun functioning as subject, the form *is* as verb and the noun phrase *one of their books* as subject complement. Note, that this bit of 'extra analysis' is not relevant for the description of the structure the clause. It will therefore not be included in Figure 6.7, which shows the structure of (37) in a tree diagram.

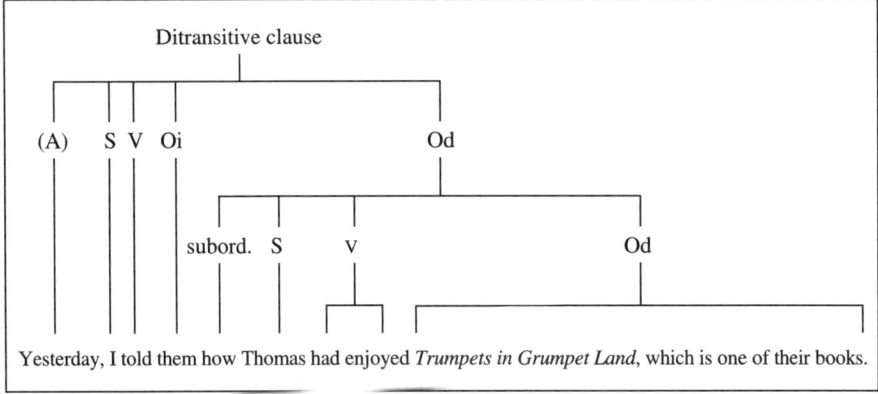

Figure 6.7: A sample analysis of the clause Yesterday, I told them how Thomas had enjoyed Trumpets in Grumpet Land, which is one of their books.

The second example is slightly more complex.

(38) It is not clear whether this is what Malachi is saying or what the people are saying. (s2a-036:050)

It makes sense to start with the whole sentence and first try to find out if we are dealing with one of the major clause patterns or a secondary clause pattern. A look at the sentence reveals that the latter is the case. More specifically, the sentence is an example of *it*-extraposition, as becomes apparent if we take a closer look at the structure of the sentence. Figure 6.4 in section 6.3 above described the relation of *it*-extraposition and its non-extraposed counterpart as follows.

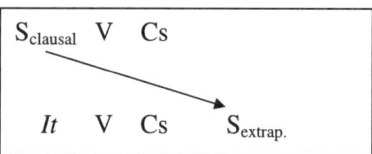

Figure 6.4: The relation of it-extraposition and its corresponding canonical clause pattern.

The example under (38) obviously fits that pattern: the verb is *is not* (we will treat the negation particle as part of the verb phrase), the subject complement is *clear*, and the extraposed subject is *whether this is what Malachi is saying or what the people are saying*. Further evidence for this analysis is provided by the fact that the whole sentence can be rewritten to match the structure described in the top line in Figure 6.3:

(38') [Whether this is what Malachi is saying or what the people are saying]$_{Sclausal}$ [is not]$_V$ clear$_{Cs}$.

The sample sentence obviously is a complex sentence since one of its constituents, in this case the subject, is a clause itself. So, we are dealing with a subordinated nominal clause, namely *whether this is what Malachi is saying or what the people are saying*. This clause, of course, can be analysed just like any other clause that we have discussed in this chapter.

First we try to identify the form of the clause. The subordinating conjunction *whether* tells us that this subordinating clause is a *wh*-clause. The clause itself has the structure SVC, with *this* as subject, *is* as verb and *what Malachi is saying or what the people are saying* as subject complement. The clausal subject can, thus, be described as follows:

(37") Whether$_{subord.}$ this$_S$ is$_V$ [what Malachi is saying or what the people are saying]$_{Cs}$.

The subject complement in (37") consists of two co-ordinated clauses, linked by the co-ordinator *or*. Each of the clauses is a *wh*-clause. The structure of each of these being simple: the verb *say* is a monotransitive verb, i.e. it demands a subject (the person that says something) and a direct object (something that is said). With the first co-ordinated clause the subject is *Malachi* and with the second it is *the people*. In both cases, the direct object of the clause is *what*. The complete analysis of this sample sentence, thus, looks like this:

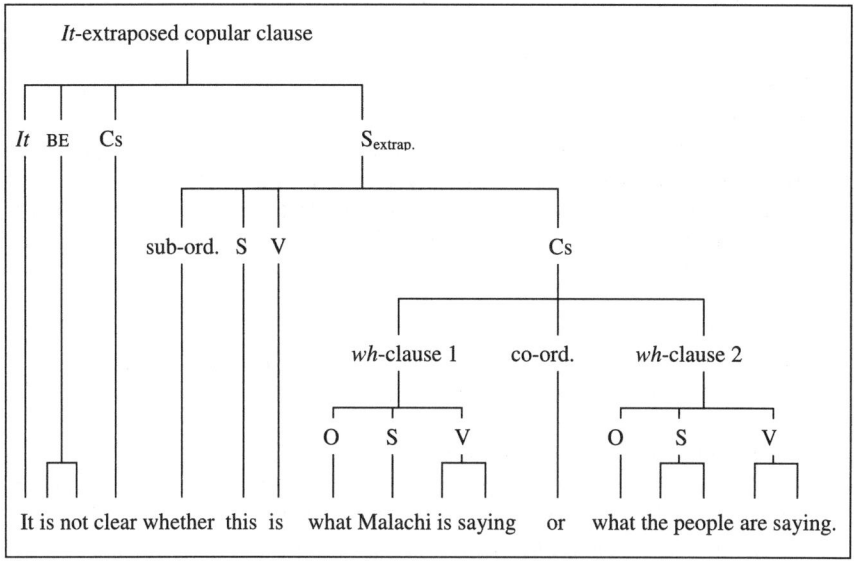

Figure 6.8: A sample analysis of the clause It is not clear whether this is what Malachi is saying or what the people are saying.

6.6 Further reading

Quirk et al. (1985: 49-59) provide an excellent survey of the major clause types and systematic correspondences between them. In addition, pages 987 to 991 are an accessible discussion of complex and compound sentences.

Aarts (1997: 66-82) provides a good overview of the different formal realisations of clause constituents.

Biber et al. (1999: 895-964) provide a detailed outline of non-canonical and secondary clause patterns, their frequencies in different genres and factors that influence their use.

6.7 Study questions

1. Name and explain the seven criteria of subject-hood presented in this chapter.
2. Which is the subject in the following clause? Which of the seven criteria can be used to substantiate your claim?
   Yesterday we went on one cable car up to the mountain. (w1b-009:017)

3. Is the underlined phrase in the following sentence a subject complement or a direct object? Why?
   He was apparently a very popular person. (s1a-003:053)
4. Name the three kinds of adverbials discussed in this chapter, explain their functions and give one illustrative example each.
5. How many transitive verb types does the English language have, and what are the corresponding clause types? Give examples of each.
6. Do the examples below instantiate two different verbs or only one verb? Substantiate your claim with the help of your knowledge of the clause patterns of English.
   Harold moved.
   Harold moved the table. (cf. Aarts 1997: 16)
7. Use *it*-clefts to highlight all of the constituents in the sentences below.
   a) *With great reluctance Iraq's given the UN figures of civilian casualties.*
   b) *Peter was sitting in the garden.*
   c) *I put my leg onto the top shelf.*
8. Explain the distinction of complex and compound sentences. Give examples.
9. Analyse the following clauses similarly to the analyses given in section 6.5.
   a) *He told them that he found it very fascinating to watch birds.*
   b) *Under the present circumstances, people should not be given influenza vaccination shots.*
   c) *I put my leg onto the top shelf because Peter told me to do it.*

7 Indeterminacy: Multiple Analysis, Fuzziness and Gradience

The previous chapters were concerned with the analysis of syntactic structures. As we have seen, syntactic analysis basically means that we assign a linguistic element or strings of linguistic elements to certain linguistic categories. For instance, the clause *I find it fascinating* (s1a-002:035) was assigned the structure 'SVOdCo' and labelled a complex-transitive clause. With regard to clause constituents we would assign the label 'subject' to the word form *I*, the label 'verb' to *find*, the label 'direct object' to *it*, and the label 'object complement' to *fascinating*. The next step, then, would take us to the level of formal realisations of the individual clause constituents: while this is unproblematic for subject, object and verb (realised by noun phrases (more specifically pronouns) and a verb) we saw in section 2.2.4 that word forms like *fascinating* are not easy to deal with. We know that the English language has a verb FASCINATE, and we also know that verbs have an -*ing*-participle form, which in this case would be *fascinating*. The word form *fascinating* could, thus, be formally categorised as a verb. However, we also know from section 6.1.4 that complements are usually realised by adjectives, i.e. this verb form occurs in a position typically associated with adjectives. In addition, the verb form is not used to describe an action but a feature (in this case, of the object); a function that is usually also fulfilled by adjectives. In 2.2.4 we solved problems like these by drawing a division between 'parts of speech', i.e. labels like 'noun', 'verb', 'adjective' and so on and the actual use of word forms. The part-of-speech classification was reserved for the lexical unit (e.g. FASCINATE is a verb), and we allowed individual word forms (in this case *fascinating*) to fulfil functions usually associated with other word forms.

This example (and many others in the last six chapters) goes to show that syntactic analysis often is not as easy as the first part of this book may have suggested. This is due to the fact that language, just as any other natural phenomenon, does not always coincide with the strict categories imposed on it by human experts. "All grammars leak" is a famous dictum by Edward Sapir (1921: 38), which maybe most grammarians and syntacticians would subscribe to. No matter how precise our model and our categories, there will always be cases of indeterminacy: the odd one out, the one case that may fit two or three categories to some extent but none of them fully, or the one token that seems to call for a category of its own. In other cases, it may seem difficult to draw a clear dividing line between categories A and B. In the most part of the previous chapters it was suggested that syntactic analysis is a case of either-or, black-or-white. At some points the reader may have got an idea of examples where the boxes and categories that the text suggested are not fully satisfactory. This chapter is devoted to such in-between cases and the grey areas of syntax, thereby putting into perspective the descriptive categories we have come up with so far in the course of this book.

7.1 Multiple analysis

At the beginning of this chapter it was said that syntactic analysis basically means to assign a linguistic element to a certain category. In many cases, however, we find that the same linguistic element may be assigned to different categories; this is what we refer to as 'multiple analysis'. It seems reasonable to distinguish three kinds of multiple analysis, namely 'pseudo multiple analysis', 'quasi multiple analysis' and 'multiple analysis proper'. Pseudo multiple analysis is concerned with different schools or different approaches. Here we find different analyses, since each approach comes up with its own categories, and these need not coincide. In the case of quasi multiple analysis we are concerned with categories within one and the same model of description, but the categories relate to different (non-overlapping) areas of description. With multiple analysis proper we are confronted with cases where one and the same linguistic element (or string of elements) can be assigned to two (or more) categories that relate to the same area of description. We will discuss each of these cases in turn below.

An example of pseudo multiple analysis is the discussion of the sentence *The man had locked the briefcase in the boot* (w2f-018:006) in section 1.2. There we saw that (at least) four different structural analyses are possible.

(1) a) [The man] had [locked [the briefcase] [in [the boot]]]
    b) [The man] [had [locked [the briefcase] [in [the boot]]]]
    c) [The man]$_{Subject}$ [had locked the briefcase in the boot]$_{Predicate}$
    d) [The man]$_{Subject}$ [had locked]$_{Verb}$ [the briefcase]$_{Object}$ [in the boot]$_{Adverbial}$

We found that the different analyses are due to different aspects that different approaches focus on. The dissimilarities between (1a) and (1b), for instance, can be explained by the fact that the analysis under (1b) subscribes to the tenet of binary branching (i.e. each constituent can be split into exactly two constituents), whereas the analysis under (1a) does not. The two analyses in (1c) and (1d) are more concerned with semantic and functional aspects of the clause, with the ancient distinction between subject and predicate in (1c) and the functional constituents analysis in (1d) (which was also introduced in chapter 6). Note that some of the above analyses are in fact irreconcilable. That is, adherents to binary branching would argue against all of the other suggestions with the exception of (1c) with its binary distinction of subject and predicate, which (to some extent) can be subsumed under the binary-branching approach. Of course conflicts of this kind, which are due to different models of grammar or syntax, do not come as a surprise. Hence, the term 'pseudo multiple analysis', indicating that it is not a real case of multiple analysis, but something to be expected taking into account that different models work with different premises.

The analyses (1a), (1c) and (1d), however, can exist alongside each other in the model that has been followed and described in this book – they are a case of quasi multiple analysis. (1a) was the result of the constituency tests that we applied in chapter 1. The fact that the auxiliary *had* occurs as a constituent of its own does justice to the special role of the operator discussed in section 3.2. The distinction of subject and predicate in (1c) was discussed in section 6.1.2 in the context of the aboutness criterion that is fulfilled by many subjects. Finally, the description given under (1d) derives from the kind of sentence analysis introduced in section 6.2. Obviously, the different analyses make reference to different facets of the same sentence, all of which are equally important: while the focus in (1a) is on structural aspects, (1c) and (1d) highlight semantic and functional ones. The term 'quasi multiple analysis' makes reference to the fact that contrasting analyses are the result of a focus on different aspects, all of which are relevant to a given model of grammar. But with regard to each of the individual aspects there is just one single analysis possible. In the above examples, the different analyses are not in conflict because each highlights an aspect that leaves untouched the aspects highlighted in the other analyses.

Finally, with 'multiple analysis proper', one aspect can be analysed in different ways, thus leading to two or more analyses. Here, however, the analyses are actually conflicting and there are arguments for each of them. A case in point is what Quirk et al (1985: 1155) call 'prepositional verbs', which consist of "a lexical verb followed by a preposition with which it is semantically and/or syntactically associated". The example discussed by the authors is the sequence *look after*, meaning 'to tend', as in the sentences below:

(2) So, foster carers look after the children. (s2b-038:095)

The question with this example is whether the preposition *after* is part of the verb or whether it heads a prepositional phrase consisting of the preposition and the following noun phrase. The two alternatives lead to different analyses of the clause structure:

(2') So, [foster carers]$_S$ [look after]$_V$ [the children]$_{Od}$.
(2")So, [foster carers]$_S$ look$_V$ [after the children]$_A$.

As you can see, in the first case, the resulting clause pattern is of the SVO type. In the second case, the resulting clause type (according to Quirk et al. 1985) is of the SVA type, with the adverbial realised by the prepositional phrase *after the children*. The problem is that there are arguments for both analyses. For instance, the fact that (2) can undergo passive transformation indicates that the noun phrase *the children* is indeed the object of the clause, which makes *look after* a transitive verb. This analysis is supported by a substitution or replacement test (see section 1.1): the string *look after* can be substituted by a form of the transitive verb TEND:

(3') So, the children are looked after by foster carers.
   So, foster carers tend the children.

On the other hand, however, a co-ordination test lends support to both analyses.

(4') So, foster carers look after the children and the pets.
(4") So, foster carers look after the children and after the pets.

Similarly, *it*-clefts seem to be able to highlight both the direct object *the children* and the adverbial *after the children*.

(5') So, it is the children that the foster carers look after (, not the pets).
(5") So, it is after the children that the foster carers look (, not after the pets).

Finally, and also supporting both analyses is the fact that in questions both the direct object and the adverbial can be fronted:

(6') Who do the foster carers look after? ~ The children.
(6") After whom do the foster carers look? ~ After the children.

Although the multi-word verb analysis presented in (2') wins out with a slight margin, we also find a number of reasons that support the analysis which treats *look* as the verb followed by the adverbial *after the children*. As a consequence, we are left with two alternative analyses of the same string, both of which are plausible.

As we have seen, multiple analysis has to do with the fact that a given linguistic element can be assigned to more than one category, i.e. researchers may have a number of different categories to choose from in their analysis. With this concept, therefore, the focus is on the act of assigning a given string of elements to one of the possible categories. In what follows, we will take a look at the nature of the categories themselves.

7.2 Fuzziness

Traditional grammatical categories are influenced by the classical view of categorization which dates back as far as Aristotle and his *Categories*. In his view categories are strictly and clearly defined, and each member of a category is as good a member as any other member. Aristotle writes:

> Substance, it seems, does not admit of a more and a less. [...] any given substance is not called more, or less, that which it is. For example, if this substance is a man, it will not be more a man or less a man either than itself or than another man. For one man is not more a man than another, as one pale thing is more pale than another and one beautiful thing more beautiful than another. (Aristotle 1963 [c. 330 BC]: 10)

The idea behind this claim is the following: any object can be thought of as a bundle of co-occurring features (cf. section 1.3). Some of these features are necessary some are non-necessary, or essential and accidental in Aristotle's words. For instance, defining features for humans are that they have speech, whereas the colour of their skin is not a defining feature. The point is that a category (and its members) can be defined by focussing on the essential features of objects and abstracting away from non-essential or accidental features. For instance, the category EVEN NUMBER is defined by the fact that even numbers do not leave a residue if they are divided by 2. This is true for the numbers 2, 4, 6, 8, 10, 12, and so on. Some of these numbers have the additional quality that they do not leave a residue if they are divided by 3, namely 6, 12, 18, etc. However, this feature is not regarded as essential for the category EVEN NUMBER, i.e. it is abstracted away from. To take another example, the category BOY is defined by the necessary features 'human', 'male' and 'non-adult'. Here, we see that if a given entity fails to show one of these features it is not a member of this category. For instance, if the feature 'human' is not given but the feature 'horse', the resulting category is COLT, a young male horse. If we have the feature 'female' instead of 'male', we are talking about the category GIRL, and if we substitute the feature 'non-adult' by 'adult', the resulting category is MAN. Each of the three features is necessary for the definition of the category BOY. At the same time, these three features are collectively sufficient to warrant membership in this category: any living being that shares the features 'human', 'male' and 'non-adult' is a boy, regardless of non-essential features that are not shared by other members of the same category. So, we find that while each of the essential features on its own is necessary for membership in a category, they are jointly sufficient to describe this given category (see Evans & Green 2006: 251). As a consequence, categories are homogeneous, they do not have any internal structure. If a group of objects all share the same essential features, then all of these objects are members of that given category to the same extent – no member is better than any other member. This traditional view on categorisation is illustrated in Figure 7.1 below: the circle represents a category, understood as a bundle of necessary features, which are represented by the little crosses. The areas marked by the broken lines represent members of the category, A and B. The two members are not identical, since A contains a feature (on the upper left-hand corner) which B does not have, and B contains two features (the two crosses on the right), which A does not have. With regard to the necessary features of the category, however, the two are identical – each of the two members has all features that are necessary for membership.

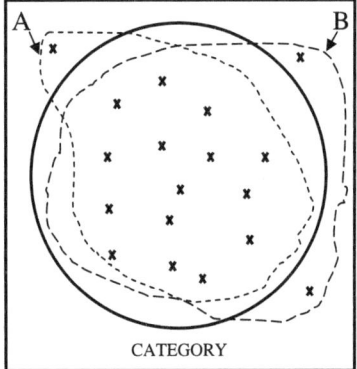

Figure 7.1: Categories in the Aristotelian sense.

However, it has been shown that this conception of categories and categorisation is not unproblematic. In some cases, for instance, it is difficult to find a single feature that is shared by all members of a category. A famous example is Wittgenstein's discussion of the category GAMES and his claim that "if you look at them you will not see something that is common to *all*" (cited in Aarts et al. 2004: 41). Also, natural categories do have members which are exceptional in some way or other: there are humans, for instance, who cannot speak and write. Still, we would consider them as members of this category. In addition, prototype theory (e.g. Rosch 1978 or Rosch et al. 1976) has shown that categories are usually not homogenous but show what is called 'typicality effects'. Asking informants to rate particular instances of one category with regard to their representativeness of this category will usually reveal an asymmetry between different members of the same category. For instance, while robin and sparrows are considered typical birds, a swan or an ostrich are considered less typical. Interestingly, these 'typicality effects' also arise with clear-cut mathematical concepts, such as that of 'even number' discussed above. Evans and Green (2006: 254) point to experiments by Armstrong et al. (1983), which shows that numbers like '2', '4' and '6' are rated better examples than '98' or '10,002'. Note that this category is a very simple one where members are defined by just one necessary feature, namely 'leaves no remainder if divided by 2'. It follows that typicality effects of the kind above pose a serious threat to the classical way of defining category membership. Instead of homogenous categories, these findings suggest that categories do in fact permit of variation, as shown in Figure 7.2. Again, each of the areas delimited by the broken lines indicates a member of the category (represented by the circle). Note that member A only shows three features whereas B and C exhibit six and seven features, respectively. A would be regarded as the least representative member of the category, and C as the most representative member. Note also that A and C do not share any features, as in the examples of the category GAMES mentioned above. The category is 'fuzzy' in that its members are representative of the category to different extents.

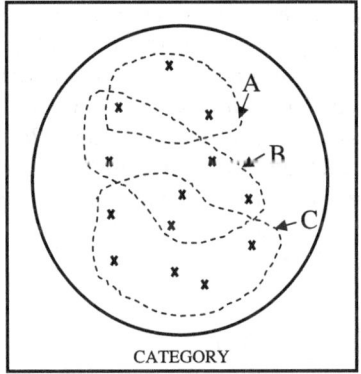

Figure 7.2: A fuzzy category.

The Aristotelian view of categorisation has also found its way into linguistics, as can be witnessed in componential approaches to phonology (see, for instance, the Prague School approach to phonology, Trubetzkoy (1939), or Pilch's (1964) *Phonemtheorie*), and generative theories of semantics and syntax (see, for instance, Chomsky's (1965) selectional restriction rules or Katz and Fodor's 1963 projection rules). But, as we saw in the first part of this book, linguistic phenomena often do not seem to be describable in such terms. Linguistic categories are not so much similar to what we see in Figure 7.1 but rather to what we find in Figure 7.2: linguistic categories are often fuzzy, i.e. they do show a certain amount of variation within the categories.

An illustrative example is the category ADJECTIVE. Aarts (2007) suggests that adjectives should be described with regard to five central properties, illustrated in (7a to e) below (see also section 2.2.4).

(7) a) a happy woman (attributive position)
 b) she is happy (predicative position)
 c) very happy (intensification)
 d) happy/happier/happiest (gradability)
 e) unhappy (*un-* prefixation) (cf. Aarts 2007: 106)

(7a) shows *happy* in attributive position, i.e. as a premodification of a noun. In (7b), the adjective functions as a subject complement, it is in predicative position. Example c) shows that *happy* can be intensified by an adverb phrase, while d) illustrates that happy can be graded. Finally, in (7e) *happy* is prefixed with the affix *un-*, meaning 'not', a feature that is common with many adjectives.

However, a look at the adjectives of the English language makes clear that not all of them exhibit all of the five properties above. The adjective *thin* shows most of the features that *happy* shows, apart from prefixation with *un-* (*unthin), which does not work with *alive* and *utter* either (*unalive, *unutter). In addition, *alive* only occurs in predicative but not in attributive position (*the hamster is alive* vs. *an alive hamster[5]), is difficult to grade (?*alive - more alive - most alive*), although it can be intensified (*this man is hardly alive*). *Utter* occurs in attributive position (*utter nonsense, complete and utter horror*) but fails to satisfy any of the other criteria. A synopsis of which criteria are met by which adjective is given in Table 7.1 below.

Table 7.1: Degrees of adjective-hood.

	attributive position	predicative position	intensification	gradability	prefix *un-*
happy	+	+	+	+	+
thin	+	+	+	+	-
alive	-	+	+	-	-
utter	+	-	-	-	-

---

[5] Note, however, that Aarts (2007: 107) provides one attested example of *alive* in attributive position: "Snow, who lives in Kentish Town, has an *alive* presence [...]."

From Table 7.1 above, we would have to conclude that 'some adjectives are better adjectives than others'. While *happy* would be considered a prototypical example, *utter* would only be thought of as a peripheral member of the category, with *thin* being close to the centre and *alive* closer to the periphery.

This finding is by no means exceptional. On the contrary, what we find here for the category ADJECTIVE holds for most of the syntactic categories of the English language (and most probably of any language). Another example to be discussed here is that of the category SUBJECT. In section 6.1.2 we identified seven features that are indicative of subject-hood, repeated in Table 7.2 below (note, by the way, that this would count as a case of 'quasi multiple analysis' since the first two features make reference to semantic aspects, while the last five refer to structural ones).

Table 7.2: Characteristic features of subjects.

The subject of a clause ...
is the agent
is what the clause is about
is a noun phrase
is the first noun phrase
is in number concord with the verb
is repeated as a pronoun in tag-questions
occurs after the operator in *yes-no* questions

Consider the examples below.

(8) a) **He** loves the company. (s1a-017:295)
   b) **Their comments** were described by Harry Fletcher. (w2c-001:074)
   c) Last night **I** was ready to tip beer over one of them. (w1b-005:144)
   d) **To list and describe them all** would take too much space here and would be confusing. (w2a-037:055)
   e) This evening **the unions** were told of the impact on jobs. (s2b-002:071)
   f) **There** is drugs in the book. (s1b-024:123)

Recall that we found in section 6.1.2 that all subjects fulfil the three last criteria, in the discussion of the above examples we will therefore focus on the first four of the above features. Only the pronoun *he* in (8a) shows all of these characteristics: it denotes the agent, the sentence is about the person referred to by *he*, and the pronoun is a noun phrase and the first noun phrase is the clause. The subject of

(8b) shares all of these features apart from the agent criterion, since the agent in that case occurs in the *by*-phrase at the end of the clause. In (8c) we find that the subject *I* is the agent and it is an NP, but it is not the first agent and it is not clear whether the clause is about *last night* or about the person referred to by the pronoun. With (8d) both the agent and the aboutness criterion are met, but the subject is a clause, so the two noun phrase criteria are not met. (8e) is similar to (8b) in that the subject *the unions* is not the agent of the clause, and it is similar to (8c) because it is not the first noun phrase in the clause and we cannot be sure whether the clause is about the subject or the initial adverbial. Finally, the subject in example (8f) does not fulfil any of the subject criteria except those that are fulfilled by all of them: *there* is not an agent, the clause is not about *there*, and *there* would be best described as an adverb phrase. Table 7.3 sums up the above analysis.

Table 7.3: Degrees of subject-hood.

Example	agent	aboutness	NP	1st NP	verb concord	tag question	*yes-no* question
(7a)	+	+	+	+	+	+	+
(7b)	-	+	+	+	+	+	+
(7c)	+	?	+	-	+	+	+
(7d)	+	+	-	-	+	+	+
(7e)	-	?	+	-	+	+	+
(7f)	-	-	-	-	+	+	+

Table 7.3 makes clear that the category SUBJECT, like the category ADJECTIVE, is fuzzy in that it allows for degrees of subject-hood: some subjects are more subject-like than other subjects. The Aristotelian way of categorisation seems to fail here. However, one might want to argue that this failure is due to the fact that the list of essential features merely is too long. After all, if we focus on the last three features only, we do have an Aristotelian category. While this approach may seem appealing at first sight (at least we would not have to put up with inconsistencies in our categories) it is undesirable if we recall from section 1.3 that categorisation is a means that helps humans to reduce the complexity of the world to manageable portions by grouping together those things that share a number of features. The choice of categories is driven by considerations of efficiency, including the degree of informativity of the individual categories. If the category SUBJECT was only described by the last three criteria, the category

would not be very informative. We would ignore bits of information that, although not for all subjects, hold for most of the subjects: most of the subjects are agents, most of the subjects refer to what the clause is about, most of the subjects are noun phrases and most subjects are the first noun phrase in the clause. With regard to efficiency it is reasonable to include these features as characteristics of subjects and to cope with the downside of a category showing degrees of representativity and exceptions to the rule. Fuzzy but generally informative categories are better than Aristotelian but relatively uninformative ones.

7.3 Gradience

While I used the term 'fuzziness' to refer to indeterminacy within one category of description, the term 'gradience' is used here to denote the merging of two categories in one another. These two categories are understood as the endpoints of a 'gradient', as Quirk et al. make clear:

> A gradient is a scale which relates two categories of description (for example two word classes) in terms of degrees of similarity and contrast. At the ends of the scale are items which belong clearly to one category or to another; intermediate positions on the scale are taken by 'in-between' cases – items which fail, in different degrees, to satisfy the criteria for one or the other category. (Quirk et al. 1985: 90)

That is, we have a set of elements which clearly belong to category I and another set of elements which clearly belong to category II. In addition, there are also tokens which show features of both categories so that it is impossible to assign them to one category only. Gradience can be represented as follows:

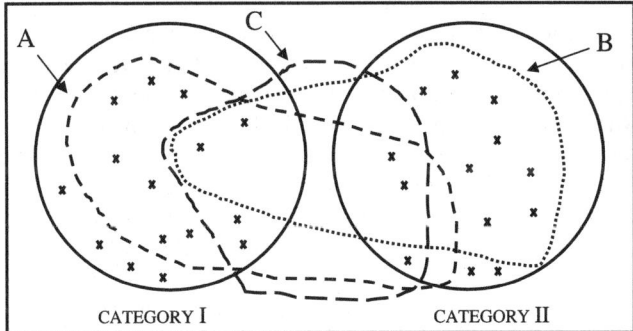

Figure 7.3: Gradience.

Note that in Figure 7.3 members that show all features of the respective categories have not been included for reasons of presentational clarity. In addition to these elements, we now also have elements that exhibit features of both categories. Element A is fairly representative of category I but it also shows some features usually associated with category II, and vice versa for element B. Element C, in contrast, obtains an intermediate position, being representative of both categories although only to a slight extent.

A nice example of phenomena of this kind is the gradient between verbs and nouns, in particular the behaviour of the *ing*-forms, which is discussed in considerable detail in Quirk et al. (1985: 1290-1291; see also Aarts 2007: 143-145 for a discussion) with the example of *painting*. Here we will only take a look at five of the fourteen examples that Quirk et al. analyse. Note that some of them are slightly adapted.

(9) a) The deft painting of Brown is as skilful as that of Gainsborough.
    b) Brown's painting of his daughter is a delight to watch.
    c) Brown's deftly painting his daughter is a delight to watch.
    d) Brown deftly painting his daughter is a delight to watch.
    e) Brown is deftly painting his daughter. (adapted from Quirk et al. 1985: 1290-1291)

First of all, one verb-related feature that we find in all examples is, of course, the form of the word form itself, since the ending *-ing* indicates the progressive aspect of verbs. Apart from that, (9a) and (9b) would be regarded as clear instance of nouns since we find *painting* as the head of a noun phrase in these examples. In the first example, the word form is preceded by the determiner *the* and premodified by the adjective phrase *deft*. This clearly indicates the noun status of *painting*, as does the postmodifying prepositional phrase *of Brown*. In (9b) we still have a determiner (this time realised by the genitive noun phrase *Brown's*) and a postmodifying prepositional phrase (*of his daughter*) but the premodifying adjective as an indicator of noun-hood is gone. So, we have one noun-related feature less. In (9c) we see that two verb-related features have been added. Firstly, the premodifying adjective in (9a) is now a premodifying adverb in (9c). Secondly, the postmodifying prepositional phrase in (9b) has changed into a noun phrase which can be interpreted as the direct object of the verbal form *painting*. A feature indicative of noun status is the fact that the whole string *deftly painting his daughter* is introduced by a genitive noun phrase, which seems to function as a determiner. In (9d) there is nothing which indicates a possible noun status of the form *painting*, since the genitive has changed into a nominative, which then functions as the subject of the nominal clause functioning as the subject of the whole clause. In (9f), finally, the verb status of *painting* becomes even more obvious since it occurs as the main verb of a clause in the present progressive. Here, the fact that it is preceded by a form of BE is an additional indicator of the verb-hood of the form. Table 7.4 shows how the form *painting* moves from noun to verb from top to bottom of the above examples.

Table 7.4: *The noun-verb gradient with the example painting.*

Example	Noun-related features			Verb-related features			
	Premod. AdjP	Postmod. PP	Det.	Direct object	Premod. AdvP	Subject	Form of BE
(9a)	+	+	+	-	-	-	-
(9b)	-	+	+	-	-	-	-
(9c)	-	-	+	+	+	-	-
(9d)	-	-	-	+	+	+	-
(9e)	-	-	-	+	+	+	+

A look at this table, again, makes clear that it would not be feasible to be too strict with the definition of categories. If we did not allow for different degrees of representativity and for gradience we would have to come up with five individual categories just to accommodate the five examples presented here. The alternative, namely to reduce the number of categories at the expense of a grammar that leaks in some places, seems more sensible.

7.4 Further reading

Aarts (2007) is a thorough discussion of grammatical indeterminacy (although employing a different terminology – see study question 5). It compares different concepts, provides a wealth of case studies and suggests a way to formalise indeterminacy.

Aarts et al. (2004) is a collection of texts that are relevant to the study of the phenomenon of indeterminacy in all its facets.

Evans & Green (2006: 8.1 and 8.2) provides an excellent introduction to prototype theory and related phenomena.

7.5 Study questions

1. What are the three kinds of multiple analysis distinguished in this chapter? Which one is most relevant for the study of syntax?
2. Traditional approaches to categorisation define categories on the basis of necessary and jointly sufficient features. Explain this distinction with regard to the category WOMAN. What are the necessary features, why are they necessary and what does it mean that they are jointly sufficient?
3. Using Table 7.1, determine how 'adjectivy' the adjectives IGNORANT and ALONE.
4. Where on the noun-verb gradient would the following examples (cf. Quirk et al. 1985: 1290-1291) of *painting* be put?
   Painting his daughter, Brown noticed that his hand was shaking.
   I dislike Brown's deftly painting his daughter.
   The painting of Brown is as skilful as that of Gainsborough.
5. Aarts (2007: 79) distinguishes intersective gradience (IG) from subsective gradience (SG) and defines them as follows:

   > IG involves two categories α and β, and obtains where there exists a set γ of elements characterized by a subset of α-like properties and subset of β-like properties.

   > SG allows for a particular element x from category α to be closer to the prototype of α than some other element χ from the same category, and recognizes a core and periphery within the form classes of language.

   On the basis of these definitions, which term relates to what here has been called 'fuzziness' and which relates to 'gradience'?

8 Same Same but Different? Spoken and Written Syntax

8.1 Does spoken language have structure?

The above question may seem a bit odd. After all, we know that both speech and writing are based on a set of rules, which we call 'grammar'. Accordingly, we would assume that spoken language (here understood as spontaneous spoken speech, as in face-to-face or telephone conversation) shows regular structures similar to those of written language. However, the question above may seem more reasonable if we take into account the common assumption that spoken language is a more or less unrefined and formless variant of the written language. Note that some decades ago, even linguists and grammarians still were of this opinion, described by Lyons (1981: 11) as the 'bias of traditional grammar'.

> Until recently, grammarians have been concerned almost exclusively with the language of literature and have taken little account of everyday colloquial speech. All too often they have treated the norms of literary usage as the norms of correctness for the language itself and have condemned colloquial usage, in so far as it differs from literary usage, as ungrammatical, slovenly or even illogical. (Lyons 1981: 11)

Although today this bias seems to have been overcome by (hopefully) all linguists we still feel its repercussions amongst lay people. A particularly nice example of this (although maybe slightly outdated) is provided by Halliday (1989: 77), who discusses the view on spoken language expressed by an author who introduces students to the craft of writing. The author presents a transcript of a conversation between two people, which he then uses as a basis for pointing out the flaws of speech.

> 'Yer saw the *Star Trek* film, eh? What ya think of it then?'
> 'Oh, dunno. S'alright I s'pose [*shrugs expressively*] ... good effects ... yeah ... beaut effects. And they've got these things ... these spaceships ... sort of sailing along ... and the music ... wow, that was something. But it wasn't all that ... [*Waves hand disparagingly*] you know ...'
> 'Boring?'
> 'Yeah ... no ... what I mean is ... well in *Star Wars* they were really up against something, weren't they ... it got you in, didn't it? don't you reckon? Yeah, but in this film ... well, there's no one there when they

get there. Too much ... no, too little, happens ... I dunno ... give me *Star Wars*'.

Did you notice how formless, tentative and spur-of-the-moment the sample of speech [...] was? Yet, although it looks shabby in printed form, the original conversation would have seemed quite sensible to the participants (try reading it aloud). Why? Because **speech is, by its nature, usually unstructured, superficial and low in content**.
(McRoberts 1981: 4-5, quoted in Halliday 1989)

The final sentence in the above example maybe is representative of what many lay people think about speech: compared to writing, speech indeed seems to lack structure, which in a way makes writing somehow superior – a view which is mirrored in expressions like 'he or she talks like a book'. It is only recently that linguists have begun to treat spoken language as a phenomenon in its own right, which deserves analysis and description just like written language. That is, spoken and written language differ in many respects, but these differences do not entail an evaluation in terms of 'better' and 'worse'. The present chapter elaborates on characteristic features of spontaneous spoken speech and the factors that determine them.

8.2 Two modes, one descriptive apparatus?

Although both spoken and written language are based on the same core grammar, and although spontaneous spoken language is not as unstructured or formless as some people believe, this does not necessarily mean that both written and spoken language can satisfactorily be described by the same descriptive apparatus. After all, it is by judging spoken language on the basis of categories relevant to written language that spoken language sometimes appears formless and fragmentary. To some extent, a new or modified method of description is called for.

This becomes apparent if we take into consideration a central notion of syntax, namely the notion 'sentence'. A look at authentic language data shows that this is a useful concept for the description of written but not for spoken language, if, as it usually does, the term refers "to a unit of the writing system – that which extends from a capital letter following a full stop up to the next full stop" (Halliday 1989: 66). A comparable unit for spoken language might be what is called the 'tone unit', which is defined "by a nucleus, a boundary and rising or falling tone at the boundary" (Esser 1988: 3). Examples from the London-Lund Corpus (a prosodically annotated corpus of authentic spoken English) are given below. Each line represents one tone unit. The syllables in bold capitals are the stressed syllables, the arrows show the intonation contour, in this case a rise (↑), a rise-fall (↑↓), and two falls (↓):

(1) well now that you've done **THESE** ↑
and they've been so suc**CESS**ful ↑↓
we'd like you to do our **SU**per ↓
alpha**MA**tic ↓ (adapted from LLC-S.1.3:143-146)

As can be seen from this example tone units are not co-extensive with syntactic units such as clause or phrase; the last tone unit only extends over one word. All of the four tone units taken together would most likely make one written sentence.

(1') Well, now that you've done these and they've been so successful, we'd like you to do our Super Alphamatic.

It becomes clear that for a comparison of written and spoken language a concept is needed that is medium-independent, i.e. can be applied both to spoken and written data. One such concept is suggested by Halliday (1989), namely the 'clause complex'. Halliday defines it as "a sequence of clauses all structurally linked" (66). The term 'clause complex' is an umbrella term that includes what in this book has been referred to as 'complex sentence' and 'compound sentence'. In the former, clauses are structurally linked by the fact that one clause fulfils a functional role in another clause. The linkage in the latter is provided by co-ordinating conjunctions. It makes sense to include both in one term since the clause complex is a psycholinguistically relevant unit. Halliday writes:

> The clause complex is, in fact, what the sentence (in writing) comes from. The unit that was intuitively recognised by our ancestors when they first introduced the 'stop' as a punctuation mark was the clause complex. (Halliday 1989: 66)

Intonation, i.e. the tone unit, and syntax, i.e. the clause complex, are combined in the 'talk unit'. This concept, based on Euler's (1991) 'Redeeinheit' ('speech unit') was introduced by Halford (1996). She defines the talk unit as

> the maximal unit defined by syntax plus intonation. Neither may a single prosodic presentation unit [i.e. a tone unit; RK] ever be analysed as more than a talk unit nor may single self-contained syntagm ever form the base of more than one talk unit. (Halford 1996: 33)

The idea is that a spoken message contains two channels along which information is conveyed. One is the channel of syntactic structure. With regard to example (1) above, for instance, the string *well now that you've done these* tells us that more is to come, since the string is not syntactically complete; it is a syntagm which is not self-contained, i.e. cannot stand on its own. At the same time, the rising tone at the end of this unit also tells us that more will follow. In the next line, the tone unit signals potential completeness (due to the fall at the tone-unit boundary) but syntactically, the string would not be complete at this point. The third line, again, shows completeness as regards the prosodic channel but signals non-completeness at the syntactic level, since *super* is most likely to be used as a premodifying adjective and not as the head of a noun phrase. Finally, in line 4, the information provided by both channels coincides, both signal completion, i.e. we have reached the end of a talk unit.

Mukherjee (2001) provides a detailed corpus-based analysis of talk units in authentic spoken language and identifies a number of functions that the talk unit may have. One important function is that the end of a talk unit is a potential signal for turn-taking in conversation, i.e. one speaker may take over from the currently talking speaker at the end of a talk unit (see Mukherjee 2001: 132-139). This brings us to the final concept needed for the description of spoken syntax, the concept 'turn'.

The turn, i.e. everything a speaker says before another speaker takes over, can be regarded as the basic unit of spoken interaction, as Carter and McCarthy (2006: 165) make clear: "What seems more important is the production of adequate communicative units and the taking of turns rather than the transition from one sentence [i.e. clause complex] to another". Although the end of a talk unit usually is a likely candidate for turn-taking, this does not mean that all turns comply with the talk unit. This is due to the fact that turns can be much shorter than clause complexes, consisting of a phrase or a word only. In addition, "[s]peakers' turns, unlike written sentences, are not neat and tidy. The speakers regularly interrupt each other, or speak at the same time, intervene in another's contribution or overlap in their speaking turns" (Carter & McCarthy 2006: 166). Some of these features are exemplified in the following excerpt (each line preceded by a small letter is a turn. The pointed brackets mark pauses. The capital letters mark the speakers; each shift from A to B or B to A marks the end of a turn).

(2) a) A: So OK that's job one
    b)   what are the others
    c) B: And uh uh I'm doing a bit of teaching and uh
    d) A: where's that that is at
    e) B: that's University College
    f)   that's just uhm coaching a couple of lasses for BMA and they are doing some
    g)   I mean that's just very temporary <,>

h)   And uhm at the College of Speech Sciences I'm putting things in alphabetical order for them
i) A: <laugh> I see
j) B: I'm their <,> their temporary administrator
k) A: D Phil in indexing
l) B: Yes exactly in alphabetical order yes
m) A: Have you given up doing your D Phil thingy (s1a-011:001-014)

All of the grey areas show overlap in turns – four in less than 100 words. Note that the turn-taking in (2d) does not coincide with the end of a talk unit: the co-ordinator *and* indicates non-completion on the syntactic channel. Still speaker A intervenes in B's turn and asks for information which B originally had not intended to give at that point in time. B provides the asked-for information and continues with what he (supposedly) originally wanted to say in (2f). Note that the second co-ordinated clause in this turn, *they are doing some,* is not finished. In (2k) the turn by speaker A merely consists of a noun phrase, which still is a communicatively adequate unit. The excerpt also illustrates another important feature of conversation: 'back-channelling', the addressee's signalling to the speaker that he or she is still listening. An example is the string *I see* in (2i).

On the whole, we see that the notion of clause-complex alone would not be sufficient to describe the conversational interaction. It is a concept that makes reference to structural relations and dependencies only, thereby ignoring other important aspects of spoken language. It therefore makes sense to include in the description of spoken language the concept of 'tone unit' and 'talk unit', which make reference to intonation and the concept 'turn', which focuses on speaker interaction. The clause complex may be co-extensive with any of the three other units, but often it is not. On some occasions we even find that one clause complex is produced jointly by two different speakers as in the example below, taken from the same conversation. The speakers are talking about what another of the interlocutors is likely to be doing at his or her job; this is what they say:

(3) A: You're going to be photocopying
    B: And making tea and going out to get the sandwiches (S1a-011:034-035)

From a structural point of view the two turns together form a clause complex that complies with the rules of grammar and could be found in a written text. Still, the structural integration coincides with fragmentation as regards the turns which realise the clause complex.

This section has demonstrated that the description of authentic spoken language calls for new concepts that in addition to structural considerations do justice to the idiosyncrasies of spoken language, most importantly prosody and speaker interaction. All of these concepts are useful for the description of spoken language, since every single one of them highlights a characteristic aspect of spoken language and spoken interaction. Table 8.1 lists the concepts described in this section.

Table 8.1: Useful concepts in the description of spoken interaction.

Concept	Makes reference to
Tone unit	Prosody (medium-dependent)
Clause complex	Structure (medium-independent)
Talk unit	Structure and prosody
Turn	Speaker interaction

While the first two sections have explored the nature of spoken syntax at a more general and theoretical level, we will now turn to a discussion of the factors that determine spontaneous spoken language and explore in more detail how this bears on the structure of spoken language.

8.3 Principles of online production and their consequences

It is important to acknowledge that there are huge differences in the production circumstances of spoken and written language. One important aspect is that spontaneous spoken language is subject to the limitations of 'online production'. Biber et al. (1999: 1066-1067) name three principles that are characteristic in this respect.

The first is 'keep talking' and refers to the necessity "to keep the conversation moving forward". If I was talking to a person I could not treat myself to lengthy pauses in order to come up with 'perfect' statement. If pauses are too long my addressees might take this as a hint to take over or the whole communication might break down altogether.

The second principle is 'limited planning ahead'. It makes reference to the limited capacity of the human working memory.

> There is a severe limit to the amount of incomplete syntactic structure we can hold in the working memory at one time – and there is also a similar limit to the amount of planned structure we can hold in readiness for future completion. (Biber et al. 1999: 1067)

We will see below that this has a strong influence on the complexity of spoken structures.

The third principle, 'qualification of what has been said', follows from the first two: if I have to keep talking but at the same time am confronted with limits of planning, it is likely that "there may be a need to elaborate and modify the message retrospectively, that is, to 'tag on' as an afterthought some elements which in a logically structured and integrated sentence, would have been placed earlier" (1067). In the following we will see how these principles of online-production result in features characteristic of spoken language.

8.3.1 Disfluency

The fact that the speaker has to keep on talking but only has limited time to plan ahead will automatically lead to phenomena of disfluency, such as pauses, repetitions and false starts. An illustrative example of these features is given in the lengthy quotation at the beginning of this chapter. The example below shows an excerpt from a face-to-face conversation with two persons. Person A asks person B: *What personally do you get out of the integrated dance?* (s1a-001:027) and this is part of the answer of person B.

(4) a)   It think that ~~the~~ <,,> what I get out of integrated dance ~~is uhm~~ is exactly the same <,> in many ways as what I get out of other forms of dance
   b)   Uhm <,> ~~the difference~~ <,> I think the main difference that I feel <,> uhm in the work that we are doing <,> uh <,> at the moment is that <,> what sets it apart is that <,> there is a sense that nobody is left out of this group
   c)   ~~This~~ this is a dance group which does not exclude people
   d)   Uhm <,> and I think one of the things that I felt when I was studying dance <,> was I very much enjoyed the work that I was involved in
   e)   I enjoyed ~~the~~ the time that I was given ~~to~~ to study and to explore
   f)   But I also had a feeling ~~that uhm~~ <,> ~~that~~ that there were two strands. (s1a-001:028-033)

Marked in bold are what is called 'filled pauses', i.e. *uhm*, *uh*, etc. Repetitions and false starts are in bold and crossed out. The above transcription also includes silent pauses. They are not part of spoken syntax but are a very characteristic feature of spontaneous spoken language. They are represented by pointed brackets, with the number of commas in between indicating whether the pauses are short or long. We see a number of repetitions (e.g. 4c, e, and f) and false starts of, as Biber et al. (1999: 1062) call them, 'retrace-and-repair sequences'. They "occur when the speaker retraces (or notionally 'erases') what has just been said, and starts again, this time with a different word or sequence of words". An example is given in (4a). Maybe the speaker wanted to start with a statement about the differences between integrated dance and non-integrated dance (as in (4b)) but then decides to more explicitly link up to the question posed by person A. Similarly, in (4b) the speaker starts with the noun phrase *the difference* but then decides to make two changes. The first is to include a hedge (*I think*, see section 8.4 for details) and the second is to premodify the head of the noun phrase by the adjective *main*.

These features are natural in speech but we have to keep in mind that they also occur in writing. The only difference is that when we listen to online speech we also witness the planning and the drafting of the message. With a written text we just look at the end product, which, of course, does not show all of the disfluencies that occur during production.

The following example tries to give you an idea of the production 'errors' that occur in writing. The example is an account of the production of the previous paragraph. Although it does not look too bad, you should consider the fact that corrected typos are not included and that it took me approximately 8 minutes to write these 67 words. The average speed in informal conversation is about 150 words per minute (Dabrowska 2004: 13). This indicates that while writing the above passage I had many periods of silent thought, all of which were much longer than the usual hesitation pauses you find in speech.

(5) These features are natural in speech but ~~they are also~~ we have to keep in mind that they ~~are also natural~~ also occur in writing. The only difference is that when we listen to ~~speech~~ online speech we ~~always~~ also witness the planning and the drafting of the message. With a written text we just look at the end product, which, of course, does not show all of the ~~irregularities~~ disfluencies that occur ~~in the production process~~ during ~~production~~ the process of production.

So, we see that (to some extent) "if a written text is reproduced with all the planning processes left in, then it too will appear formless" (Halliday 1989: 77). The fact that in the above case the extent of formlessness is fairly low is due to very long periods of extremely careful planning. Written language, just like spoken language, also has disfluencies but we cannot see them as they do not occur in the redrafted final version of a written piece of text.

8.3.2 Structural differences

Still, even if we do take the planning process into account, written language seems more complex (i.e. more highly structured). This is what we experience when we try to understand, say, an academic text that is read aloud to us. In this respect, an attractive hypothesis (although not entirely supported by empirical data) is forwarded by Halliday (1987, 1989, 2001): written language is structured in ways that are different from the structuring of spoken language, because, as Halliday (1985: 81) argues, "written language represents phenomena as products. Spoken language represents phenomena as processes". Representing products leads to a heavy use of noun phrases, whereas processes can only be described by the use of verbs, which, in turn, leads to a large number of clauses. To substantiate his claims, Halliday takes authentic examples of written sentences and renders them in their supposedly spoken form, for instance:

(6) a) The use of this method of control leads to safer and faster train running in the most adverse weather conditions. [written]
b) If this method of control is used trains will run more safely and faster when the weather conditions are more adverse. [spoken] (adapted from Halliday 1985: 79).

Most likely, it would be more difficult for you to understand (6a) than (6b) if both were read aloud to you, and this makes clear where the complexity of written language lies: in the noun phrase. This becomes obvious if we compare the structures of the noun phrases in (6a) and (6b), as shown below (note that *train running* is analysed as a compound).

(6) a')

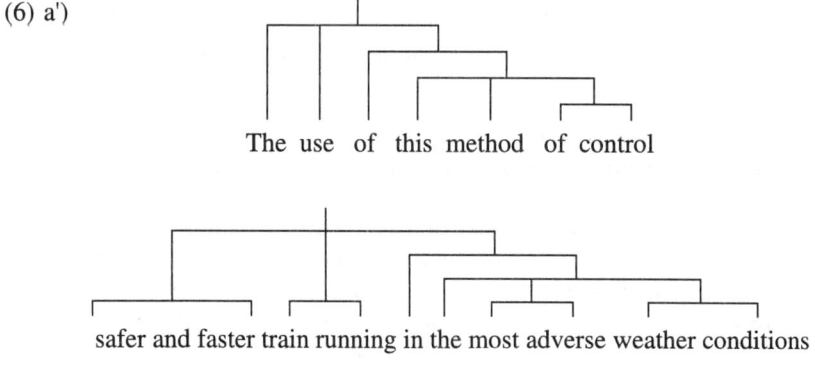

(6) b')

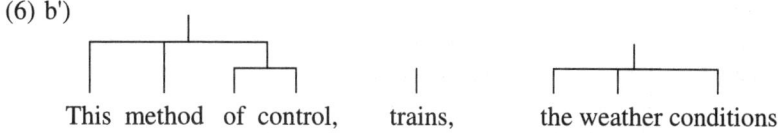

A comparison of the clause structure yields the opposite picture. (6a) is a simple SVA structure (if we treat *lead* as a copular verb), while (6b) shows subordinated clauses. (6a) is a simple sentence, whereas (6b) is complex.

(6) a")

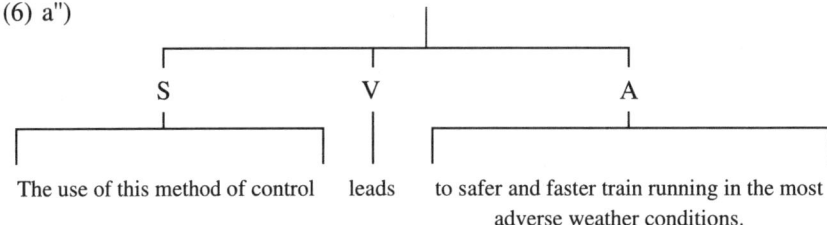

(6) b")

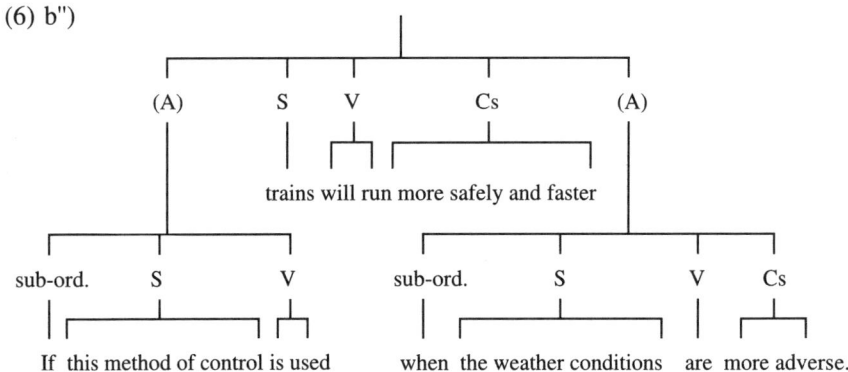

Cases like the one in (6a) can often be found in written language. Some further examples together with an analysis of clausal constituents are given below.

(7) a) [What we are witnessing]$_S$ is$_V$ [a major script revolution, in which a conscious choice of script type appears to have been made for a variety of reasons, not all of which are as yet understood]$_{Cs}$. (w2a-008:071)
  b) [Single- and three-phase electrical supplies]$_S$ [are]$_V$ generally$_{(A)}$ [available in a milking parlour where they are commonly used to power the milking vacuum pumps, and could be used to power a robot]$_{Cs}$. (w2a-033:053)
  c) [The moves towards so-called "just in time" production systems (pioneered by Japanese auto manufacturers and widely copied and adapted by the European and US majors), and closer integration of motor manufactures and suppliers resulting from this,]$_S$ have$_V$ [a number of major implications for auto component firms]$_{Od}$. (w2a-015:071)

As you can see, in all of the above cases we are dealing with simple clauses (recall that relative clauses and other kinds of postmodifying clauses are part of phrase structure and not of clause structure). The obvious complexity of these examples therefore cannot stem from clausal complexity but must reside in the individual constituents, more specifically, in the noun phrases that occur in them. Noun phrases of such high complexity are usually not found in spontaneous spoken speech, as you can see in the examples below.

(8) a) Predominantly$_{(A)}$ [what you will see]$_{Sclausal}$ is$_V$ [the lining]$_{Od}$ [because we thought [the lining would tie in with the bedhead]$_{Od\_clausal}$]$_{(A\_clausal)}$. (s1a-086:019; slightly adapted)
   b) [[I$_S$ [didn't pick]$_{V1}$ them$_{Od}$ up$_{V2}$ [till on the way home]$_{(A)}$]]$_{Clause}$ and [I$_S$ [couldn't be bothered to bring]$_{V1}$ them$_{Od}$ back$_{V2}$]$_{Clause}$ and [I$_S$ thought$_V$ [I$_S$ ['ll leave]$_V$ it$_{Od}$]$_{Od\_clausal}$]$_{Clause}$. (s1a-099:160; slightly adapted)

Instead, in the examples under (8) there seem to be more clauses in one sentence. (8a) shows a nominal clause functioning as the subject and a causal adverbial clause, which shows a nominal clause functioning as direct object. (8b) shows a coordination of three main clauses, with the last main clause showing a subordinate nominal clause functioning as direct object of the main verb *thought* (note that this example the objects of the phrasal verbs *pick up* and *bring back* occur between main verb and particle).

To sum up, Halliday claims that both written and spoken language are complex – but each in a different way. While the complexity in written language lies in the noun phrase, the complexity of spoken language is found on the clausal level, i.e. spoken language contains more clauses per clause complex and more subordination. This hypothesis is very appealing and it would provide an explanation for the fact that we experience written language as more complex, but Halliday has never given any substance to this claim in the form of empirical analyses.

Such an analysis is provided by Schäpers (2009), who sets out to explore the relation of clausal and nominal complexity in spoken and written language with the help of corpus linguistic analyses. Her findings only partly support Halliday's hypothesis. While it is true that "[n]oun phrases are more complex in written language with regard to premodification, postmodification and both pre- and postmodification" (153), Schäper's findings refute part of Halliday's hypothesis concerning clausal complexity: her spoken data, in line with Halliday's claims, show more clauses per words than the written data, which indicates that spoken language is indeed more process-oriented than written language. But, in contrast to Halliday's assumption that the complexity of spoken language resides in the clause complex, she finds that "[w]ritten language [...] uses more complex clause complexes than spoken language" (153). Schäpers also points out, however, that this result has to be taken with a grain of salt:

> Halliday [...] assumes in his concocted examples [...] that the same amount of information is carried in the clause complexes of spoken and written language. This may be possible. However, it seems untypical of spoken language. In most cases, the amount of information that a clause complex carries in spoken language is smaller than in written language. Therefore, the results are, on the whole, not surprising. (Schäpers 2009: 138)

A 'translation' of a nominally complex written sentence into a spoken sentence may result in an increase of clausal complexity if we want to transmit the same amount of information (as shown in the examples under (6)). In authentic spoken language, however, clause complexes are usually not as informationally dense as authentic written sentences: the same amount of information is usually presented in a number of structurally isolated clauses. On the whole, we find that spoken sentences are less complex than written sentences with regard to noun phrases and we find that the number of clauses per words is higher for spoken than for written sentences, i.e. written sentences are longer.

These findings tie in nicely with Chafe's (1982) distinction of 'integration' in written language as opposed to 'fragmentation' in spoken language, which is due to the production circumstances of the two modes:

> As we write down one idea, our thoughts have plenty of time to move ahead to others. [...] In writing we have time to mold a succession of ideas into a more complex, coherent, integrated whole, making use of devices we seldom use in speaking. (Chafe 1982: 37)

These "complex, coherent, integrated wholes" are the highly complex noun phrases and the more intricate clause complexes that Schäpers (2009) finds in her corpus data. Spontaneous spoken language, as we have seen, is influenced by the principles of online production, in particular 'keep talking' and 'limited planning ahead'. As a consequence,

> [i]n speaking, we normally produce one idea unit at a time. That is apparently about all we have the capacity to pay attention to, and if we try to think about much more than that we are likely to get into trouble. (Chafe 1982: 37)

As a result, spoken language will usually not be as intricately structured as written language. Rather, we often find that "[o]ne piece of information follows after another" (Carter & McCarthy 2006: 168)", which

> accounts for the basic [169/170] characteristic of spoken grammar being more like the strung-together coaches of a train or links of a chain rather than a carefully constructed hierarchy of embedded structure, one inside the other. (Carter & McCarthy 2006: 169-170).

The following excerpt nicely illustrates this fragmented and strung-together nature of spoken language.

(9) He's seventy-one
And uh they had this pink champagne which they did the toast with
It was quite a nice do otherwise
She'd got lovely food all laid
And everybody was eating something
And it was a beautiful day
And she had borrowed everybody's patio chairs and things and had them all over the lawn
It was rather nice actually cos we were all outside
It was very nice and they were you know very thrilled with it all (s1a-019:071-079)

A possible written 'rendering' of the above passage might be the following:

(9') They had a very nice party for his seventy-first birthday, with pink champagne for the toast and lovely food, which everybody enjoyed. Since it was a beautiful day we were all outside, sitting on patio chairs that they had borrowed from everybody and that were all over the lawn. It was a lovely party and they were very thrilled with it all.

Note how both versions transmit approximately the same amount of information, although condensed to different degrees. Of course, the concocted example under (9') cannot bring out all the differences between spoken and written grammar, but it can illustrate one more important characteristic of spoken language. In addition to the higher complexity of noun phrases in the written rendering, we also find that the spoken original makes use of a large number of co-ordinators, mostly *and*. Other co-ordinators that are frequent in spontaneous spoken language are *but* and *or*. Common subordinators that can be found are *so* and *because*. The latter, as in the above example, is reduced to *cos*. Note also, that *cos* in example (9) above seems to function more like a coordinator than a subordinator – a feature common for spoken language (see Carter & McCarthy 2006: 170). On the whole, these co- and sub-ordinators are far more frequent (over four times as frequent) in spoken than in written language, as Chafe (1982: 39) shows in a comparison of 9,911 word of informal spoken with 12,368 words of formal written language.

Another important feature is a special kind of construction that to a certain extent is also caused by the production circumstances of spontaneous spoken language. The story above continues with a passage about a certain Pauline: the host of the party had borrowed all her vases and Pauline didn't have any left for flowers she got sent for her birthday two days later. So Pauline came to the speaker's house but the speaker was not at home, only a person called Stuart. This is what the speaker says:

(10) but it was only Stuart here
and she didn't want to bother him with vases and things cos she didn't know where I kept them or anything cos **we were in Bromley Den and I** (s1a-019:086-087)

This passage illustrates a frequent phenomenon of spoken language, namely that of 'double (or multiple) filling' (see, for instance, Halford 1996: 70-77), where one syntactic slot is filled more than once. In this particular case, we are dealing with what is usually referred to as 'dislocation': a noun phrase in a clause is replaced by a pronoun and moved to the beginning or the end of the clause, which is referred to as 'left-dislocation' and 'right-dislocation', respectively. So, the above text shows an example of right-dislocation. Some further examples are given below; the string in bold print marks the dislocated noun phrase, the co-referential pronoun is in angular brackets:

(11) a) Has [it] got double doors **that shop**?
b) Did [they] have any, **the kids**? (Biber et al. 1999: 957)
c) I really like [him], **your dad**.
d) I gave [him] a dollar, **that man back there**.
e) I've never spoken to [her] before, **the Vice Chancellor**. (adapted from Huddleston & Pullum 2002: 1411)

The examples show that different constituents in different functions can be moved with right-dislocation: the subject in (11a and b), the direct object in (11c), the indirect object in (11d) and the prepositional complement in (11e). The function of this construction is to clarify the reference of a pronoun in the preceding clause: "I utter a pronoun and then realise it may not be clear what the pronoun is being used to refer to. I then add this information in clause-final position, as a sort of 'afterthought'" (Huddleston & Pullum 1999: 1411). In (10) above, for instance, the speaker, after having uttered the clause *we were in Bromley*, becomes aware that the reference of the pronoun *we* might not be clear to the addressees. So she clarifies it by adding *Den and I*. It is easy to see how this construction instantiates the third principle of online production 'qualification of what has been said'.

With left-dislocation a noun phrase is moved to initial position, as illustrated below.

(12) a) **Sharon** [she] plays bingo on Sunday night.
   b) **That picture of a frog**, where is [it]?
   c) **All that money**, I mean, in the end is [it] worth rescuing?
   d) "But **Anna-Luise** – what could have attracted [her] to a man in his fifties?" (Biber et al. 1999: 957)
   e) **My sister**, someone threw a rock at [her] at the beach.
   f) **The people next door**, the police have just arrested [their] son on a drugs charge. (adapted from Huddleston and Pullum 2002: 1409)

As can be seen from the first three examples, the dislocated element is usually co-referential with the subject of the clause. Co-referentiality with the object or other functional elements as shown in (12d) to (12f) is more rare. The function of this construction is to establish the topic of the sentence or even of a larger part of the discourse. Recall from section 6.1.2 that the subject usually is what the clause is about and should usually occur at the beginning of the clause. In the examples above this would only be the case with (12a). In (12b and c) a non-dislocated sentence would leave the subject in non-initial position, where it would usually not be understood as the topic of the sentence. Examples (12d to f) nicely illustrate how the use of left-dislocation can also be helpful in marking a constituent other than the subject as topic.

This function of topic-marking makes left-dislocation useful in conversations. Even though the speaker may not yet be clear about what he or she will exactly say, the speaker can at least make clear what his or her contribution will be about, and then, after a moment of thought, elaborate on the topic. Left-dislocation is a valuable means of holding the floor and of guiding a conversation with regard to its topic at the same time. Again, we see how the principles of online processing motivate the use of this construction. It is therefore no wonder that this construction is almost limited to spoken discourse only. In those case where it is found in written language it is either found in dialogical passages of prose fiction (as in (12d)) or is used to exemplify the construction as in (12e to f) or as in this book.

8.4 Spontaneous spoken language as interaction and its consequences

The examples of right- and left-dislocation have hinted at the effort that a speaker exercises to keep the conversation going. Speakers interact with their audiences while writers do not. This is captured in another useful dichotomy suggested by Chafe (1982: 45), namely the distinction between 'involvement' with and 'detachment' from the audience in spoken and written interaction, respectively. With spoken interaction, "the speaker can monitor the effect of what he or she is saying on the listener, and [...] the listener is able to signal understanding and to ask for clarification" (Chafe 1982: 45). This monitoring becomes apparent in the frequent use of 'discourse markers' in spoken language. Take a look at the excerpt below:

(13) a) A: But why should she feel that because other people have second children
 b) B: Yes I know
 c)   But **I think you know**
 d)   **I think** it is a difficult thing and if is isn't got over properly **I think** can leave a lasting problem
 e)   **I think** we should have **you know** done a bit of digging at that point **sort of you know** make her feel particularly special and find out [...] whether she thought she had to be nice to this child because again she was earning her place [...]
 f)   **I think** she feels probably that uhm **you know** unless I need her for <,,> uhm **you know** making my life happy then I don't really want her
 g)   And clearly I've got what I need to make my life happy
 h)   So she can't see a place for herself
 i) A: Yes
 j)   Well **you see I mean** rationally she's got a point
 k)   **I mean** it's a very difficult one for those of us who leave our first husbands <,> (s1a-031: 147-160)

As you see, discourse markers can be very frequent in spontaneous spoken language. They fulfil various functions. *You know*, according to Biber et al. (1999: 1077) signals that "the speaker is imparting new information to the hearer, but is also appealing to the hearer's shared knowledge or experience for the acceptance of this information". It is a means of creating a common ground between speaker and hearer and "checks that the listener is following what is being said" (Carter & McCarthy 2006: 221). *I mean* and *you see*, in contrast, signal that what follows is to be taken as an explanation or clarification of a previous part of the utterance. This is most clearly seen in (13j and k). Speaker A's first statement is *Yes* (in 13i), that is, he thinks that B's assumption about the feelings of the person that they are talking about is correct. In (13j) she provides an explanation, namely that the woman they talk about has got a point, which she then explains in (13k). *I think* as discourse marker mainly functions as a 'hedge'. While interacting with a person, you usually do not want to sound too self-assured, because the addressee might think you are arrogant. Hedges like *I think* are used "to downtone the assertiveness of a segment of discourse" (Carter & McCarthy 2006: 223).

With the exception of *I think*, the discourse markers described above are usually not integrated in the structure of the clause, they are more like stance or style adverbials (see section 6.1.5). Consider the modified version of (13k) below.

(13) f') **I think** that she feels probably that uhm **you know** *that unless I need her for <,,> uhm **you know** *that making my life happy then I don't really want her

In the example above, *think* can be thought of as a verb governing the clause *she feels probably that* .... In that case we would be dealing with an SVOd clause, with *think* as a monotransitive verb. Clausal objects are often introduced by the complementiser *that*, which sounds alright in the above example. With *you know*, in contrast, it does not make much sense to insert *that* as a complementiser. It seems reasonable to assume that the speaker does not want to express (13f') but (13f''').

(13) f'') *I think that she feels that you know that unless I need her for making my life happy then I don't really want her.
    f''') I think that she feels that unless I need her for making my life happy then I don't really want her.

The second instance of *you know* in (13f') also is outside of the structure of the clause. The speaker does not want to say *you know that making my life happy* .... Accordingly, we would not treat the instances of *know* as a monotransitive verbs that govern the clauses that follow them. Together with *you* they form a string which has a pragmatic function, but is outside of the clause itself. It would not make much sense to subject this case to an analysis in terms of the clause patterns discussed in chapter 6.

8.5 Further reading

Esser (2006: chs. 4 and 5) provides an accessible introduction into medium-independent and medium-dependent units.

A good introduction into the general features of spontaneous spoken language can be found in Biber et al. (1999: ch. 14) and Carter and McCarthy (2006: 164-175).

Pilch (1990) provides an insightful discussion of the nature of spoken syntax as opposed to written syntax.

See Miller and Weinert (1998: ch. 2) for a discussion of the concept 'sentence' with regard to spoken language.

8.6 Study questions

1. In which sense was traditional grammar biased and why does modern grammar claim to be unbiased?
2. Why is the term 'sentence' problematic with regard to the analysis of spoken language? What term is suggested instead and what does that term mean?
3. What is the basic unit of conversation?
4. Name and explain the three principles of online production. Give examples of typical spoken-language phenomena that are a consequence of these principles.
5. What is Halliday's hypothesis concerning complexity in written and spoken language? How do you evaluate his hypothesis?
6. What is right- and left-dislocation? Give examples. In what sense are these constructions motivated by the principles of online processing?
7. Which of the two strings *I think* in the following example is not used as a discourse marker? Why?
   ***I think** it is a difficult thing and if it isn't got over properly **I think** can leave a lasting problem*

9 Syntactic Variation

Although it is useful for linguistic studies to treat languages as completely homogeneous systems, it is obvious that this is not the case: any language allows for variation in many different respects or along many different dimensions. One of these, for instance, is the region a speaker comes from: a person from the south of England, for instance, will talk differently from someone from the North. Another of these dimensions is the social group one belongs to. Sociolinguistic studies report on a large number of differences between people speaking so-called lower- and upper-class English. A third dimension of variation is that which is due to the medium in which language is realised, i.e. spoken as opposed to written language: in the previous chapter we saw that spoken and written English show considerable differences with regard to the exploitation of the structural potential common to both modes, but also with regard to constructions that occur in one but not in the other. Yet another dimension concerns what is called the 'field of discourse', i.e. the subject matter with which a piece of language is concerned. For instance, the present book is about linguistics, more specifically, about syntax. Because of that there are many lexical units that you are unlikely to find, say, in a sports commentary, such as *linguistics*, *syntax* or *constituency*.

A useful distinction regarding variation is that between variation according to the user and variation according to the use of language. The first two dimensions discussed above make reference to the language user. Each user lives in a certain region and belongs to a certain social group. Such features are relatively permanent and they can only be changed by conscious effort. A speaker with a thick northern accent, for instance, might be able to switch to RP if that is necessary but it takes conscious effort on the side of the speaker. Variation according to language use is not permanent; it depends on the context of situation in which the communication takes place. At present, I make frequent use of linguistic terms, because that is what the situation demands. If I was talking to my friends about last Saturday's football matches I would be using a different vocabulary. Similarly, if I was talking to you about syntax I would be using constructions that are different from the ones that I use now when writing about it.

All of these kinds of variation are of a fairly global kind. Syntactic variation, in contrast, is situated on a more local level, i.e. within sentences or phrases. It concerns the fact that a language can provide different syntactic means to express the same propositional content, to convey the same information. Consider the examples below.

(1) Iraq's given the UN figures of civilian casualties. (s2b-018:013)
Iraq's given figures of civilian casualties to the UN.
Figures of civilian casualties have been given to the UN by Iraq.
What Iraq's given the UN is figures of civilian casualties.
It's Iraq that has given figures of civilian casualties to the UN.

The above examples are similar in that all of them have the same truth conditions, i.e. they all convey the same propositional content: if one of the above sentences is true then all of the others are true as well; if one is false, all of the others are false. Quirk et al. (1985) speak of 'systematic correspondences', the Prague School linguist Daneš (1964: 233) talks of 'allo-sentences' in this respect. The use of the prefix *allo* nicely illustrates what has been said above. Just like allophones are identical with regard to their function in a string of sounds, and just like allomorphs are identical with regard to the meaning that they express, so are allo-sentences: they convey the same meaning. But the analogy does not stop there. Allophones and allomorphs are determined by the context in which they occur; similarly, one allo-sentence is more appropriate for one situation, another for another one. The present chapter first takes stock of the different kinds of syntactic variation and, in its main part, elaborates on the ways in which the surrounding context influences the choice of one allo-sentence over another.

9.1 Kinds of syntactic variation

In 6.3 we already glanced at some constructions that are susceptible to syntactic variation. This section provides a fuller picture of the range of phenomena discussed in this context – it is basically an extended list of constructions, with a focus on sentence-level constructions.

In the description of word order phenomena it makes sense to start off with the basic clause patterns that we discussed in section 6.2. We can classify allo-sentences on the basis of their divergence from a given basic clause pattern. Two large groups can be identified. The first group are those allo-sentences where elements of the underlying basic clause pattern have been moved. With the second group additional elements have been inserted on top of the moved elements. Examples of the first group are given below.

(2) a) **Heavy NP shift**
Many French politicians take for granted a Europe in which France shares a lead. (BNC-ABF:1495)
Many French politicians take a Europe in which France shares a lead for granted.

b) **Dative alternation**
He gave the cash to the astonished owners of the house at Crosby, Merseyside. (BNC-CBF:3757)
He gave the astonished owners of the house at Crosby, Merseyside the cash.

c) **Multiple prepositional phrases**
We were having a discussion with Bob actually about the organisation of the course. (s1a-008:102)
We were having a discussion actually about the organisation of the course with Bob.

d) **Fronting (direct object)**
Maybe Thursday I could take off. (s1a-039:027)
Maybe I could take off Thursday.

e) **Fronting (indirect object)**
Everybody that cooks I ask how they make pastry. (s1a-057:131)
I ask everybody that cooks how they make pastry.

f) **Fronting (subject complement)**
Oh great that'd be. (s1a-042:132)
Oh that'd be great.

g) **Fronting (object complement)**
Distinctly brilliant I thought him (s1a-094:312)
I thought him distinctly brilliant.

h) **Fronting (adverbial)**
In my cupboard I've got lots of rejections (s1a-034.196)
I've got lots of rejections in my cupboard.

i) **Inversion (subject complement)**
Also null and void is any stipulation releasing a partner from playing an active role in running the business. (BNC-EEH:718)
Any stipulation releasing a partner from playing an active role in running the business is also null and void.

j) **Inversion (adverbial; also: 'locative inversion')**
Behind the plate is a chiselled cavity. (BNC-J13:3401)
A chiselled cavity is behind the plate.

In the cases (2a to c) we see that none of the alternatives is more or less grammatical *per se*. Every single one is just as grammatical and as standard as its counterpart. Note also that the movement only concerns postverbal elements. The subject and the verb remain the first constituents and they occur in their usual order. This is different with the remaining examples under (2). With the cases of fronting in (2d to h), a post-verbal constituent occurs in a position at the beginning of the clause. That is, the important first position in the clause (see below for details as to why this is so important) has changed. On the whole, we can say that this kind of word-order change is more 'drastic' than the one under (2a to c), and will also draw more attention. Finally, with **full-verb inversion** as exemplified in (2i and j) two constituents are moved: the subject and a postverbal constituent swap place while the verb stays in its position. This phenomenon is usually restricted to clauses with copular verbs, i.e. the structures SVC or SVA.

In addition to the allo-sentences that only involve movement, we also find those cases where movement co-occurs with the insertion of additional material. Consider the examples below.

(3) a) **Passive**
One of the ads is placed by the S.F. Zoo. (w1b-011:056)
The S.F. Zoo places one of the ads.
b) **Existential-*there* sentence**
There are references to political exile and hostages taken in Adomnan's 'life of Columba'. (w1a-002:098)
References to political exile and hostages taken are (given) in Adomnan's 'life of Columba'.
c) ***It*-extraposition**
It's always rather surprising when people actually come and hear what one has to say. (s2a-039:003)
When people actually come and hear what one has to say is always rather surprising.
d) **Cleft sentence**
It is the species composition of this layer which determines the treatment efficiency. (w2a-021:009)
The species composition of this layer determines the treatment efficiency.
e) ***Wh*-cleft**
What I'm obviously talking about here is the classic phenomena of bureaucracy. (s2a-049:065)
I'm obviously talking about the classic phenomena of bureaucracy here.
f) ***Wh*-cleft (reversed)**
That's what the pigment does. (s1b-015:125)
What the pigment does is that.

Above it was said that although all variants are identical with regard to the semantics, i.e. the truth-conditional value, they are different with regard to their appropriateness in different contexts or situations. What are these contexts and situations? What are the factors that make the reader choose one constructional alternative over the other?

9.2 Factors that influence syntactic variation

9.2.1 Syntactic complexity

The idea that syntactic complexity or weight influences the order of constituents in a clause is fairly old. As early as 1909, the German linguistic Otto Behaghel talks of the *Gesetz der wachsenden Glieder* (Law of growing elements; see also Behaghel 1932: 6; cf. Wasow & Arnold 2003), which describes a tendency for shorter elements to occur before longer elements. At present the same intuition is discussed under the term 'the principle of end-weight' (among many other terms).

Underlying this principle are concerns about processing complexity. Biber et al. claim that complying with the principle of end-weight "eases comprehension by the receiver, who does not then have the burden of retaining complex information from earlier in a clause in short-term memory while processing the remainder" (1999: 898). In addition, "[t]here is a severe limit to the amount of incomplete syntactic structure we can hold in the working memory at one time" (1067). A more technical version of the principle of end-weight does justice to these two aspects, namely Hawkins' (1994) principle of Early Immediate Constituents (EIC). It states that

> words and constituents occur in the orders they do so that syntactic groupings and their immediate constituents (ICs) can be recognized (and produced) as rapidly and efficiently as possible in language performance. Different orderings of elements result in more or less rapid IC recognition. (Hawkins 1994: 57)

What this means becomes apparent if we look at the following example of what is usually referred to as heavy-NP shift and its non-shifted counterpart.

(4) a) I $_{VP}$[gave $_{NP}$[the valuable book that was extremely difficult to find] $_{PP}$[to Mary]].
  b) I $_{VP}$[gave $_{PP}$[to Mary] $_{NP}$[the valuable book that was extremely difficult to find]]. (Hawkins 1994: 57)

The focus in this example is on the verb phrase. To understand this sentence, the hearer or reader has to do a syntactic analysis of some kind or another. Part of this syntactic analysis is to get the structure of the verb phrase right. On the most basic level, this means that the recipient has to find out what the immediate constituents of the verb phrase are. In the above example we have three such constituents, namely the verb *gave* itself, the noun phrase *the valuable book that was extremely difficult to find* and the prepositional phrase *to Mary*. An important step in the analysis of this verb phrase, thus, is to recognise that the verb phrase contains these three elements. The recipient recognises the verb as soon as he or she comes across the verb form *gave*. The noun phrase is recognised when the recipient encounters the direct article *the*, since *the* as a central determiner introduces a noun phrase. Similarly, the preposition *to* will tell the recipient that a prepositional phrase has begun. If we now take a closer look at example (4a), we see that the recipient has to process 11 words of the verb phrase until the preposition *to* has been reached. That is, it is only after having processed 11 words that the recipient can be certain as to the structure of the verb phrase, i.e. 'V + NP + PP'. In contrast, in (4b) the hearer or reader only needs to process 4 words. At that point he or she will have reached the direct article, which constructs a noun phrase, and he or she will have found out that the structure of the verb phrase is 'V + PP + NP'. In (4a) the structure of the verb phrase remains incomplete for 10 words, in (4b) the incompletion only lasts 3 words. From a processing perspective, then, (4b) is to be preferred over (4a).

The principle of end-weight, or its newer formulation in the principle of EIC, account for a number of the syntactic-variation phenomena presented above. Hawkins' example of heavy-NP shift, for instance, shows that the shifting of a heavy, i.e. long and complex, noun phrase usually results in an ordering of constituents that is preferable with regard to syntactic processing. The same holds for the example under (2a), here repeated as (5a and b).

(5) a) Many French politicians $_{VP}$[take $_{PP}$[for granted] $_{NP}$[a Europe in which France shares a lead]]. (BNC-ABF:1495)
  b) Many French politicians $_{VP}$[take $_{NP}$[a Europe in which France shares a lead] $_{PP}$[for granted]].

In (5a) the heavy noun phrase *a Europe in which France shares a lead* occurs in final position. Because of that the structure of the verb phrase, i.e. 'V + PP + NP', becomes obvious after the fourth word in the VP. In case of (5b), 10 words of the verb phrase have to be processed to be sure about its structure.

Similarly, the cases of dative alternative in (2b) (here repeated as 6a and b) can be accounted for by end-weight or EIC.

(6) a) He $_{VP}$[gave $_{NP}$[the cash] $_{PP}$[to the astonished owners of the house at Crosby, Merseyside]]. (BNC-CBF:3757)
  b) He $_{VP}$[gave $_{NP}$[the astonished owners of the house at Crosby, Merseyside] $_{NP}$[the cash]].

In (6a) the immediate constituents of the verb phrase are recognised after the fourth word in the verb phrase, the preposition *to*, whereas in (6b) it takes 11 words until the hearer or reader has reached the direct article *the*, which betrays the final noun phrase.

The same explanation also accounts for structures other than the verb phrase. Consider (2i), here repeated as (7a and b), where we can apply the idea of EIC to the structure of the clause as a whole.

(7) a) $_{Cs}$[Also null and void] $_V$is $_S$[any stipulation releasing a partner from playing an active role in running the business]. (BNC-EEH:718)
b) $_S$[Any stipulation releasing a partner from playing an active role in running the business] $_V$is $_{Cs}$[also null and void].

Again, in (7a) the hearer or reader has to process six words to recognise the clause type SVCs, whereas in (7b) it takes 16 words to arrive at the same conclusion.

It is important to note that the influence of weight is of a gradient nature. That is, if the shifting of constituents results in a big processing advantage, constituents are more likely to be shifted than if the advantage is only small. In addition, some tokens cannot be explained by considerations of weight, either because a shifting of constituents does not lead to a faster recognition of structures or because a canonical word order would even be preferable as regards the distribution of weight; consider example (2j), here repeated as (8a and b), and example (9a and b).

(8) a) $_A$[Behind the plate] $_V$is $_S$[a chiselled cavity]. (BNC-J13:3401)
b) $_S$[A chiselled cavity] $_V$is $_A$[behind the plate].

(9) a) $_{Cs}$[Related to this question of pedagogic/pragmatic research as an integrated element of classroom practice] $_V$is $_S$[the matter of teacher formation]. (BNC-CBR:613-615)
b) $_S$[The matter of teacher formation] $_V$is $_{Cs}$[related to this question of pedagogic/pragmatic research as an integrated element of classroom practice].

(8a) and (8b) are identical with regard to end-weight or Early Immediate Constituents: in both cases, the reader has to process five words to arrive at the structure of the clause. The inverted construction in (9a) results in an order that is not in line with what we would expect from EIC. This order makes the reader or hearer process 17 words to understand the structure of the clause, whereas in (9b) he or she only needs seven words to arrive at the SVC structure. The question that arises from examples like these is why the author felt inclined to change the order of constituents in the first place. If this cannot be explained by processing advantages it is likely to assume that there are other factors at work.

One extremely important one is the distribution of old and new information in the clause. The next section discusses this aspect in some detail.

9.2.2 The distribution of information in the clause

More than a century ago the French-German linguist Henri Weil suggested that a clause proceeds from information that is given, i.e. known to the reader or hearer, to information that is new, i.e. unknown to the hearer or reader. He proposed that in order to communicate successfully it is

> necessary to lean on something present and known, in order to reach out to something less present, nearer, or unknown. There is then a point of departure, an initial notion which is equally present to him who speaks and to him who hears, which forms, as it were, the ground upon which the two intelligences meet; and another part of discourse which forms the statement [...], properly so called. ([1844] 1978: 29)

From then on, this assumption has been the topic of uncountable treatises. It was brought up, for instance, in Gabelentz's (1901: 365-373) notions of 'psychological subject' and 'psychological predicate', in Behaghel's (1932) Second Law ('That which is less important (or known to the reader) is placed before that which is important') and in the Prague-School concept of 'Functional Sentence Perspective' (see, for instance, Mathesius 1929 and [1961] 1975 or Daneš 1974).

Put simply, the basic idea is that the distribution of given and new information in the clause is such that it eases the processing of the content of the clause. More specifically, the recipient of the message already has a certain amount of knowledge stored in his or her memory. The speaker wants to add something to this stock of knowledge, i.e. the new information. To make it easier for the receiver to integrate this new information, it makes sense to tell the recipient where in the existing stock of knowledge the new information should be integrated. This is what the old information does: it provides a link to what the recipient already knows. Obviously, it is preferable, from the side of the recipient, to tell him or her as soon as possible where the new information should go. This is similar to what was said about weight in section 9.2.1 above: just as processing difficulties arise from keeping incomplete syntactic structure active in working memory, we are likely to encounter processing difficulties if we have to keep active in working memory bits of information while we are waiting to be told where to put them in our stock of knowledge. These considerations have been captured in Clark and Clark's (1977) 'Given-New Contract' (see also Clark & Haviland 1977 and Haviland & Clark 1974):

> The speaker agrees (a) to use given information to refer to information she thinks the listener can uniquely identify from what he already knows and (b) to use new information to refer to information she believes to be true but is not already known to the listener. (Clark & Clark 1977: 92)

This 'contract' allows the recipient to follow the 'given-new strategy' (95-97): he or she understands those parts of the utterance that are marked 'given information' as details on where in the stock of knowledge the new information should be integrated.

With regard to syntactic variation, as in the examples above, it thus makes sense to assume that in those cases where the producer has a choice between two or more constructions, he or she will choose that construction which complies with the idea of 'given-before-new'. This is also important with regard to the understanding of texts. While reading a text, the reader, on the basis of the information conveyed in each of the sentences, creates a textual world, and every new sentence provides another facet of this textual world. Just as new information has to be integrated into the existing stock of knowledge, so the information provided by a sentence has to be integrated into the structure of the previous text, into the image of the textual world created by the reader. This rationale is expressed in what Kreyer (2006a) calls the Principle of 'Immediate Textual Integration' (ITI):

> There is a general tendency in clause construction to prefer those structures that allow to integrate the content of the clause as soon as possible into the already existing text structure. (Kreyer 2006a: 199)

The progression from given to new information is the most economical way of presenting information considering the recipient's need to integrate new information into the structure of the text so far and into the already existing stock of knowledge. In some cases, this need may even override the influence of Early Immediate Constituents. So, the distribution of information in the clause could be a plausible explanation for the violation of end-weight in example (9), here repeated with some additional context.

(9) a) $_{613}$The question then arises as to how this pragmatic enterprise differs, if it differs at all, from the kinds of activity which are customarily carried out under the name of research. $_{614}$*Related to this question of pedagogic/pragmatic research as an integrated element of classroom practice is the matter of teacher formation.* $_{615}$What kind of preparation or priming do teachers need in order to exploit their classroom experience in the manner I have suggested? (CBR:613-615)

a') $_{613}$The question then arises as to how this pragmatic enterprise differs, if it differs at all, from the kinds of activity which are customarily carried out under the name of research. $_{614}$*The matter of teacher formation is related to this question of pedagogic/pragmatic research as an integrated element of classroom practice.* (CBR:613-614; modified)

The inverted clause in sentence 614 of (9a) provides a link to the previous discourse (and, hence, to the stock of knowledge of the recipient) through the preposed subject complement *related to this question of ... classroom practice*, because *this question* refers back to the question discussed in sentence 613. So, the reader is told immediately how the new information *the matter of teacher formation*, to be discussed from 615 onwards, fits in the whole text. If we compare this version with the non-inverted counterpart in (9a'), we see that the new information is already introduced in the text without making explicit how it relates to what came before. The reader will have to keep this information active in his or her working memory until further on in the clause. With regard to the integration of information the first variant seems preferable. The same accounts for a number of the examples above. Consider example (2i) in its context.

(10) $_{715}$Partnership contracts must contain, inter alia, the individual financial or in specie contributions of the members. $_{716}$Government agencies may also participate in partnerships. $_{717}$Contributions become partnership property unless the contract provides otherwise, and any stipulation providing for interest or other financial benefit for a partner in consideration of his contribution is null and void. $_{718}$*Also null and void is any stipulation releasing a partner from playing an active role in running the business.* (BNC-EEH:715-718)

In sentence 717 of example (10) the writer tells the reader that a particular kind of stipulation is *null and void*. In the next sentence, the writer wants to introduce another stipulation which is also null and void. Notice how the order of constituents facilitates processing on the part of the reader: the first part of the clause links up to the previous discourse and to the stock of knowledge in the reader's head. The function of this part could be glossed as 'what follows now should also be grouped in the set of things that are null and void'. So, the reader is first told where the new bit of information should be integrated and only then is the new information introduced.

A note is in order here concerning the nature of the link to the previous discourse. In example (10) above, we see that the link *also null and void* describes a state, namely that of being null and void, which is part of the previous discourse. So, this bit of information is given or old in its strictest sense – the same kind of information has already occurred in the previous discourse. However, the link to the previous discourse need not be given or old in that restricted understanding. In (9a) above, for instance, the link *Related to this question of pedagogic/pragmatic research as an integrated element of classroom practice* is not fully given in the previous discourse. But a part of this link, namely *this question*, refers back to the question posed in the immediately preceding sentence. This part of the preposed constituent suffices to link the new information to the previous discourse.

Finally, consider the next example.

(11) $_{310}$An exemption clause is a term of the contract intended to exclude or restrict the liability of one of the parties, usually the seller. $_{311}$Sometimes a seller is so financially powerful that he can blatantly insist on such a clause being included in the contract; he can adopt a "take it or leave it" attitude. $_{312}$*More common is the seller who, having inserted an exclusion clause into his conditions of sale, relies on his buyer not bothering to read (or not understanding) the small print*; ... (BNC-H7U:310-312)

Here, the preposed subject complement *more common* does not occur in the previous discourse in any shape or form. In a strict understanding, we would have to classify this as new information. However, we see that the phrase is indirectly related to the previous discourse: the adverb *sometimes* in sentence 311 evokes the idea of a scale of frequency, and the reader finds out that a particular kind of seller is not very frequent. The preposed constituent in 312 denotes another point further up on the same scale, where another kind of seller is positioned. Even in that case, the construction serves the integration of new information into the stock of knowledge held by the reader, although the recipient may have to work a little harder.

To sum up, in all of these cases the reader is enabled to integrate the new information. All of the preposed constituents have a general potential to serve as a link, but they differ in the way in which this link works – in some cases (as in example (11)), establishing the link demands some effort on the part of the recipient. In light of these observations it makes sense to formulate the influence of information status on syntactic variation as follows:

The influence of information status on syntactic variation
In those cases of syntactic variation where only one constituent provides a link to the previous discourse, that constructional variant will usually be chosen which puts this constituent at the beginning of the clause.

However, not in all cases of syntactic variation does this or a similar 'rule' explain why a non-canonical variant has been chosen. Consider example (2d), here repeated as (12) with additional context, where the speaker is thinking about when he or she should buy Christmas presents.

(12) a) I'm going to have to go this Saturday.
b) I'm going to have to say to myself Christmas shopping on Friday.
c) Maybe I'll take the afternoon off.
d) I can't take Friday afternoon off.
e) *Maybe Thursday I could take off.* (s1a-039:022-027)

It could be argued that all parts of the inverted clause are somehow given in the previous discourse. The mention of Saturday and Friday in (12a and b) evokes the idea of week days, one of which is Thursday. So, the preposed constituent is given to some extent. On the other hand, sentences (12c and d) talk about taking a day off and use the personal pronoun *I*, which means that the rest of the inverted clause is also given to a certain extent. In that case, it does not make much sense to assume that information status plays a decisive role in the choice of construction. With regard to this factor, any order would be acceptable – another explanation is called for....

9.2.3 Emphasis, text structuring and artistic concerns

While the factors of weight and information status are the usual suspects with regard to syntactic variation, we saw above that they cannot explain every instance satisfactorily. This hints at other factors that may influence the choice of construction. First of all, it should be taken into account that the secondary clause patterns as well as the instances of non-canonical word order all are fairly rare in actual language use. As a consequence, each occurrence of these will normally be conspicuous and will hit the eye of the reader and the ear of the hearer. This can be exploited to achieve an effect of emphasis on the message in general and the unusually positioned constituent in particular. An illustrative example of this is example (12) above. Because of the unusual word order, particular emphasis is placed on *Thursday*, which helps to emphasise the contrast between Friday, when the speaker is not allowed to take off, and Thursday, when he or she is. A similar case is illustrated in (2g), here shown with some more context. The speaker talks about the qualities of a guide that showed the speaker a church.

(13) I had listened to him. And he went through this very exact. He was very exact. He was masterly at it and made it pleasant and lots really of humour. [...]
Distinctly brilliant I thought him. (s1a-094:295-312)

Again, the function of the preposed construction in example (13) does not seem to lie in establishing a smooth transition from given to new information. Rather, the aim appears to lie in emphasising that the person the speaker talks about was in fact brilliant. This is an instance of what Mathesius (1975 [1961]: 156) refers to as 'subjective order', which "[i]n normal speech [...] occurs only in emotionally coloured utterances in which the speaker pays no regard to the hearer, starting with what is most important for himself".

Other examples make clear that non-canonical word order can also be motivated by considerations of text-structuring. The word order in (2e), here repeated with context as (14), stresses the fact that the speaker asked *everybody that cooks*. This is important for the following discourse as the context shows.

(14) Well I've been doing a lot of research into this and *everybody that cooks I ask how they make pastry you see.*
And they all say well it's very difficult.
That's about the only information I've ever got.
Nobody can tell me how to make pastry like <unclear-word> used to make and I'd never get it either. (s1a-057:131-134)

The main topic of this stretch of discourse is the fact that people that cook and chefs cannot really say how to make good pastries. Since the speaker has stressed that *everybody that cooks* has been asked, the statements in 132 to 134 become more powerful: it is really difficult to find a person that can tell you how to make pastries.

The discussion so far has been concerned with the initial element in non-canonical word order constructions (we disregard the initial placement of the adverb *maybe* in example (2d)). However, we have to be aware that non-canonical word order often results in a final element that usually would not occur in this position. A case in point is full-verb inversion. In many cases, this construction serves to introduce a new topic into the discourse, thus fulfilling an important text-structuring function, as in example (15) below.

(15) $_{508}$Sergei Kolchinsky was the stereotyped image of a chain smoker. $_{509}$Early fifties, thinning black hair, the unmistakeable signs of middle-age spread and the sort of doleful features that gave the impression he was carrying the troubles of the world on his shoulders. $_{510}$The strange thing was that he derived no real enjoyment from smoking. $_{511}$It had just become a costly, and addictive, habit. $_{512}$Yet behind those melancholy eyes lay a brilliant tactical mind. $_{513}$Following a distinguished career with the KGB, including sixteen years as a military attache in a succession of western countries, he was appointed as Deputy Director of UNACO after his predecessor had been sent back to Russia in disgrace for spying. $_{514}$He had been with UNACO now

for three years and although he still suffered from bouts of homesickness he never allowed those feelings to interfere with his work. $_{515}$His clinical approach to his job had always been one of complete professionalism. (BNC-ECK:508-515)

The whole excerpt describes a person named Sergei Kolchinsky. After a more general description, the inverted construction in sentence 512 is used to introduce the *brilliant tactical mind* of Kolchinsky as a new discourse topic. The following sentences provide evidence for the claim that he has a brilliant tactical mind. That is, the postposed constituent serves as a topic for three following sentences.

A similar explanation may hold for the use of the *wh*-cleft in (3e), here repeated as (16).

(16) $_{63}$Any organisation has a kind of a memory. $_{64}$At least it learns processes and then procedurises them and keeps them going. $_{65}$*What I'm obviously talking about here is the classic phenomena of bureaucracy.* $_{66}$What bureaucracy is is finding something that works and then setting up stable conditions and procedures and rules and rulebooks and working practices and so on that reliably and economically and punctually repeat that performance because it's something that's useful to do. $_{67}$And it keeps going on. (s2a-049:063-066)

The *wh*-cleft serves to introduce the topic of bureaucracy into the discourse. Note how a basic clause pattern is less efficient in this respect, since it does not draw as much attention to the clause itself (and its content) as does the secondary clause pattern.

(17) $_{63}$Any organisation has a kind of a memory. $_{64}$At least it learns processes and then procedurises them and keeps them going. $_{65}$*I'm obviously talking about the classic phenomena of bureaucracy here.* $_{66}$What bureaucracy is is finding something that works ...

In addition to these text-structuring uses we also find that non-canonical word order can be exploited to achieve certain aesthetic effects. An illustrative example in this respect is the use of full-verb inversion as a means of mirroring natural perception in prose-fictional texts. What does 'natural' mean in this context? The term is used to refer to the fact that perception is usually 'smooth' and proceeds from one item to another item. The important point is that the second item is located in relation to the first. That is, a perceiver sees an item A, locates an item B in relation to item A, then locates an item C in relation to item B, and so on. Inverted constructions are a useful means to describe the transition from one item to the next. This effect has been described under various terms, such as 'imaginary guided tour' (Drubig 1988), 'camera movement' (Dorgeloh 1997) or 'immediate-observer effect' (Kreyer 2006a and b). The main point is that the extralinguistic world is portrayed and described in an iconic way, which creates the illusion of immediacy on the part of the reader. As a result, it is easier for the reader to immerse him- or herself in the narrative. Note how this effect works in the following passage where several inverted constructions occur in a row.

(18) From below his sternum to his waist, Quinn's front was occupied by a flat wooden box that had once contained liqueur chocolates. The bonbons were gone, along with the box's lid. The tray of the box formed a flat container strapped with surgical tape across his chest. *In the centre was the velour package of diamonds, framed on each side by a half-pound block of tacky beige substance. Jammed into one of the blocks was a bright-green electrical wire, the other end of which ran to one of the jaws of the wooden clothes-peg Quinn held aloft in his left hand.* It went through a tiny hole bored in the wood, to emerge inside the jaws of the peg. *Also in the chocolate-box was a PP3 nine-volt battery, wired to another bright-green flex.* (BNC-CAM:1406-1412)

The reader looks at a bomb through the eyes of a character in narrative. The inverted constructions mirror the transition from one object to another object: the centre of the box – the package of diamonds and the beige substance – the electrical wire; and; the box – a PP3 nine-volt battery.

An even better example of this effect is given example (2j) and its immediate context.

(19) Ludo is conscientious. He bends closely to his work. He unscrews the plate and removes it from the door. *Behind the plate is a chiselled cavity. Inside the cavity is a polythene bag. Inside the bag are several smaller bags. Inside each of them is a single ounce of heroin.* (BNC-J13:3398-3404)

The succession of four inversions creates a strong impression of immediacy: the reader participates in the process of discovering the heroin by recreating one step of this discovery after another in their natural order. Note how this effect is destroyed if the full-verb inversions are changed into canonical sentences.

(19') Ludo is conscientious. He bends closely to his work. He unscrews the plate and removes it from the door. *A chiselled cavity is behind the plate. A polythene bag is inside the cavity. Several smaller bags are inside the bag. A single ounce of heroin is inside each of them.*

In addition to fictional prose, we often find this use of inversion in radio sports commentaries, where the recipient has to (re-)create a series of actions only on the basis of oral input. The following example is taken from a horse race commentary.

(20) And behind Ballyhane comes Blue Dart.
Behind Blue Dart is Team Challenge.
And then comes Durham Edition.
And towards the centre of the course is Seagram still there. (s2a-005:105-108)

Again, the skilful use of inverted constructions in this example helps the hearer to create a vivid representation of the scene that is described.

9.2.4 A note on interactions and interdependencies of individual factors

The previous sections introduced a number of factors that may influence the choice of word order. Concerns of syntactic complexity, as we have seen, apply to the clause in isolation, i.e. which order guarantees the fastest and easiest processing of the syntagm. Information status, in contrast, focuses on the clause at issue and its relation to the previous discourse (and the stock of knowledge of the recipient). In this respect it is important that the clause can be linked up to the previous text and to the recipient's knowledge as quickly as possible, so that the bits of new information at the end of the clause can be integrated into already existing knowledge. The aspect of emphasis is not concerned with the processability of the clause or with the integration of the clause's content. The form of the message draws attention to the message itself, resulting in a deeper impression on the part of the recipient, which can be exploited to express contrasts among other things. This chapter has also shown how syntactic variation can be influenced by purposes of text-structuring. In these cases, the final constituent usually is in the focus of attention, as it serves to introduce a new topic into the discourse. Finally, we have seen that non-canonical word order can also be exploited to create the illusion of immediacy, thereby helping the reader to immerse him- or herself into a narrative. That is, non-canonical word order can be used for aesthetic effects as well. Table 9.1 sums up the factors discussed in this chapter.

Table 9.1: Factors that influence syntactic variation.

Factor	Motivation
End-weight, Early Immediate Constituents	Facilitation of processing of the clause in isolation
Given-before-new, Immediate Textual Integration	Facilitation of integration of new information into existing knowledge structures
Emphasis	Contrast, topic introduction
Text structuring	Topic introduction
Artistic concerns	Illusion of immediacy, immersion into the narrative

So far, these factors have been discussed in isolation. In authentic use, however, usually more than one factor exert their influence at the same time: factors interact, thereby focussing on different aspects of the whole utterance. It is reasonable to assume that the producer is concerned with many aspects at one time: he or she may want the clause to be easily processible while at the same time following the demands of information integration and text-structuring. The inverted construction in (11), here repeated as (21), for instance, can be interpreted as following the principle of end-weight and given-before-new at the same time.

(21) $_{311}$Sometimes a seller is so financially powerful that he can blatantly insist on such a clause being included in the contract; he can adopt a "take it or leave it" attitude. $_{312}$*More common is the seller who, having inserted an exclusion clause into his conditions of sale, relies on his buyer not bothering to read (or not understanding) the small print*; ... (H7U:311-312)

In other cases, factors may pull in different directions, as in (9), here repeated as (22), where end-weight is violated for reasons of integration of information and text structuring.

(22) $_{613}$The question then arises as to how this pragmatic enterprise differs, if it differs at all, from the kinds of activity which are customarily carried out under the name of research. $_{614}$*Related to this question of pedagogic/pragmatic research as an integrated element of classroom practice is the matter of teacher formation.* $_{615}$What kind of preparation or priming do

teachers need in order to exploit their classroom experience in the manner I have suggested? (CBR:613-615)

Finally, we also find that factors are interdependent, i.e. factors correlate to a certain extent. Many authors, for instance, have drawn attention to the fact that phrases conveying new information are likely to be longer than those that convey old information, as in the following example.

(23) We met a charming young man who was trying to write on the back of as far as I could tell an envelope one or two amendments to the Union constitution. (s2b-047:023)

The given information is represented in the first noun phrase, which is realised by the simple personal pronoun *we*. The noun phrase that conveys new information (indicated by the indefinite article *a*), in contrast, is a long and complex noun phrase, showing a lot of modification. Since the degree of informativity ('given' versus 'new') correlates with the length and complexity of phrases, following the 'given-before-new' principle will often result in compliance with the principle of end-weight, as in the above example.

Similarly, we can assume that an order of given-before-new elements is concomitant with text-structural and aesthetic exploitations of syntactic structures. For instance, if an inverted construction is used to introduce a topic into the discourse, then the postposed constituent can be expected to convey new information since it would not make much sense to introduce the postposed constituent as a topic otherwise. At the same time, we can expect the preposed constituent to contain a link to the previous discourse, as it is useful to know how a newly introduced topic relates to what has been discussed before. The same holds for constructions used to simulate natural perception. If the initial constituent represents the item in relation to which the final constituent is located, then, of course, the initial constituent should contain given information. Otherwise, it could not serve as a point of reference for locating the second item.

These observations show that the study of factors that influence syntactic variation is far from trivial. Factors usually don't occur in isolation. They interact and are interdependent. Accordingly, an analysis of these aspects should always take into consideration several factors simultaneously.

9.3 Further reading

Esser (1995) provides an exhaustive overview of allo-sentences.
Quirk et al. (1985: ch. 18) provide a discussion of syntactic variation and its relation to aspects of information processing.

See Wasow and Arnold (2003) for a detailed study on factor interaction in post-verbal constituent ordering in English.

Birner and Ward (1998) is an influential attempt to account for a range of word order phenomena in terms of information status.

Givón (2009) is a book-length exploration of syntactic complexity, including aspects of language acquisition and change, neuro-biology and evolution.

9.4 Study questions

1. In what sense is semantics relevant to the study of syntactic variation?
2. Name and give examples of the three kinds of syntactic variation distinguished in this chapter.
3. Explain in your own words the basic idea underlying principles that make reference to syntactic complexity and those making reference to the distribution of information in the clause.
4. Apply the Principle of Early Immediate Constituents to show which of the two alternatives given in (2c) (repeated below) is easier to process.
    We were having a discussion with Bob actually about the organisation of the course. (s1a-008:102)
    We were having a discussion actually about the organisation of the course with Bob.
5. Which principles are violated in the underlined clause? How could that clause be adapted to be more in line with them?
    A conspicuous opaque spot is found near the costal margin of the wing in many insects, and is termed the stigma or pterostigma (Fig. 25). It is present, for example, in the fore wings of the Psocoptera and most Hymenoptera, and in both pairs of wings of the Odonata. <u>A more or less clearly defined blood sinus through which haemocytes move from the lacuna of the costa into other veins is within the stigma (Arnold, 1963)</u>. (adapted from BNC-EVW:510-512)
6. How can the non-canonical word order in example (2f) above, given here with its context, be explained?
    A: *Have you got his album?*
    B: *Yeah*
    A: *I'd really love to tape it from you if you didn't mind*
    B: *Yeah.*
        If you give me a tape I've got a tape to tape and I can run it off.
    A: <u>*Oh great that'd be.*</u> (s1a-042:127-132)
7. Explain in your own words why compliance with the principle of end-weight often results from the principle of given-before-new.

8. The example below illustrates a special kind of 'postponement', namely deferring the postmodification of a noun phrase head to the end of the clause, which results in a discontinuous noun phrase.

   However, the basis exists for speculating that in some people oxidation might be more tightly coupled than in others. (w2a-024:059)

   How could this phenomenon be explained in the light of the Principle of Early Immediate Constituents?

10 Syntax and Meaning

It might seem strange in a book on syntax to include a chapter on the relationship of syntax and meaning. These two aspects are usually relegated to different disciplines of the linguistic enterprise, which can be seen in the table of contents of most introductory textbooks into linguistics: usually we will find separate chapters on syntax, the study of the linear arrangement of words, and semantics, the study of meaning conveyed through language. Nevertheless, the two aspects are interrelated in many ways. The aim of the present chapter is to look at these interrelations in more detail.

10.1 Generative syntax and semantics

The idea underlying a classical generative grammar is the following: if we find a set of rules, i.e. a grammar, that can generate all of the grammatical sentences of a language without generating any of the non-grammatical languages, then we have found an adequate description of this language. One part of the descriptive apparatus of generative grammars is what is called 'phrase structure rules' or 'rewrite rules'. These rules state the number and order of constituents that a superordinate constituent can consist of. For instance, we know that a sentence can consist of a noun phrase, followed by a verb phrase, followed by another noun phrase, as in the example $_{NP}[$That $_{VP}[_V$was $_{NP}[$an interesting period$]]$ (s1a-001:049). A rewrite rule that describes this sentence on the level of its immediate constituents would be the following:

(1) S → NP VP

Further rules are of course needed for the constituents on the lower levels.

(2) NP → ProN
(3) VP → V NP
(4) NP → Det (Adj) N

In addition, we also need a 'lexicon' which tells us how the constituents at the lowest level can be realised lexically.

(5) ProN → *that*   (8) Adj → *interesting*
(6) V → *was*   (9) N → *period*
(7) Det → *an*

Figure 10.1 below shows where in the generation of the above sentence the individual rules come in.

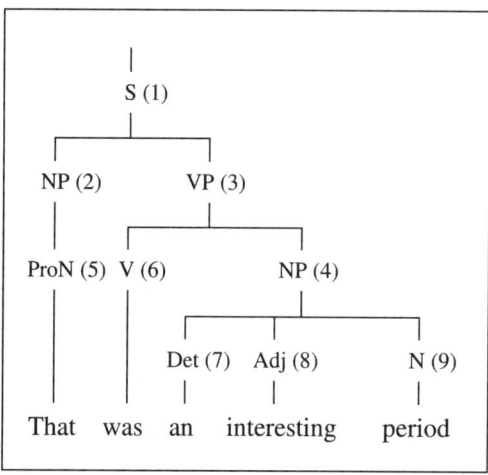

Figure 10.1: The phrase marker of the sentence <u>That was an interesting period</u>.

Figure 10.1 also makes clear why we talk of rewrite rules. If we want to generate a sentence, we can follow rule (1) and rewrite the symbol 'S' by the sequence 'NP VP'. The symbol 'NP', according to rule (2), can be rewritten by the symbol 'ProN', which can be rewritten by the lexical item *that*, following rule (5), and so on. Applying the same rules we could generate sentences like *An interesting period was that* or *An interesting period was an interesting period* or *That was that*, all of which would be grammatical according to the grammar laid out in rules (1) to (9).

In this model, we see a distinction between two kinds of rules. The first kind is called 'categorical rules'; they apply to syntactic categories and generate the abstract syntactic structure. The second kind, the 'lexical rules', is less abstract: they provide information as regards the lexical filling of the slots provided by the first set of rules. That is, the phrase structure rules generate the string 'ProN + V + Det + Adj + N', which consists of syntactic categories only. Obviously, this string does not have any meaning. The meaning is contributed by the lexicon, which tells us how the individual elements in the above string can be lexically realised. So, we end up with a clear division of labour between a syntactic and a semantic component of language, a division which cannot be held up on closer scrutiny.

Syntax and Meaning

Problems arise as soon as our lexicon becomes a little larger.

(5') ProN → *that, we, you, they, it, ...*
(6') V → *was, read, sit, devours, smiled, drank, eats, were,...*
(7') Det → *an, their, his, its, the, ...*
(8') Adj → *interesting, red, awful, boring, tasty, hungry ...*
(9') N → *period, book, car, cat, house, man, husband, wife, ...*

The problems we are facing are of two kinds, as the examples below show.

(10) a) We smiled the boring book.
  b) I laugh the interesting man.
  c) They sit their red car.

(11) a) He devours his new car.
  b) He drank the cat.
  c) It is a hungry book.

Note that all of the above sentences have the same structure as the sentence shown in Figure 10.1. Still, all of them are problematic. The first three examples are ungrammatical (on the basis of English grammar) since the clause contains elements that are not licensed by the verb. The verbs SMILE and LAUGH are intransitive, but in the above example they are followed by a noun phrase, which could be understood as a direct object. Example (10c) shows the copular verb SIT. It needs a locative adverbial, usually realised by a prepositional phrase and not by a noun phrase. These three examples show errors that clearly pertain to the realm of syntax, they violate the verb complementation rules of English language, also called 'subcategorisation rules' (see chapter 12.1 for details).

The errors in (11a to c), in contrast, are of another kind. Here we have the verbs EAT, DRINK and BE. The first two are monotransitive verbs and they are followed by noun phrases, which could function as their direct objects. The last verb is a copular verb followed by a noun phrase which could function as the obligatory subject complement. Syntactically speaking, the three clauses are fine. Still, the words that co-occur do not really fit: we cannot eat cars, we do not drink cats and books are not hungry, at least not in a normal, non-metaphorical sense. Although the above examples are in line with the subcategorisation rules, they violate what has been termed 'selectional rules' (see chapter 12.1 for details). Other famous examples of such violations are the following (note that (12b) is not treated as an example of object fronting; the noun *golf*, here, is understood as the subject of the clause).

(12) a) colorless green ideas sleep furiously
   b) golf plays John
   c) the boy may frighten sincerity (Chomsky 1965: 149)

All of these violations reside in the meaning of the words that are used, i.e. they are clearly of a semantic kind: if something is green it cannot at the same time be colourless, ideas cannot sleep and something cannot sleep furiously, etc.

Note that the two kinds of rules are of a different nature and that their violation results in deviations of different degrees (cf. Chomsky 1965: 148-160). The examples under (10) would be marked as ungrammatical in the strict sense and they can usually not be given a sensible interpretation. The 'errors' in (11), in contrast, are somewhat less categorical, and "we shall usually try to 'make sense' of the sentence by looking for a context in which it might be used" (Palmer 1976: 116-117). Many of these examples, for instance, might be interpreted as metaphorical expressions. The person described in (11a) likes his new car so much that he might actually eat it, or the book in (11c) is so fascinating that it demands the full attention of the reader and draws him or her in to such an extent that it appears hungry. Regarding (11b), those of us who have seen the American TV series *ALF* (short for 'alien life form') know that the main character Gordon Shumway is a furry extraterrestrial life form from the planet of Melmac, where cats happen to be the favourite dish and cat juice is a much-liked beverage. Given this cultural background, the sentence under (11b) would be perfectly alright. Metaphor and cultural knowledge, however, are not part of syntax but make reference to semantics (culture to some degree depends on meaning). So, the selectional rules discussed above demonstrate that syntax and semantics are interdependent to a certain extent and interact in intricate ways.

10.2 The open-choice principle and the idiom principle

What we have discussed so far has fittingly been referred to as the 'slot-and-filler model' of language. This relates to what Sinclair (1991) calls the 'open-choice principle', namely

> a way of seeing language text as the result of a very large number of complex choices. At each point where a unit is completed (a word, phrase, or clause), a large range of choice opens up and the only restraint is grammaticalness. It is often called a 'slot-and-filler' model, envisaging texts as a series of slots which have to be filled from a lexicon which satisfies local restraints. At each slot, virtually any word can occur. (Sinclair 1991: 109)

Syntax and Meaning

In contrast to that, Sinclair claims that language use is dominated by the 'idiom principle', which says that

> a language user has available to him or her a large number of semi-preconstructed phrases that constitute single choices, even though they might appear to be analysable into segments. (Sinclair 1991: 110)

Since we are dealing with the linear organisation of words we would have to concede that the idiom principle is somehow related to syntax. However, in contrast to what traditionally is assumed to be syntax-related, the idiom principle is not so much based on the arrangement of abstract categories (as for instance the phrase-structure rules discussed above) but rather makes reference to individual and concrete lexical items, and in that respect pertains to the realm of semantics. These next sub-sections elaborate on concepts relating to the idiom principle.

10.2.1 Collocation

The concept of selectional rules is captured *ex negativo*, i.e. it is based on the fact that categories of words are not allowed to co-occur with words from particular other categories, as this co-occurrence would lead to more or less meaningless sentences. This is also expressed in the alternative term 'selectional restrictions': it makes clear that the language user is restricted in his or her lexical choices once one lexical item has been chosen. The '*ex positivo*' counterpart is the notion of 'collocation'; it is concerned with the tendencies of words (we will discuss later what enters into collocational relationships, i.e. word forms, lexical units, etc.) to co-occur often. That is, collocation is not concerned with what is possible but rather with what is probable and what co-occurs characteristically. This also entails important differences with regard to the data that corpus linguistics deals with. While models in the generative paradigm are usually based on invented examples, many corpus linguists emphasise that their findings and theories not only are based on naturally occurring data but driven by the patterns that show up in large amounts of authentic text – a distinction captured by the terms 'corpus-based' and 'corpus-driven'. The concepts to be discussed in the following sections, to a large extent, are the outcome of corpus-driven research.

The term 'collocation' is multi-faceted and used differently by different authors. A frequent understanding of the term has been suggested by Firth. He writes:

> The habitual collocations in which words under study appear are quite simply the mere word accompaniment, the other word-material in

which they are most commonly or most characteristically embedded. (Firth 1968 [1957]: 180)

As the quotation makes clear, collocation has to do with the degree to which the occurrence of a given word is associated with the occurrence of another word. For instance, *example* would collocate with *of*; the two word forms co-occur so frequently that they are strongly associated with one another. Similarly, we have a strong association between *naked* and *eye* (discussed in detail be Sinclair 1996; see section 10.2.3. Some examples of the two word forms co-occurring are given below.

(13) The mite is just visible to the **naked eye** and feeds on honey bees. (BNC-AJB:111)
Because the creatures of the plankton individually are small, they are not always visible to the **naked eye**. (BNC-AMS:892)
But the loss of these marine plants, which the **naked eye** may hardly perceive, would spell the end for almost all animals. (BNC-AMS:896)
The human egg is just visible to the **naked eye**. (BNC-ASL:76)
He showed some incredible coloured slides giving close-up detail of petal formation and patterns not often seen by the **naked eye**. (BNC-B03:1863)

Collocational relations have to do with expectations: the occurrence of one member of a collocational relationship (one collocate) leads us to expect the occurrence of another collocate somewhere in its vicinity. Partington (1998: 16) speaks of "[t]he habitual associations of a word with other items". This habitual association is not merely based on frequent co-occurrence but on characteristic co-occurrence; hence the part "most commonly or most characteristically embedded" in the above quotation from Firth. A look at the case of *naked eye* is revealing in that respect. The 100-million-words British National Corpus shows a total of 148 instances of this string of words. The string *my father*, however, is much more frequent, it occurs 3502 times. While in the first case we have a much lower frequency of co-occurrence than in the second case, *naked* and *eye* co-occur more characteristically with each other. That is, the occurrence of *naked* leads us to expect the occurrence of *eye* much more than the occurrence of *my* leads us to expect *father*. This is due to the fact that *my* co-occurs frequently with a lot of other word forms. For instance, *my mother* occurs 3334 times and the string *my own* 4781 times. Although *my* co-occurs frequently with *father*, this co-occurrence is not characteristic. In contrast, *naked* occurs almost three times as frequently with *eye* than with the second-strongest collocate *body*, which again is more than two times as frequent as the third-strongest collocate *woman*.

The string *naked eye* as a whole also stands in collocational relations; usually with elements to its left. All of the above examples show the definite article *the* immediately to the left (in short: N-1, standing for 1 word to the left of the node, in this case *naked eye*) of the lexical string. This is in line with observations made by Sinclair (1996), who finds that *the* immediately precedes *naked eye* in 95% of his examples. We will find later that *naked eye* attracts not only particular words but also syntactic categories and semantically defined sets of lexical items.

Collocates need not be adjacent – there can be intervening material between them (see, among others, Sinclair 1991: 115). The strongest collocate of *heavy* in the BNC, for instance, is *rain*. The corpus lists 274 cases of the two collocates, 225 of which form the string *heavy rain*. Some examples of where the two words are separated by intervening word forms are given below.

(14) The **rain** was so **heavy** it was 'like a swimming pool'. (BNC-CAN:896)
With the first **heavy** drops of **rain**, Mungo started to run. (BNC-ACV:776)
[...] in times of **heavy** and prolonged **rain**. (BNC-B31:112)
Unfortunately **heavy** monsoon **rain** caused our first game to be abandoned against Singapore. (BNC-BN9:1443)
Cloudy in Scotland and Northern Ireland with **rain**, **heavy** at times especially over the hills. (BNC-CF5:198)

Although the two collocates are not adjacent, they still occur in one another's vicinity, raising the language user's expectancy to encounter one collocate when he or she has encountered the other one.

Above I already hinted at the question of what kind of elements enter into collocational relations. So far we have only been looking at word forms, and there are good reasons to do so, because one word form of a lexical unit may behave differently than another word form. While *rain* is the top collocate of *heavy*, the plural *rains* is not listed among the collocates. A similar observation about *eye* and *eyes* is made by Sinclair:

> [M]ost uses of the form *eye* are not in a singular/plural relationship with *eyes*. [...] there is shown to be very little overlap between the "top twenty" collocates of the two word forms; *blue* and *brown* collocate only with *eyes*, while *caught* and *mind* collocate only with *eye* [...]. (Sinclair 1996: 84)

On the other hand, in some cases, expectancies are not between individual word forms but between lexical units and (sometimes) between their derivations. Altenberg and Eeg-Olofsson (1990: 3-4), for instance, observe that *drink heavily*, *heavy drinker*, *heavy drinking*, and *drink/drinks/drank/drinking heavily* are all instantiations of one collocational relationship, namely that between the adjective HEAVY and the verb DRINK together with the derived noun DRINKER. The same opinion is reflected in Lipka (2002: 182), when he claims that the sentence "*A bullfighter fights bulls at a bullfight* [...] contains three instances of collocation of *fight* and *bull*".

This section has shown how in many cases the occurrence of one lexical item leads to a higher likelihood of occurrence for particular other lexical items. The influence of expectancies of this kind, however, does not stop at the level of word forms or lexical units, as becomes clear in the next section.

10.2.2 Colligation

Corpus linguistic research has found that in addition to expectancies relating to lexical items, similar relationships also hold between individual words (in the broad sense) and syntactic categories or constructions. Relationships of this kind are called 'colligation'. Sinclair (1996), for instance, reports on interesting findings regarding the string *naked eye*: in 90 % of all cases, the word on N-2, i.e. two words to the left of the string, is a preposition; compare with the examples under (13). That is, we see that a string of lexical items – a semantic entity – attracts a specific word class – a syntactic entity. Hunston and Francis (e.g. 2000) have done a lot of work on the interdependencies of lexical items and syntactic constructions under the heading of 'pattern grammar'. Its basic tenet has been formulated as follows:

> [...] syntactic structures and lexical items (or strings of lexical items) are co-selected, and [...] it is impossible to look at one independently of the other. Particular syntactic structures tend to co-occur with particular lexical items, and – the other side of the coin – lexical items seem to occur in a limited range of structures. The interdependence of syntax and lexis is such that they are ultimately inseparable [...].
> (Francis 1993: 143)

Instead of two clearly demarcated components syntax (or grammar) and semantics (or lexis), the pattern grammar contends that the two components are interdependent to such an extent that it makes more sense to speak of lexicogrammar instead. Pattern grammar tries to do justice to this interdependence. It is an attempt to describe "the interaction between the particular lexical items in [... a corpus] and the grammatical patterns that they form a part of" (Hunston & Francis 2000: 1). The identification of patterns is essentially lexically based and starts off from a particular lexical item and the words and phrases that usually co-occur together with it. Accordingly, patterns are defined as "all the words and structures which are regularly associated with the word and which contribute to its meaning". (37) Below some examples are given of the patterns in which the verb DIVIDE occurs (note that the code 'pl-n' refers to any noun-like element that makes reference to more than one entity, e.g. *the dogs* or *the dog and the cat*).

(15) a) '*divide* n *between/among* pl-n'
   Drain the noodles and **divide them among the individual serving bowls**. (cf. Francis et al. 1996: 361)
   b) 'be *divide-ed between/among* pl-n'
   The tips **are divided up equally between the staff**, and then added on to their wage packet. (cf. Francis et al. 1996: 361)
   c) '*divide* n adv/prep'
   Such a system would **divide the country on tribal lines**.
   (cf. Francis et al. 1996: 324)

With the examples above, the idea of co-selection of lexical and syntactical/grammatical items becomes apparent. In (15a), for instance, the pattern consists of the lexical items *divide* and *between* or *among* and the syntactic categories singular and plural noun. In addition, the individual elements occur in a certain order – a feature also pertaining to syntax. The same holds for the other examples. On the whole, we witness the complex interactions of syntax and semantics. Patterns are instances of the "semi-preconstructed phrases that constitute single choices" Sinclair talks of.

A further look at authentic data reveals that other verbs also enter into the same patterns as the verb DIVIDE. Francis et al. (1996) reports on many tokens where other verbs occur in the verb slot of the pattern illustrated in (15a).

(16) a) Election coverage on radio and television **will be split between the party in power and the opposition parties**.
   b) The programme aims to **forge links between higher education and small businesses**.
   c) The liquid crystal is **sandwiched between two glass plates**, each of which carries a polarising filter.
   d) He **numbered several Americans among his friends**.
   (cf. Francis et al. 1996: 361-362)

In the light of these examples, it makes sense to assume a more general pattern, namely 'V n *between/among* pl-n', which is instantiated by more concrete patterns where the V slot is instantiated by individual verbs, such as DIVIDE, SPLIT UP, FORGE, etc. In addition, Hunston and Francis (2000) identify an intermediate level of patterns: "particular patterns will tend to be associated with lexical items that have particular meanings" (Hunston & Francis 2000: 83). More precisely, a slot in a particular pattern attracts items that can be assigned to a fairly restricted number of meaning groups. Examples (16a) to (16d) exemplify four such groups, namely the 'divide', the 'forge', the 'sandwich' and the 'number' group. The 'divide' group, for instance, in addition to *divide* and *split*, contains the verbs *distribute*, *split up*, and *share out*. All of these verbs, according to Francis et al. (1996: 361) share the fact that they are "concerned with dividing something up between two or more people or groups". To give another example, the 'sandwich' group, containing *sandwich*, *interpose* and *intersperse*, encompasses verbs that are "concerned with putting something between two or more things, either physically or metaphorically" (361).

So we see that, similarly to syntactic constructions, patterns form hierarchies organised in different levels of specificity or generality. Figure 10.2 shows such a hierarchy for the patterns discussed above.

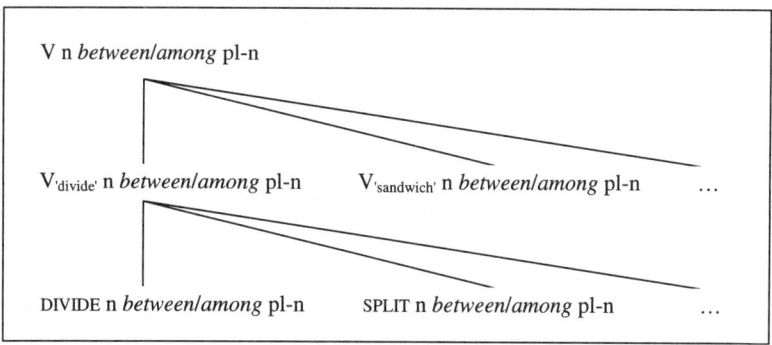

Figure 10.2: The hierarchical organisation of patterns of the 'V n <u>between/among</u> pl-n' group.

Having discussed the co-selection of lexical items and lexical items as well as of lexical items and syntactic constructions we now turn to the co-selection of lexical items and classes of lexical items defined by a given semantic feature.

10.2.3 Semantic preferences and prosodies

In his analysis of the string *naked eye*, Sinclair (1996) finds that in addition to collocations and colligations in N-1 and N-2, respectively, words that occur (mostly; see 17c below) at the third slot to the left usually have a particular meaning component:

Whatever the word class, whatever the collocation, almost all of the instances with a preposition at N-2 have a word or phrase to do with visibility either at N-3 or nearby. (Sinclair 1996: 86)

A look at the data under (13), here repeated as (17), corroborates this conclusion.

(17) a) The mite is just <u>visible</u> to the **naked eye** and feeds on honey bees. (BNC-AJB:111)
   b) Because the creatures of the plankton individually are small, they are not always <u>visible</u> to the **naked eye**. (BNC-AMS:892)
   c) But the loss of these marine plants, which the **naked eye** may hardly <u>perceive</u>, would spell the end for almost all animals. (BNC-AMS:896)
   d) The human egg is just <u>visible</u> to the **naked eye**. (BNC-ASL:76)
   e) He showed some incredible coloured slides giving close-up detail of petal formation and patterns not often <u>seen</u> by the **naked eye**. (BNC-B03:1863)

In (17a, b, and d), the semantic aspect of visibility is realised in the adjective *visible*, in (17c and e) it is the verb forms *perceive* and *seen*. This shows that semantic preferences cut across word classes (cf. Esser 1999: 158).

Related to the idea of semantic preferences is the notion 'semantic prosody'. The term was introduced by Louw (1993) and describes the fact that some elements attract lexical items that describe 'negative' things, features, actions, etc., while others show a characteristic co-occurrence with 'positive' elements. Louw (1993: 160), for instance, observes that the adverb "*utterly* has an overwhelmingly 'bad' prosody: there are few 'good' right-collocates". Typical examples include phrases like *utterly meaningless to himself, utterly stupid,* and *utterly terrified.*

The same holds for the *naked-eye* examples under (17), repeated here for convenience, this time with those items underlined that express semantic prosody.

(17) a) The mite is <u>just</u> visible to the **naked eye** and feeds on honey bees. (BNC-AJB:111)
   b) Because the creatures of the plankton individually are small, they are <u>not always</u> visible to the **naked eye**. (BNC-AMS:892)
   c) But the loss of these marine plants, which the **naked eye** may <u>hardly</u> perceive, would spell the end for almost all animals. (BNC-AMS:896)
   d) The human egg is <u>just</u> visible to the **naked eye**. (BNC-ASL:76)
   e) He showed some incredible coloured slides giving close-up detail of petal formation and patterns <u>not often</u> seen by the **naked eye**. (BNC-B03:1863)

We see the adverb *just*, and the strings *not always*, *may hardly* and *not often*. Together with Sinclair (1996) we can conclude that the pattern 'visibility + preposition + *the* + *naked* + *eye*' has

> a *semantic prosody* of 'difficulty', which is evident in 85% of the instances. It may be shown by a word such as *small, faint, weak, difficult* with *see* [...] and *barely, rarely, just* with *visible* [...] or by a negative with 'visibility' or *invisible* itself; or it may just be hinted at by a modal verb such as *can* or *could*. (Sinclair 1996: 87)

The discussion in section 10.2 has revealed that the linear arrangement of word forms is not only driven by considerations of syntax, i.e. the question which word classes can co-occur with which. Rather, we find all kinds of semantic effects influencing the 'generation' of syntagmatic strings of word forms. This influence may be from one word form to another, from a word form to more or less syntactic patterns, and from word forms to semantic features. On the basis of these findings, it makes sense to dispense with the strict division of syntax/grammar and semantics/lexis and get used to the idea of a lexico-grammar, in which lexical items and syntactic constructions are co-selected.

10.3 Constructions

The discussion of patterns in 10.2.2 (partly) dealt with the influence of semantics on the choice of syntactic constructions and showed that syntax and semantics are interdependent to a certain extent. Bold as this claim may seem, a lot stronger is the claim that syntactic constructions themselves have meaning, a claim put forward by construction grammar. A look at the data below indicates that this view should not be discarded too eagerly.

(18) a) Caroline had tried to **talk her way into** being permitted to enter a summer class that was already under way. (BNC-JY7:5806)
b) The family – without plane tickets and passports – had to **talk their way past** airport officials on their homeward journey. (BNC-CH2:11928)
c) All those murderous little thugs in Grimm who cheated and stole and **lied their way to** the princess and half the kingdom? (BNC-CFK:2042)
d) Let's just **discuss our way round** a couple of other things. (BNC-KGU:949)

All of the above cases instantiate the pattern 'V *way* prep/adv'. According to Hunston and Francis (2000) cases like the ones above indicate that "someone uses clever, devious, or forceful language to achieve a goal, usually extricating themselves from a difficult situation, or getting into a desirable situation" (100). The verbs in the above examples (maybe with the exception of *lied*) do not insinuate such behaviour. It seems in this case that the pattern itself contributes this particular meaning aspect. This is what construction grammar is about.

According to Taylor (1998), the rise of construction grammar can be seen to some extent in attempts to account for the idiomatic expressions of a language, which were impossible to capture in more traditional approaches (apart from merely listing them). A case in point is the famous *let-alone* construction discussed in Fillmore et al. (1988). Some authentic examples are given below.

(19) a) Most policemen and women at Easton have not even **drawn their gun**, *let alone* **fired it**. (BNC-A5Y-502)
b) Mrs Tanqueray, was extremely displeased at having to share **Jessie**, *let alone* **a dressing-room**. (BNC-A0D:1344)
c) Official statistics become less and less use as a basis **for rational debate**, *let alone* **for good decisions**. (BNC-A44:8)
d) Neither alternative was anywhere near implemented **by 1926**, *let alone* **in 1922**. (BNC-A64:1680)

The construction is regular to a certain degree. First of all, all of the tokens contain the string *let alone*, which gives the construction its name. We also see that the construction is somehow similar to coordination, in that two elements are related to each other. However, in this case these two elements (marked in bold print) are focused and contrasted. That is, (19a) contrasts *drawn their gun* with *fire it*, (19b) contrasts *Jessie* with *a dressing room*, (19c) contrasts *for rational debate* with *for good decisions* and so on. In addition to the lexical string *let alone* and the two focused elements there is additional material which is not involved in the contrast. But this additional material is restricted in that it needs to describe a negative context. In (19a) this is expressed by the use of the negation particle *not*, in (19b) by the morpheme *dis-*, in (19c) by the coordinated adverbs *less and less*, and in (19d) by the string *anywhere near*. On the basis of these observations we can in first approximation (which will suffice for the present purposes) describe the construction as follows.

(20) $X_{negative}$ A   *let alone* B,

Again, we see how in that construction rule-based abstract strings are mixed with fixed lexical items, i.e. syntax and lexis are co-selected. So far this is what we already know from pattern grammar. Above, it was said that the most important feature of construction grammar is the claim that constructions themselves have a meaning. What, then, is the meaning of the *let alone* construction? Fillmore et al. (1988) describe it as follows:

Stronger proposition *a fortiori* weaker proposition. That is, whatever reason we have to believe, state, impere, suggest, etc., the stronger proposition, we have even stronger reason to so express the weaker proposition. (Fillmore et al. 1988: 528)

Let us take a closer look at (19a) to see what that means. This example conveys two propositions, namely: 1) 'most policemen and women at Easton have not even drawn their gun', and 2) 'most policemen and women at Easton have not even fired their gun'. The first is the stronger proposition in the sense that it is easier to draw a weapon than to fire it. It is, therefore, a stronger to claim that, say, 90% of the police force have never drawn a weapon than to claim that 90% have never fired a weapon. Also, we see that the first proposition entails the second since in order to fire a gun you first have to draw it. This is part of what the *let alone* construction expresses. But this could also be expressed in other ways, as shown in (19a').

(19) a') Since most policemen and women have not even drawn their gun they have not fired it.

Compared to (19a), (19a') sounds somewhat weak. More specifically, it does not as clearly emphasise the fact that guns have not yet been fired by most of the police. This is the extra meaning conveyed by the *let alone* construction: it places special emphasis on the weaker proposition: if it is true that most policemen have never even drawn their guns then, of course, it must also be true that they have never fired them. As a consequence the assumption that policemen and women fire their guns regularly is rejected more forcefully than it would in other constructions.

Admittedly, this is a somewhat special type of construction and maybe would not qualify as a syntactic construction in a strict understanding of the term. Let us therefore take a look at the following cases.

(20) a) **I could paint you an exact copy**. (BNC-FR6:2294)
   b) A black family moves in – **the neighbours bake them a cake**. (BNC-G0F:2182)
   c) **British Gas** do that and **drop you a line** when the engineer's coming. (BNC-K9S:863)

All of the above examples are ditransitive clauses, i.e. they are of the form SVOiOd – a syntactic constructions in any possible understanding of the term. The following argument will show that constructions of this kind also have meaning. Let us first focus on the verbs. The verb PAINT, according to LDOCE, has the basic meanings 'to put paint on a surface', 'to make a picture', or 'to describe someone or something in a particular way'. Neither of these meanings that *LDOCE* provides contains a meaning of transfer. This, however, is exactly what the sentence under (20a) says: the person referred to by *I* transfers an exact copy to the person referred to by *you*. Similarly, the verb BAKE; LDOCE lists two meaning, namely 'to cook something using dry heat' and 'to make something become hard by heating it'. Again, neither of the two meanings implies a transfer of any kind, but this meaning is expressed in the sentence under (20b). Without going into any further detail, (20c) works similarly.

If the transfer meaning conveyed in all of the above examples does not reside in the verb (as for example with GIVE), and if it does not come from other lexical items in the sentence (which obviously it does not), the only possible source of the transfer meaning that is left is the construction itself, i.e. the clause pattern SVOiOd, called the 'ditransitive construction' in Goldberg (1995). The basic meaning of this construction is 'X CAUSES Y to RECEIVE Z' (Goldberg 1995: 49). And it is this basic meaning that lets us understand a transfer meaning even though this is nowhere in the wording of the utterance.

As a final example let us consider what Goldberg calls the 'caused-motion construction', i.e. the sequence SVOdAo, illustrated below.

(21) a) **The Spirit urged Jesus into the desert.** (BNC-CCE:469)
  b) Mr Hobbs unpacked a nightdress and together **we helped her out of her clothes**. (BNC-CEX:1324)
  c) Isn't it about time **this silly nonsense was laughed out of court**, and have done with it. (BNC-KGP:86)

As before, we find that the whole sentence contains a motion meaning that we do not find in the semantics of the three verbs. This time, however, the situation is slightly more complicated, since we always have a directional expression, i.e. *into the desert*, *out of her clothes* and *out of court*. So it might be argued that in this case the motion aspect resides in the directional prepositions. However, Goldberg (1995: 158) provides examples where the same motion meaning evolves even though instead of a directional expression the sentence contains a locational one:

(22) a) Sam squeezed the rubber ball inside the jar.
  b) Sam urged Bill outside of the house. (Goldberg 1995: 158)

In other contexts the phrases *inside the jar* and *outside of the house* have a clear locational meaning. We would usually not come up with a directional interpretation of the examples below.

(23) a) The wasp was flying inside the jar.
　　b) The children were running outside of the house.

Accordingly, we can assume that "the locative terms [... are] coerced into having a directional meaning by the caused-motion construction itself" (Goldberg 1995: 159), which warrants a meaning which the construction has independently of the lexis that fills it, namely 'X CAUSES Y to MOVE Z'.

On the whole, the last two examples have shown that even very basic, 'run-of-the-mill' syntactic constructions like clause patterns do have a meaning on their own. Accordingly, a view which draws a clear dividing line between syntax and semantics cannot be upheld anymore. Not only are syntax and semantics interdependent, resulting in co-selection of lexical items and syntactic categories, syntactic constructions can have a meaning of their own.

Goldberg (1995) lists a number of advantages of assigning meanings to constructions. One of them is that the "constructional approach avoids the problem of positing implausible verb senses" (9). For instance, if we would not assume the existence of the ditransitive construction in (20b), *the neighbours bake them a cake*, we would have to claim that the verb BAKE has "a sense which involves something like 'X INTENDS to CAUSE Y to HAVE Z'" (9). Obviously, this is not very plausible.

Related to this is the problem of proliferation of senses. Consider some of the examples of the uses of the verb KICK provided by Goldberg.

(24) a) The horse kicks.
　　b) Pat kicked the wall.
　　c) Pat kicked Bob black and blue.
　　d) Pat kicked the football into the stadium. (cf. Goldberg 1995: 11)

On the basis of these sentences (Goldberg lists four more) we would have to come up with different senses of KICK. There seems to be a basic sense common to all examples which denotes a particular kind of movement of feet and legs. (24a) is an instantiation of this basic sense, but at the same time it also describes a particular 'mental' disposition of the horse: the meaning of *kick* in this example might be paraphrased as 'showing aggression by a particular kind of movement of feet and legs'. With regard to (24b) we would also have to include a monotransitive sense 'hitting something through a particular kind of movement of feet and legs'. (24c) shows a complex transitive sense which might be paraphrased as 'initiating a change of state by a particular kind of movement of feet and legs', and the complex transitive sense instantiated in (24d) could be described by 'transferring something somewhere by a particular kind of movement of feet and legs'. In addition to the fact that not all of these senses seem plausible, we also find that the size of the lexicon would increase dramatically, if we posited such a multiplicity of senses whenever a verb occurs in different constructions. Instead, it seems more reasonable, for instance, to posit a transfer meaning for the caused-motion construction (as in (24d)) and not attribute the transfer meaning to an additional sense that the verb has if it occurs in that construction. This way, construction grammar provides a more elegant way than other approaches of treating the phenomenon that verbs seem to show untypical senses in some cases.

10.4 Further reading

For more information on the corpus linguistic concepts discussed in this chapter take a look at Sinclair (1991) and Sinclair (2004). Another interesting read in this respect is Hoey (2005), who argues that "lexis is complexly and systematically structured and that grammar is an outcome of this lexical structure" (1), i.e. a reversal of the relative position of lexis and grammar.

The main book on pattern grammar is Hunston and Francis (2000). It is also worthwhile to take a look at the pattern dictionaries published by Collins (Francis et al. 1996 and 1998), as they show a markedly different approach to syntactic patterns and their relation to semantics.

Good introductions into construction grammar are given in Evans and Green (2006: chs. 19 and 20) and Croft and Cruse (2004: chs. 9 and 10). Since there are many different types of construction grammars there are a number of books on the individual models, some of them quite technical. Maybe the most easily accessible one is that developed in Goldberg (1995, see also 2006).

10.5 Study questions

1. What phrase structure rules would you need to generate the sentence *I brought you a present* (w2f-002:220)?
2. Describe what part of the generation of sentences subcategorization rules and selectional rules organise.
3. Which rules (subcategorization or selectional) do the following examples violate:
    He read the newspaper to the table.
    Mary bought some cruel water.
    The noisy idea slept the book.
4. Explain the concept 'slot-and-filler model' in your own words and illustrate it with examples.
5. What would you think is the semantic prosody of the verb CAUSE? Can you cause good things?

11 Major Approaches to Syntactic Description: An Overview

In the previous chapter we already took a glance at the ways different approaches incorporate semantic aspects into syntactic description. This chapter intends to take a closer look at some major approaches to syntax which have been extremely influential over the past decades and therefore warrant at least a short cursory discussion. In particular, we will be looking at theories developed in the generative framework and at construction grammar.

11.1 The standard theory of generative-transformational syntax

With the term 'standard theory' we refer to the generative-transformational model introduced by Chomsky in his *Syntactic Structures* from 1957 and his *Aspects of the Theory of Syntax* from 1965. This model has undergone major changes over the last four decades but it makes sense to start our discussion at this point since it allows us to introduce basic concepts and assumptions in this framework that pave the way for a discussion of the more recent approaches.

As pointed out in section 10.1 the term 'generative' refers to the fact that a description of a language is understood to be correct and valid if it generates all grammatical sentences of a language and no ungrammatical sentences. A generative grammar, therefore, can be likened to an algorithm or a machine that produces all of, and only, the grammatical sentences of a language. Above, we saw that phrase structure rules form one important component of such a grammar. These phrase structure rules describe how the syntactic skeleton of a sentence is generated by providing 'algorithms' that make explicit what constituents an element consists of and in which order these constituents occur. That is, each element is rewritten as a sequence of its constituents, hence the term 'rewrite rules'. Above, for instance, we saw that a sentence can be re-written as a noun phrase followed by a verb phrase, i.e.

(1) S → NP + VP

Depending on the number and kinds of obligatory constituents that the verb demands, we arrive at different phrase structure rules for the 'VP' element, as the (incomplete) list below shows. Note that the term 'VP' is used differently from the use in chapter 3: in the context of generative-transformational grammar it is understood in the sense of 'predicate', i.e. the verb and the postverbal constituents.

(2) VP → V   (intransitive)
(3) VP → V NP   (monotransitive or copular)
(4) VP → V PP   (copular)
(5) VP → V NP NP   (ditransitive or complex-transitive)

In a similar fashion, we can describe the structure of the noun phrase.

(6)   NP → N   (*people*)
(7)   NP → Det N   (*these people*)
(8)   NP → AdjP N   (*nice people*)
(9)   NP → N PP   (*people in Germany*)
(10) NP → Det AdjP N   (*these nice people*)
(11) NP → Det N PP   (*these people in Germany*)
(12) NP → AdjP N PP   (*nice people in Germany*)
(13) NP → Det AdjP N PP   (*these nice people in Germany*)

The above examples make clear how the number of possible combinations that the English language allows can easily lead to a proliferation of phrase structure rules. Usually, individual rules are combined in one rule which states obligatory and optional constituents. The rules from (6) to (13) can be subsumed under one single rule, namely

(14) NP → (Det) (AdjP) N (PP)

This rule indicates that each NP must have a noun (i.e. the head) and in addition may have a determiner, a premodifying adjective phrase or a postmodifying prepositional phrase (or any combination thereof).

Especially interesting is the prepositional phrase since it draws attention to an important phenomenon of natural languages – 'recursiveness'. The PP is rewritten as follows.

(15) PP → P NP

As you can see in (15), the symbol 'NP' occurs to the right of the arrow. In rule (14), the symbol 'PP' occurs on the right-hand side. As a consequence, we can produce noun phrases like the following:

(16)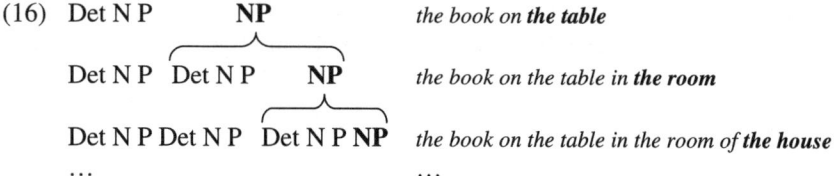

The complexity results from the application of rule (15) on the output of rule (9), to which then we can again apply rule (15) and so on. This phenomenon is called 'recursiveness': at a certain point you go back to where you started your journey. In the above case, we have a noun phrase that contains a prepositional phrase that contains a noun phrase that contains a prepositional phrase and so on. A nice (non-linguistic) example of recursiveness is found in *Wikipedia* (http://en.wikipedia.org/wiki/Recursion; accessed on 17.01.2010) where under the lemma 'recursion' we also find the following two 'definitions'.

(17) **Recursion**   **Recursion**
     See 'Recursion'.   If you still don't get it, see 'Recursion'.

Recursiveness is one reason why it is impossible to list all grammatical sentences, because I can always add one more element to a recursive cycle. Maybe the most famous example of recursiveness (though not usually known under that heading by the non-linguist) is the nursery rhyme *The house that Jack built*, part of which is shown under (18)

(18) This is the dog
     that worried the cat
     that killed the rat
     that ate the malt
     that lay in the house
     that Jack built.

The rules underlying this recursiveness could be formulated as follows:

(19) NP → Det N S_{rel}
(20) S_{rel} → *that* V NP

As in the examples above, the output of rule (20) leads us back to rule (19) – and we can start all over again.

The set of rules that generate the bare syntactic tree are called 'categorical' rules. In section 10.1 we saw that another component serves to 'attach' leaves to the syntactic tree, namely the 'lexical rules'. In this context, we also talked about 'subcategorization rules' and 'selectional restrictions'. These are what are called context-sensitive rules and they can solve the problem of generating a sentence like (21).

(21) The boy laughs the man.

The sentence structure 'NP V NP' usually results from monotransitive verbs and is generated by rule (3) above. Obviously, LAUGH is not a monotransitive verb but an intransitive one. How can we specify this in our grammar? The answer lies in the V element of the VP. A lexicon entry as the one under (22) is too general.

(22) V → LAUGH, READ, GIVE, CONSIDER, ...

Instead, it is necessary to distinguish different kinds of verbs in the lexicon, as shown in (23).

(23) $V_{intransitive}$ → LAUGH, LIVE, EXIST, ...
      $V_{monotransitive}$ → DRINK, READ, WRITE, WATCH, ...
      $V_{ditransitive}$ → GIVE, HAND, TELL, ...

In addition, we need context-sensitive rules as the ones in (24).

(24) V → $V_{intransitive}$ / ___
      V → $V_{monotransitive}$ / ___ NP
      V → $V_{ditransitive}$ / ___ NP NP

This rule can be paraphrased as 'rewrite V as a monotransitive verb if it is immediately followed by a noun phrase'. That is, in the context of a following NP, a verb can be rewritten as a monotransitive verb. Let us assume that we want to generate a sentence and arrive at the string 'NP V NP'. If we want to rewrite the V element, rule (24) states that, in the context in which the symbol appears, V has to be rewritten as $V_{montransitive}$, which then can be rewritten as any verb in the second row in the list under (23). An intransitive verb like LAUGH is not possible, as this is restricted to a different context.

In a similar fashion, selectional rules can be handled. Here, the context does not consist of syntactic categories but of semantic features. For instance, a verb like DRINK can only be used in a context in which the following noun phrase denotes something that can be drunk. A possible context-sensitive rule is shown below.

(25) $V_{monotransitive}$ → DRINK / ___ [+drinkable]

This would keep the grammar from generating a sentence like *He drank the cat*, since the lexical unit CAT does not have the semantic feature [+drinkable] (unless you are from the planet Melmac).).

The two components described so far, the categorical rules and the lexical rules, enable the grammar to generate a phrase structure together with the meaning that it has. We could say that such a phrase structure represents the proposition of the sentence, i.e. that part of the sentence that is responsible for the truth value of the sentence. As we saw in the many instances of syntactic variation discussed in chapter 9, the English language provides different ways of expressing the same proposition. A text-producer can choose between different allo-sentences. The phenomenon that the same content can be expressed in different ways is captured in the distinction between 'deep structure' and 'surface structure'. In the deep structure we find the sentence as generated by the categorical and lexical rules of the grammar together with the meaning that arises from the syntactic tree and its words. The deep structure sentence is then subjected to transformations, i.e. rules that "operate [...] on a given string (or [...] on a set of strings) with a given constituent structure and convert [...] it into a new string with a new derived constituent structure" (Chomsky 1957: 44). Hence the term 'generative-transformational grammar'. Consider the following example.

(26) a) Iraq's given the UN figures of civilian casualties. (s2b-018:013)
     b) Figures of civilian casualties have been given to the UN by Iraq.

Although both sentences look different, they express the same meaning in a truth-conditional sense: if (26a) is true then (26b) is true and vice versa, and if (26a) is false, (26b) is false and vice versa. In generative-transformational words we would say that both sentences have the same deep structure (which accounts for the identity of meaning) but a different surface structure. This difference is due to the application of the 'passive transformation', which is described by Chomsky (1957: 43) as follows:

(27) $NP_1 - Aux - V - NP_2$
        $NP_2 - Aux + be + en - V - by + NP_1$

This is similar to part of what is expressed in Figure 6.2 in section 6.3, here repeated as Figure 11.1.

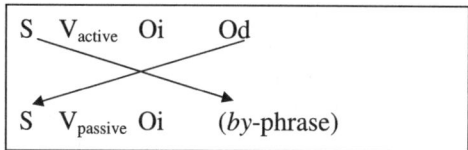

Figure 11.1: The relation of active and passive sentences (= Figure 6.2 in 6.3).

The distinction between deep and surface structure solves some puzzles regarding homonymy and polysemy of syntactic strings. Each of the following 'versions' of (26a) has the same deep structure, which accounts for their identity in meaning.

(26) a) Iraq's given the UN figures of civilian casualties. (s2b-018:013)
 b) Iraq's given figures of civilian casualties to the UN.
 c) Figures of civilian casualties have been given to the UN by Iraq.
 d) What Iraq's given the UN is figures of civilian casualties.
 e) It is Iraq that has given figures of civilian casualties to the UN.

The differences in appearance are merely due to transformations that have been (or have not been) applied to the deep structure. These, however, leave the meaning untouched. That is, concepts like 'systematic correspondence' or 'allosentence' as discussed in chapter 9 are accounted for by transformations in the standard model of generative grammar.

Different meanings of identical strings are accounted for by different deep structures. A well-known example is the sentence *The man saw the boy with the telescope*. With one reading the prepositional phrase *with the telescope* works as a postmodifier to the noun phrase head *boy*, in the other reading the telescope functions as an adjunct that describes the manner of the verbal action. So, we have one surface structure, i.e. one string of items, which is related to the two different deep structures shown below. This is often referred to as 'structural homonymy'.

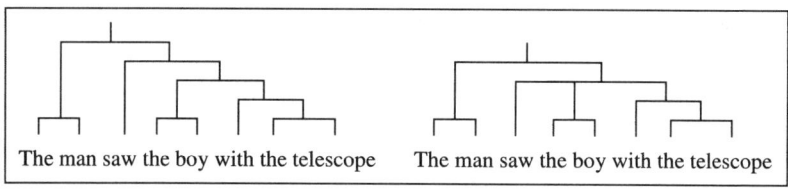

Figure 11.2: The two deep structures of the strings <u>The man saw the boy with the telescope</u>.

So far we have discussed categorical and lexical rules and transformations. The first two are also called the 'base' and they generate 'base phrase markers', "the elementary units of which deep structures are constituted" (Chomsky 1965: 17). Together with the transformations, the base forms the 'syntactic component' of a generative-transformational grammar. In addition to this, the grammar needs a semantic component which assigns a meaning to the deep structures generated by the base and a phonological component which assigns a string of phonological elements to the surface structures yielded by the transformations. On the whole, then, the standard model of generative-transformational grammar looks as follows.

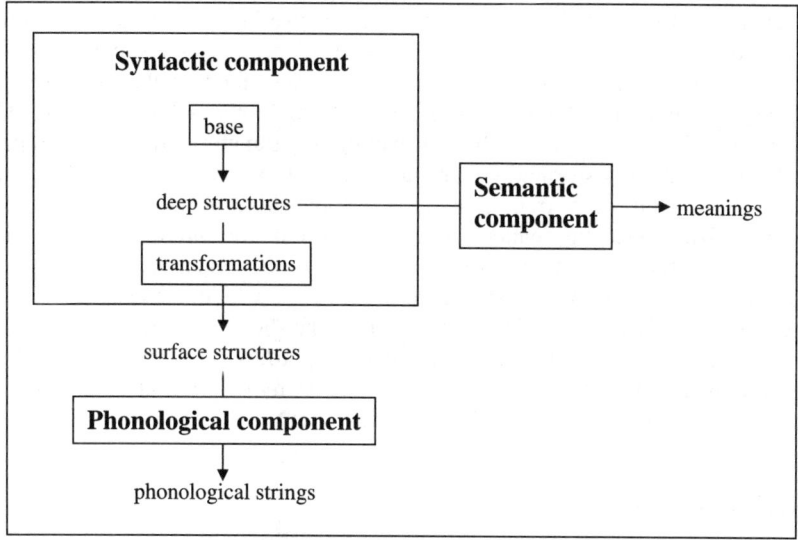

Figure 11.3: The standard model of generative-transformational grammar (see Chomsky 1965: 15-18, cf. Klenk 2003: 77)

The standard model has been subjected to a number of major revisions over the last few decades, even to such an extent that it is not always easy to find similarities to more recent theories in the framework. Significant changes have been made to the transformational component. It has been argued, for instance, that the transformations posited in the standard model can be understood as consisting of a sequence of more general transformations. An example is the passive transformation: one thing that happens is that noun phrases are moved, a process that can also be found with other phenomena. Consider the examples of passive and raising shown in (28a) and (28b) below:

(28) a) Mary was given the ball by Peter.
   (← Peter gave Mary the ball.)
(28) b) Mary seems to have solved the problem.
   (← It seems that Mary has solved the problem)

Instead of interpreting these as results of two individual transformations (as in Chomsky's earlier works), we now find that both constructions can be related to one kind of elementary transformation (plus other transformations): in both cases it is an NP that is moved out of its original position (either as indirect object in (28a) or as subject of an embedded clause in (28b)) to a position in the front of the clause. In both cases, the moved NP occupies the subject position of the resulting clause. This process is usually described as the 'NP-movement' transformation, "in which an NP is moved to an empty subject position" (Haegeman ^{2}1994: 305). Instead, then, of having one transformation for each pair of allo-sentences, transformations are now understood as consisting of chains of more basic elementary transformations. Another kind of movement transformation is *Wh*-movement, which (in part) accounts for interrogative or relative clause structures. On the most general level, all movement transformations can be captured under the transformation 'Move α', which merely means "move something" (Haegeman ^{2}1994: 305). This (very short) overview has shown that substantive generalisations have been made regarding the transformational component of the model. The next section looks in more detail at modifications of the phrase-structure rules, i.e. the base component.

11.2 X'-Theory

X'-theory (read: x-bar theory) is a modification of the base component of the grammar. It was instigated by Chomsky's influential 1970 paper "Remarks on Nominalization", further developed in Jackendoff's (1977) monograph *X'-Syntax. A Study of Phrase Structure* and has since then been subject to major revisions by other researchers. The following account of X'-theory will dispense with unnecessary technicalities but nevertheless hopes to provide information on the basic claims and underlying arguments of X'-theory.

The major achievement of X'-theory is that it has shown that all phrases in English grammar can be described by the following set of three phrase structure rules (Haegeman ^{2}1994: 104):

(29) a) XP   → Spec X'
    b) X'*   → X' YP
    c) X'   → X YP

'X' refers to any lexical category, 'YP' to complement phrases and 'Spec' to the so-called specifier (the terms will become clear further below); the asterisk in the second rewrite rule shows that more than one X' can occur in one XP.

At first sight, it seems impossible that all the phrase structures that have been described in this book should be describable with just three rewrite rules. What is more, X'-theory claims that sentences, both superordinate and subordinate, can be subsumed under the above schema. The following discussion shows that this is indeed possible. Let us consider phrases first.

(30) a) the assumption that you are being understood (w1b-007:128)
    b) much cheaper than anybody else (s1a-010:036)
    c) even faster than we can possibly hope to pursue them (s2a-031:032)
    d) straight into the next day (s1a-005:152)
    e) not read books (s1b-046:052)

With the above examples, it is useful with most phrases to distinguish three parts: the head, that which comes before the head, and that which comes after the head. Focussing on the strings that come after the heads for the moment, we find that each of them are in some way or other obligatory (in case the same information is not provided somewhere in the context), just like some postverbal elements are obligatory for the completion of the sentence. In (30a) the noun *assumption* needs the *that*-clause: if we hear the noun we want to know what assumption in particular we are talking about. Similarly, in (30b), if something is *cheaper*, we need to know what the basis of comparison is, just like (30c). The preposition *into* in (30d) expresses a direction and the following noun phrase provides the goal of this direction, and, finally, the head *read*, being a monotransitive verb, demands a direct object. In X'-theory such strings are called 'complements'. Note that the term is used differently from the use in this book, where 'complement' denotes a particular kind of obligatory post-verbal constituent. In X'-theory the term is used in a broader sense to encompass any kind of syntactic element that is demanded by another element. In this sense, for instance, direct and indirect objects, obligatory adverbials and also phrase elements as presented above are complements. They have to be distinguished from 'adjuncts', which are non-obligatory (see below for further detail).

If we take a look at the elements preceding the head, we find that they seem to 'modify' the sequence of head and complement. In (30a), for instance, it is not *any assumption that you are being understood* but one particular assumption, hence the use of the definite article *the*. (30b) describes a person or a shop not as *a little* or *somewhat cheaper than anybody else* but as *much cheaper than anybody else*, and so on. In that sense, we can say that the pre-head material specifies the head together with its complement, hence the term 'specifier' (note, however, that in some cases the use of the term is not motivated semantically but by considerations of model-inherent restrictions; see Radford 1997: 89-93).

On the whole, then, we end up with an extremely abstract tripartite structure consisting of specifier, head and complement. This structure is hierarchical in that head and complement together are 'specified' by the specifier, as shown in Figure 11.4 below.

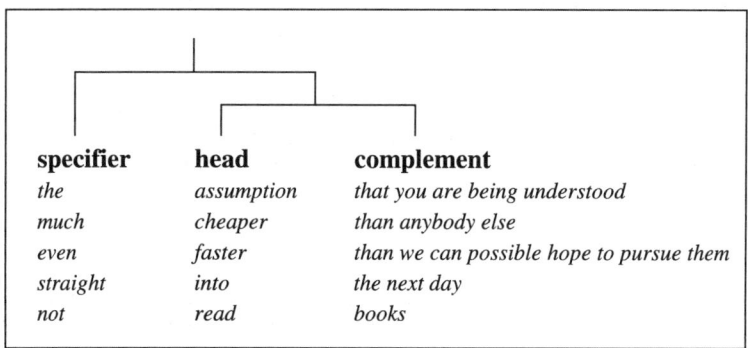

Figure 11.4: The basic structure of phrases.

Figure 11.4 above shows the structure of what is called an 'XP', i.e. an 'X-phrase', where the 'X' can be understood as a variable that stands for the five main word classes, i.e. noun, adjective, adverb, preposition and verb. The head is referred to as 'X', since the head gives the phrase its name. The complement is usually referred to as 'YP', where 'Y' is another variable. That is, so far we have the following labelled tree diagram.

Major Approaches to Syntactic Description: An Overview   217

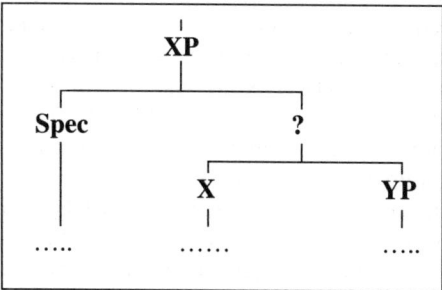

Figure 11.5: The structure of the XP (incomplete).

The question now is as to the nature of the intermediate constituent marked by the question mark in Figure 11.5. Obviously, the head X is still the main element in this intermediate constituent. On the other hand, the constituent is smaller than the XP itself. Being intermediate between the head X and the phrase XP, this constituent is usually referred to as X'. So, the combination of X and its complement YP is called X'. The complete structure of the XP thus looks like this.

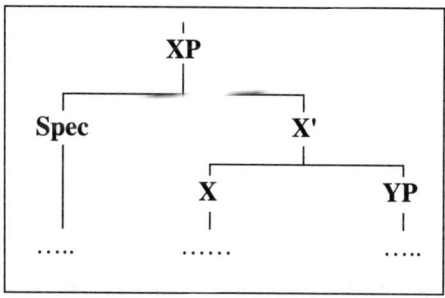

Figure 11.6: The structure of the XP (complete).

We say that the node XP is the 'maximal projection' of the node X, whereas X' is called an 'intermediate projection'. Note that the first and the last rewrite rule given at the beginning of this section under (28), here repeated as (31), generate the structure under Figure 11.6.

(31) a) XP   → Spec X'
     b) X'*   → X' YP
     c) X'   → X YP

Which specifiers and complements are possible for a given XP depends on the word class of the head. Typical specifiers for nouns are determiners, and possible complements are the kinds of modification discussed in chapters 3 to 5. Specifiers for AdjPs, AdvPs and PPs are adverbs. In VPs, negative elements such as *not* or *never* occupy that slot (cf. Aarts 1997:103). The complements in a VP are the obligatory postverbal elements, e.g. noun phrases functioning as object, complement or obligatory adverbial.

For the description of the examples above rule (31b) was not needed, but it is necessary to describe structures like *the new interest in hearing voices* (s2b-038:46) discussed in section 5.4. Recall from the description of phrases in chapters 3 to 5 of this book that we stuck to flat, non-hierarchical structures. A description of the given phrase in these terms would be 'det + premodifying adjective + head + postmodifying prepositional phrase'. It was only in section 5.4 that we looked into the hierarchical relations within phrases. The structural description in terms of X'-syntax is superior in that respect, as it provides the hierarchies together with the structure. The X'-description of the string *the new interest in hearing voices* looks as follows:

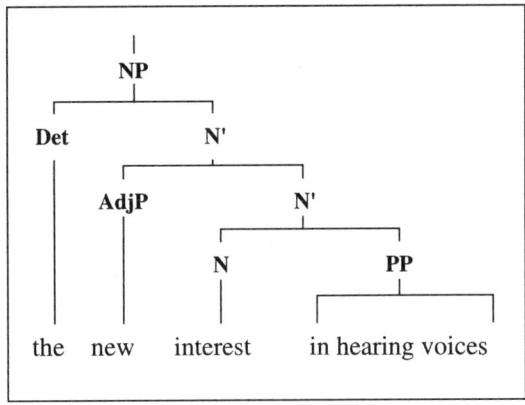

Figure 11.7: The X'-description of <u>the new interest in hearing voices</u>.

The first N'-node is generated by an instantiation of rule (31c), namely 'N' → N PP'. Following rule (31b) we arrive at the second N'-node. Finally, the NP-node is generated by rule (31a).

Figure 11.7 makes explicit the semantic relation of the individual elements in the noun phrase: we are dealing with an interest in hearing voices, and this particular interest is new. This is what the diagram expresses. Figure 11.7 also illustrates that the specifier always is the sister to the highest X'-node. In addition, it demonstrates nicely the difference between complements and adjuncts in phrases. With the noun *interest* we want to know what the interest is in. So, *in hearing voices* is a complement of the head. In contrast to that, the noun *interest* does not lead us to ask whether this interest is new or old. That is, the premodifying adjective *new* only provides additional information which is not necessary to the same extent that the information provided by the complement is. Such bits of information are called 'adjuncts' in X'-theory. The difference between complements and adjuncts also becomes apparent in the phrase marker: a complement is a sister to the head, i.e. the complement and the head share the same mother node X'. An adjunct, in contrast, always is a sister to an X'-node. This also helps us to understand the rule under (31b) (X'* → X' YP). It states that we can have more than one adjunct, as in the example *an ideal democratic society* (s1b-011:171). Here we have two adjuncts but no complement. Still, neither of the adjuncts is immediately attached to X. Following convention, we always have at least one intermediate projection X' in the tree diagram to which adjuncts can attach. Accordingly, the structure of *an ideal democratic society* looks as follows.

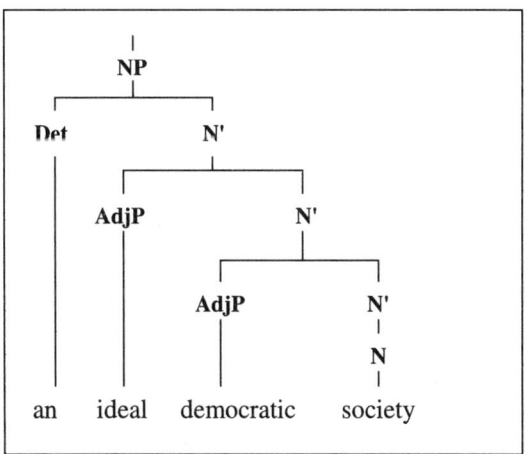

Figure 11.8: The structure of the phrase <u>an ideal democratic society</u>.

So far, we have seen that the X'-approach manages to account for all kinds of phrases in a very elegant and simple system. But X'-syntax not only generalises over phrasal structures but is also able to accommodate sentence structure in the same basic schema, as will be illustrated with the simple sentence *The cat will attack anyone* (s1a-019:162).

The rationale underlying the description of phrases in X'-theory is that the head of the phrase, the X, characterises the whole phrase. For instance, it is the noun and its features which determines how the noun phrase can be used, where it can occur and so on. What could be a similar element for the sentence? Some of the most characteristic features of the whole sentence, such as tense, voice and aspect are related to the finite element in the verb phrase (Klenk 2003: 86). This element, therefore, is assumed to function as the head X of a sentence. It is denoted by the symbol 'I' (for 'inflection'), and sentences, accordingly, are understood as IPs. In the above example, the auxiliary *will* is the I. Since the auxiliary needs the VP *attack anyone*, this VP is understood as the complementation of the node I. The subject *the cat* is understood as the specifier within the IP. The sentence *The cat will attack anyone* can thus be described as follows in the X'-schema (note that we are not concerned with the internal structures of the VPs and NPs at this moment).

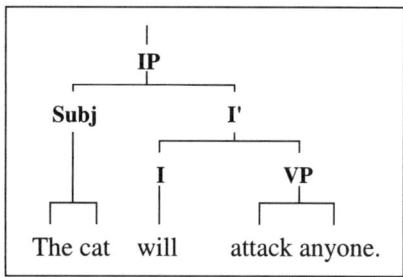

Figure 11.9: The structure of the sentence The cat will attack anyone.

The next question, then, is what to do with sentences like the following: *He saw a flicker of recognition* (w2f-012:118). This sentence does not contain an auxiliary. A possible candidate for the 'I' element might be the verb *saw* since it contains the information which would be provided by the auxiliary if the sentence had one. However, the lexical verb cannot function as the 'I' element, since as a 'V' element it already projects the VP. The solution to this problem is an abstract element 'I', which contains the information expressed in the inflected verb form, i.e. [+past]. The 'V' element, then, simply is the uninflected form *see*, and our tree looks like this (disregarding the internal structure of the NP).

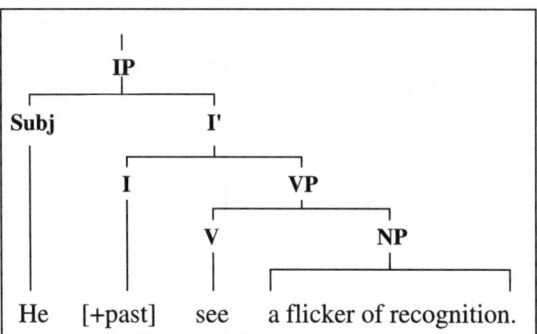

Figure 11.10: The structure of the sentence <u>He saw a flicker of recognition.</u>

On the whole, we have seen how X'-theory provides an elegant way of generalising over phrase and clause structure with a powerful descriptive apparatus that only consists of three basic categorical rules. Note, however, that the high degree of abstraction in X'-theory leads to a blurring of differences and regards elements as essentially identical although they do not seem to have a lot in common at first sight. An illustrative example is the category 'I', which contains concrete auxiliary verbs like *will* or *may* but also abstract features like [+past] or [+3rd person]. In some cases, the nature of the generative algorithm demands categories that may appear counter-intuitive to the layman and even the linguist.

11.3 Construction Grammar

In section 10.3 we already glanced at constructions (in the construction grammar sense) with a focus on the relation of syntax and semantics. The present section takes a closer look at construction grammar as a syntactic theory, contrasting this fairly recent approach to the other models described so far. Despite a fair amount of heterogeneity within the different theories, all of them "conform to three essential principles [...]: the independent existence of constructions as symbolic units, the uniform representation of all grammatical structures, and the taxonomic organization of constructions in grammar" (Croft & Cruse 2004: 265).

Regarding the first principle we find that at the heart of construction grammar lies the idea of constructions as symbolic units, i.e. constructions are regarded as signs in the Saussurean sense: they contain a form side and a meaning side, which are mapped onto each other. Consider Figure 11.11 (taken from Croft & Cruse 2004: 258).

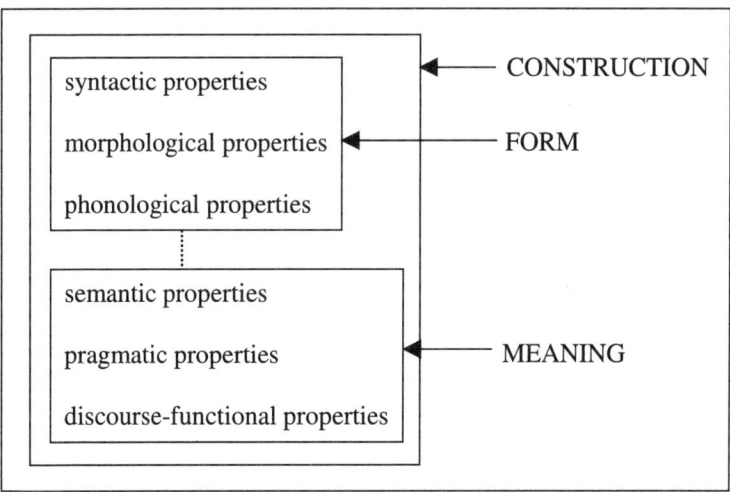

Figure 11.11: Form and meaning in constructions (cf. Croft & Cruse 2004: 258).

Note that 'meaning' as used in construction grammar approaches is not restricted to lexical or semantic meaning but involves pragmatic and discourse-functional properties. The string *How are you?*, for instance, would be considered as a construction in construction grammar. It has obvious formal properties and in addition to the semantic meaning side also has pragmatic meaning, namely that of 'greeting', and may have the discourse function of initiating a conversation; note that the latter cannot be derived from the components in the string.

In construction grammar we witness an expansion of the notion of sign since, as we saw in 10.3, meaning is not only ascribed to morphemes and words but also to syntactic constructions (in the traditional sense). So, constructions range from morphemes, over words and phrases, to complete sentences. According to Goldberg (2005: 17) "[c]onstructions are posited whenever there is evidence that speakers cannot predict some aspect of their form, function, or use from other knowledge of language (i.e., from other constructions already posited to exist". The clause *the neighbours bake them a cake* (BNC-G0F:2182), as was argued in 10.3, suggests the existence of a ditransitive construction which accounts for the transfer meaning that cannot be found in any of the other constructions in that sentence.

The second principle, the uniform representation of all grammatical structures, claims that "grammar consists of constructions" (Goldberg 2005: 18). This is an extremely strong claim: it does away with rules governing the sequencing of words and phrases, such as the rewrite rules and the transformations that were discussed in the previous two sections. As Taylor (1998: 186) points out, "[e]xpressions are sanctioned by the constructions that they instantiate, rather than by their conformity with general principles". This view is also appealing if we take into account that "most children begin language acquisition by learning some unparsed adult expressions as holophrases – such expressions as *I-wanna-do-it, Lemme-see,* and *Where-the-bottle*" (Tomasello 2003: 38). These phrases have a semantic and pragmatic meaning as a whole and it is likely that they are not treated as strings consisting of smaller elements by the child, but as unanalysable units. In the construction grammar view, language acquisition consists of deriving more and more abstract schemas (or constructions) from the input that a child is exposed to.

As a consequence, a grammar does not consist of rules induced into a set of data but of schematic representations abstracted from the data. This process of abstraction leaves the more concrete units untouched, they may still be part of the knowledge of the speaker. Langacker writes:

> [T]he rule is viewed simply as a schematic characterization of [... input] units. Speakers do not necessarily forget the forms they already know once the rule is extracted, nor does the rule preclude their learning additional forms as established units. Consequently, particular statements (specific forms) coexist with general statements (rules accounting for those forms) in a speaker's representation of linguistic convention, which incorporates a huge inventory of specific forms learned as units (conventional expressions). (Langacker 1987: 46)

When Langacker in the above quote talks of "schematic characterization" he makes reference to the notion of abstraction that we discussed in section 1.3. Consider the sentences below.

(32) a) And they give us a couple of tapes. (s1a-008:076)
  b) Charles could tell him the story. (s1a-018:167)
  c) That will give the panel a chance to expand on what they've been saying (s1b-036:066)
  d) He offered Tony Crossland the Chancellorship of the Exchequer. (s1b-40:034)
  e) That now earns Manchester United another corner kick. (s2a-003:025)
  f) You sent us some stuff then. (s1b-080:256)
  g) These problems would cause the programmer considerable differences. (w2a-038:039)

Abstracting away from the lexis and just focusing on the phrases that are used, we find that all of these examples instantiate the following pattern:

(33)   NP V NP NP

And this sequence becomes associated with the meaning of transfer, since in all of the above cases this sequence expresses just this meaning. On a less abstract level, we can find further patterns, such as the following:

(34)   NP GIVE NP NP

This is a 'particular statement' in the sense of the Langacker quote (although still fairly general). It expresses the language user's knowledge that the verb GIVE is associated with the ditransitive pattern. There is good reason to believe that through the use of the verb GIVE, the infant actually acquires the ditransitive construction (see in this context Tomasello's 1992 'verb island hypothesis').

We see that constructions (on different levels of specificity) are distillations of patterns that are encountered in actual language data. They are restricted by what Langacker (1988: 12) calls the "content requirement", which ensures that the grammar of a language only contains units that occur overtly, i.e. instantiating expressions, or units that are schemas, i.e. abstractions of instantiating expressions, or describe relations that exist between schemas and instantiating expressions. Construction grammar thus tries to "ensure the naturalness of description" (13) in ruling out

> the use of "dummies" having neither semantic nor phonological content, invoked solely to drive the machinery of formal syntax. [...] It further precludes the derivation of an overt structure from a hypothetical underlying structure of radically different character (e.g. the derivation of a passive from an underlying active). (Langacker 1988: 12)

An element like the 'I' element in X'-theory, which may just 'represent' tense and aspect features without a formal realisation, does not exist in construction grammar. Similarly, as the quotation above shows, there is no distinction between a deep structure and a surface structure. Construction grammars, therefore, are often called 'monostratal' grammars.

Examples (33) and (34) already hint at the third principle, the taxonomic organization of constructions in grammar. We have seen that constructions are related by schematicity: an abstract construction is instantiated by a number of less abstract constructions, each of which is again instantiated by less abstract constructions, and so on. Another example of this kind of organisation is given below.

(35)   [Verb Phrase]
    |
   [Verb Obj]
    |
   [*kick* Obj]
    |
   [*kick* [*the bucket*]] (Croft & Cruse 2004: 263)

The top-level construction, [Verb Phrase], has a meaning that could be glossed with 'action' or 'doing something', whereas the construction on the second level specifies that something is done to somebody or something, i.e. part of its meaning is the existence of a patient. The next construction [*kick* Obj] is warranted by the fact that it provides information on the argument structure of the verb KICK and, finally, the last construction is idiomatic, i.e. its meaning cannot be derived from any other construction.

The hierarchy under (35) shows how grammatical knowledge is accommodated in a network of constructions. Croft and Cruse (2004: 263) point out that the first two levels replace a rewrite rule like 'VP → V + NP': a verb phrase can be instantiated by a verb followed by an object. The construction on the third level provides the same information as the subcategorisation rules discussed in 11.1; it tells us that the verb KICK needs a direct object, information which would be part of the lexicon. Similarly, the last construction, being an idiom, would also be captured in the lexical component of traditional approaches. This way of description differs markedly in two ways from more traditional approaches: 1) it includes those aspects that are fully regular (like phrase structure rules) as well as those that are more idiosyncratic and peripheral (such as idioms) in one model, using the same descriptive tool for both; 2) it dispenses with the distinction of lexis and syntax and treats what is regarded as two distinct modules in traditional approaches as a continuum from fully concrete lexical to fully abstract syntactic elements (see also section 10.3).

11.4 Further reading

See Klenk (2003) for an accessible yet thorough introduction into different models of syntax in the generative framework (written in German).

Ten Hacken (2007) is a discussion of the Chomskyan paradigm with a focus on epistemological questions.

Aarts (1997: ch. 7) provides a very good account of X'-syntax.

Useful overviews of construction grammars and their theoretical grounding can be found in Croft and Cruse (2004; chs. 9 and 10) and Evans and Green (2006: chs. 17, 19 and 20).

11.5 Study questions

1. What is the difference between categorical and lexical rules? Give examples.
2. What problems do context-sensitive rules solve? Give examples.
3. Provide one grammar (i.e. a set of categorical and lexical rules) that generates the deep structure on the left of Figure 11.3, and one grammar that generates the deep structure on the right.
4. Provide context-sensitive rules that keep a grammar from generating the sentences below.
    He read the newspaper to the table.
    Mary bought some cruel water.
    The noisy idea slept the book.
5. Formulate a transformational rule that describes cases of dative alternation such as the one below.
    Iraq's given the UN figures of civilian casualties. (s2b-018:013)
    Iraq's given figures of civilian casualties to the UN.
6. What is the difference between complements and adjuncts in X'-theory terms and how does it show in the phrase markers?
7. Provide an X'-description of the following two noun phrases (there is no need to give a detailed description of the post-head material).
    the assumption that linguistics is difficult
    the assumption that I am talking about
8. Describe the three basic principles that characterise all construction grammars.
9. In what sense is the ditransitive construction described in section 10.3 a sign in the Saussurean sense? More specifically, what is its form, what is the meaning, and how are components of the form side related to components of the meaning side?

12 Psycholinguistic Aspects of Syntax

So far we have looked at syntax as a closed system. That is, we have been focussing on how the structures that the English language provides can be described and what problems may arise in the description of these structures. We have discussed the interrelations of syntax with other levels of linguistic description and we have taken a look at different models of syntactic description. Chapter 9, on syntactic variation, was a slight exception. Here, reference was made in passing to notions that are best understood with regard to psychological processes: underlying the principle of end-weight is the assumption that end-weight eases processing and comprehension of sentences. Among other things it makes reference to limitations of working memory. All these are concepts that pertain to the realm of psychology. Similarly, the principle of 'given-before-new', as described, among others, in Weil ([1844] 1978), Gabelentz (1901) or Mathesius (1929), makes reference to processes in the mind of the speaker or listener. It is based on assumptions regarding knowledge structures in the mind of the listener and how these need to be addressed in order to successfully integrate new information. Such assumptions are of a psychological nature, as becomes obvious, for instance, when Gabelentz (1901: 365-373) talks of 'psychological subject' and 'psychological predicate' in this respect.

This final chapter will take a closer look at the psychology of syntax. However, while in chapter 9 the approach was from the linguistic side, chapter 12 approaches the topic from a decidedly psychological perspective. This might make the chapter a slightly more demanding read, as the focus will not only be on psycholinguistic findings that are relevant for a theory of syntax but also on the nature of the psycholinguistic approach to language itself. In particular, the chapter aims at giving the reader an idea how questions regarding syntax can (or cannot) be answered with the help of psychological experiments. This involves a somewhat detailed look at the setup of the experiments, at the procedures involved and at the interpretation of experimental data. With regard to the latter, the chapter will point out pitfalls and caveats and it will also draw attention to experiments that have incorrectly been taken to shed light on processes relevant to syntax.

Before, however, a comment is in order regarding the fact that we can never be really sure what the results of such experiments actually tell us. In this respect consider the lengthy quote from Lamb about a joke that is being told at Texas A&M University.

> [It] is about a science class at Texas A&M in which each student selected a science project to work on. One student decided to investigate

what he called 'the toothpaste problem'. Having observed, as we all do, that toothpaste comes from the tube in a flexible cylindrical shape, with the cylinder having a diameter of about one centimetre [...], he decided to measure the length of the whole cylinder [...]. He carefully laid out the cylinder from a tube of toothpaste onto a long continuous stretch of paper towels and then carefully measured. I forgot what the total length was, let's say 3.45 meters. Of course he observed that tubes of different sizes evidently hold cylinders of different lengths. Now came the really difficult theoretical phase of the project: to determine how they get that long cylinder into that short tube. After weeks of stewing over this problem he finally decided that, since it is quite flexible, it could be folded up and/or coiled, and then there must be a small mechanism near the output end of the tube which straightens it out just before it gets to that output unit. As the teacher was a graduate of Texas A&M, he gave the student an A. (Lamb 2000: 87-88)

As this story makes clear, we have to be aware of the fact that the 'structure' of behaviour does not necessarily mirror the 'structure' of the mechanisms and units responsible for that behaviour. Experiments yield behavioural data and the researcher has to come up with models that explain this behaviour. With regard to the joke above, one candidate for such a model is the one described in the joke, i.e. toothpaste is stored as one long coiled-up cylinder in the tube and straightened by a mechanism near the output unit. Another candidate is the hypothesis that toothpaste is stored as an amorphous mass in the tube and brought into shape by the shape of the opening of the tube. If you do not look inside the tube you cannot answer the question of which model is the correct one with absolute certainty. In choosing between alternative models we usually make reference to what is referred to as Occam's razor, which basically says that we choose the simpler model, that model which makes fewer assumptions. In the above case, we would therefore prefer the second model, since the first assumes a particular shape of the toothpaste in the tube and an extra straightening mechanism towards the end of the output unit. The second model can do without these additional assumptions; it is the more elegant of the two. Which of these models is actually true can only be found out by cutting open the toothpaste tube and examine what it looks inside. Obviously, we still cannot look very far into the minds of humans. All we have is experimental data and these can only be the basis of our model but they are never the model itself. We should keep this in mind for the rest of this chapter.

12.1 The derivational theory of complexity

An illustration of the difficulties in developing models on the basis of experimental data is experiments in the field of derivational theory of complexity. The term 'derivational' refers to the derivation of surface-structure sentences from deep-structure sentences through transformations. The derivational theory of complexity, thus, concerns itself with the validation of the transformational component of Chomsky's generative-transformational grammar described in section 11.1. At first sight this seems plausible since Chomsky himself claims the model of generative-transformational grammar to be psychologically real (at least to a certain extent). After all, "[a] grammar of a language purports to be a description of the ideal speaker-hearer's intrinsic competence", i.e. "the speaker-hearer's knowledge of his language" (1965: 4). Note, however, that Chomsky complains that his suggestions have given rise to "a continuing misunderstanding" (9), namely that his model of competence might be taken as a model of language use, an idea that he opposes strongly:

> It [a grammar] attempts to characterize in the most neutral possible terms the knowledge of the language that provides the basis for actual use of language by a speaker-hearer. When we speak of a grammar as generating a sentence with a certain structural description, we mean simply that the grammar assigns this structural description to this sentence. When we say that a sentence has a certain derivation with respect to a particular generative grammar, we say nothing about how the speaker or hearer might proceed, in some practical or efficient way, to construct such a derivation. These questions belong to the theory of language use – the theory of performance. (Chomsky 1965: 9)

Psycholinguistic experiments, however, are always based on language use, i.e. on performance. Experimental data are the outcome of the knowledge that a speaker-hearer has of his or her language, but we can have different models that describe how the experimental data come into existence (see above). Still, as Prideaux points out:

> [T]he derivational theory of complexity is such a natural projection of grammatical theory onto the domain of language use that it would be absurd not to explore it. If it could be shown that the theory is empirically justified, we would have learned a great deal about language processing, and we would also have discovered that our theory construction has been on the right track. (Prideaux 1984: 104)

The basic assumption of the derivational-theory-of-complexity approach is that the processing complexity of a sentence is related to the number of transformations that the sentence has undergone from its deep structure to the surface structure. This assumption was tested with sets of sentences of the following kind.

(1) a) The dog chased the cat. (no transformation)
  b) The cat was chased by the dog. (Passive)
  c) The dog did not chase the cat. (Negation)
  d) Did the dog chase the cat? (Question)
  e) The cat was not chased by the dog. (Passive + Negation)
  f) Was the cat chased by the dog? (Passive + Question)
  g) Didn't the dog chase the cat? (Negation + Question)
  h) Wasn't the cat chased by the dog? (Passive + Negation + Question)

The sentences above all have the same deep structure and only differ in the number and kinds of transformations that have been applied. With regard to the number of transformations we find that (1a) is the least complex sentence whereas (1h) is the most complex one, with the other sentences in between. If transformations influenced processing complexity we would have to assume that sentence (1a) is the easiest to process, followed by sentences (1b to d), followed by (1e to g). (1h) with its three transformations would be the most difficult to process. In short: the more transformations, the more difficult to process. One way of measuring processing difficulty is to measure the time it takes to process a sentence. One experiment designed by Miller and McKean (1964) was to present their subjects with sentences like the ones under (1) above. One of the experimental tasks was "to find the sentence that means the same thing [...] but in a different form" (302). That is, subjects had to identify sentences with the same deep structure, and Miller and McKean measured the time that it took the subjects to complete this task.

If transformations were psychologically real we would assume that identification time depends on the number of transformations between the stimulus and the target sentence. And this is exactly what the experiment yielded. Identification times were linearly related to the number of transformations involved: the more transformations involved, the longer it took subjects to complete the task. In addition, the experiment also showed differences in complexity between individual transformations. For instance, to match a non-transformed sentence to a passive sentence took an average of 0.91 seconds whereas it took only 0.41 seconds to do the same with negative sentences. Again, this is exactly what we would expect on the basis of transformational theory. As we saw in chapter 11, the passive transformation is fairly complex. It involves movement and insertion of elements. Negation, in contrast, is very simple: you just have to insert the negation particle *not* after the first auxiliary or insert a form of DO plus *not*. Finally, combinations of passive and negation took an average of 1.53 seconds, which also seems plausible. It takes slightly longer (0.11 seconds) than both passive and negation taken together, which could be explained by the fact that the succession of two transformations puts an extra strain on the human processor.

So, these are (some of) the experimental facts. One way to account for them is to assume that the transformational component as described in section 11.1 is a psychological reality. After all, the existence of transformations has been empirically validated, hasn't it? There are at least two caveats that need to be considered. Firstly, there are alternative explanations, i.e. alternative models. The difference in the time needed for the completion of the task can also be explained by mere length of the sentences involved, as Prideaux (1984: 107) points out. The negated sentence in (1c) is shorter than the passive sentence in (1b), which again is shorter than the combination of both in (1e). Maybe the differences in identification times are just due to the length of the sentences involved. So, now we have two possible models to account for the facts and, following Occam's razor, we should go for the second explanation, namely: identification times are merely due to differences in sentence length.

The second caveat concerns the experimental task itself. Harley (^{3}2008) writes:

> If we ask participants explicitly to detransform sentences [i.e. relate a transformed sentence to its non-transformed counterpart], it is not surprising that the time it takes to do this reflects the number of transformations involved. However, it is not a task that we necessarily routinely do in language comprehension. (Harley ^{3}2008: 293)

The experiment analyses a conscious process. However, Chomsky makes clear that knowledge of a grammar and consciousness of the rules involved are two quite different things:

> Obviously, every speaker of a language has mastered and internalized a generative grammar that expresses his knowledge of his language. This is not to say that he is aware of the rules of the grammar or even that he can become aware of them, or that his statements about his intuitive knowledge of the language are necessarily accurate. Any interesting generative grammar will be dealing, for the most part, with mental processes that are far beyond the level of actual or even potential consciousness [...]. (Chomsky 1965: 8)

A more indirect and 'natural' task was used in an experiment by Savin and Perchonok (1965). Participants were aurally presented with sentences like the ones under (1) and a list of unrelated lexical items. They had to memorise the sentence and as many of the lexical items as possible. If they recalled the sentence correctly, the number of accurately recalled words was counted. The underlying assumption of this experimental design is the following: each of the transformations takes up space in memory. A sentence with no transformation, thus, leaves more space to memorise words than a sentence involving two or three transformations. Again, the results of the experiment are in line with what we would expect if transformations were psychologically real: the recall rate was inversely related to the number of transformations, i.e. the more transformations involved, the lower the number of words recalled correctly and vice versa. However, we have to ask again whether this experiment really tells us something about the processing of sentences. Prideaux criticises that

> there is an obvious potential confounding here between processing and memory. This particular experiment really focuses on some notion of memory space into which both a processed sentence and the list of words is placed, with the assumption that this is a fixed space. (Prideaux 1984: 108)

Similarly, Harley (^{3}2008) argues:

> Memory measures are not an on-line measure of what is happening in sentence processing; at best they are reflecting a side-effect. What we remember of a sentence need have no relation with how we actually processed that sentence. (Harley ^{3}2008: 293).

In addition, even though the results by Savon and Perchonok (1965) seem to be in line with those by Miller and McKean (1964) on a general level, they diverge on the processing demands of the negative and the passive transformation (Prideaux 1984: 108). While Miller and McKean showed passives to result in longer processing times than negations, participants in Savon and Perchonok's study were able to recall more words with passive than with negated sentences. A possible reason for this diversion might be that the two experiments actually tap different processes.

On the whole, we have seen that it is far from trivial to design experiments that really tell us something about language processing. In addition, we have seen how results that at first sight seem to clearly support a particular theory may have to be interpreted differently on closer inspection. With regard to the derivational theory of complexity we can conclude that although the results of the experiments seemed promising at first, "[t]he heady success of the early studies was shortly tarnished" (Prideaux 1984: 111), and "later experiments provided little support for the psychological reality of transformational grammar" (Harley ^{3}2008: 293).

12.2 The psychological reality of syntactic units

Half of this book has been about the description of the major syntactic elements and units, i.e. words, phrases and clauses. We have seen how constituency tests and other criteria license the existence of such units. It makes sense to posit them in our description of the language system. But does that necessarily mean that they are psychologically real? This section will take a closer look at experiments that are concerned with the reality of clauses and sentences. Again, the topic is approached from a psycholinguistic perspective and one aim is to draw attention to pitfalls in the interpretation of experimental data.

One paradigm in the study of clauses and sentences is what has been referred to as 'click migration' or 'click displacement'. The underlying idea is that "major processing units resist interruption: we finish what we are doing, and then process other material at the first suitable opportunity" (Harley [3]2008: 294). If a constituent is interrupted by a noise, this noise is perceived as having occurred after (or before) the presentation of the constituent. In the context of such experiments 'other material' refers to a click superimposed on a sentence that was presented over the auditory channel. A study of this kind is reported in Fodor and Bever (1965), who tested the following hypothesis:

> Noise heard during speech should tend to shift perceptually towards the boundaries of constituents. This shift should occur in such a fashion as to minimize the number of constituents the noise is perceived as interrupting. (Fodor & Bever 1965: 416)

What this means becomes clear if we take a closer look at one of the test sentences that they used, namely *That he was happy was evident from the way he smiled*. A tree diagram is given in Figure 12.1 below. Note that details of the structure of the adjective phrase are omitted, as they are irrelevant for the argument.

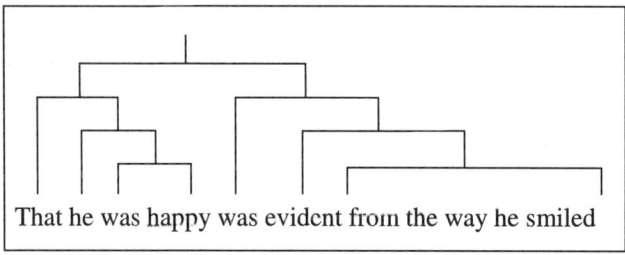

Figure 12.1: The syntactic structure of That he was happy was evident from the way he smiled.

Let us assume that while people hear this sentence a click was presented during the word *happy*. What would happen if the hypothesis stated above was correct? It is claimed that subjects would not perceive the click as being presented simultaneously with the word *happy* but it would be perceived as having occurred at a constituent boundary. The two nearest boundaries would be immediately to the left and the right of *happy*. In the first case the click would not be perceived as disrupting the processing of the word form *happy* but it would still get in the way of the processing of three constituents, namely the verb phrase (in the generative sense) *was happy*, the subordinate clause without subordinator *he was happy* and the clause with its subordinator *that he was happy*. If the click was moved to the right of *happy* it would appear to be less disruptive since all these constituents would already have been processed by then.

The authors placed clicks at various positions in sentences like the one in Figure 12.1 above. One of these clicks was placed after the major boundary (immediately following *happy* in Figure 12.1), four to the left and four to the right of this boundary. The participants were presented with a spoken version of the sentences through one ear and a click at one of the nine positions in the other ear. The subjects then had to write down the entire sentence and mark the position where they think the click had occurred.

As was argued above, clicks should be moved in the direction of the major constituent boundary or into the constituent boundary itself (marked by 'x'); see below.

(2) That he was happy, ‖ was evident from the way he smiled.

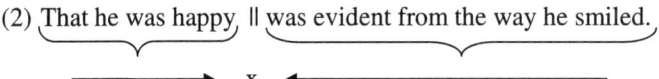

This is exactly what the data yielded: clicks that occurred to the left of the major boundary were usually perceived as having occurred further to the right and clicks that were placed to the right were perceived as being further to the left. In addition the authors found that clicks were least likely to be moved if they already occurred in the position of the major boundary. These findings suggest that this position is special as regards the processing of the sentence, i.e. the subject clause (*That he was happy* in example (2)) seems to have been validated as a psychologically real unit.

However, as Harley ([3]2008) points out:

> This interpretation is premature. The participants' task is a complex one: they have to perceive the sentence, parse it, understand it, remember it, and give their response. Click migration could occur at any of these points, not just perception of parsing. (Harley [3]2008: 294)

So, the experiment may tell us nothing about syntactic processing but instead it may only tell us something about how our memory works. Again, we are confronted with different plausible explanations and we have to come up with further data to be able to choose from those on offer. Other studies suggest that the dislocation of the clicks does not occur during processing but during the participants' response (i.e. writing down the sentence and marking the position of the click there). For instance, Harley points to a study by Wingfield and Klein (1971) who found that "the size of the migration effect is greatly reduced if participants can point to places in the sentence on a visual display at the same time as they hear them, rather than having to remember them" (Harley ^{3}2008: 295). As a consequence, the experiment conducted by Fodor and Bever (1965) should not be counted as evidence for the psychological status of clauses, although, at first sight, their interpretation seems plausible.

Nevertheless, the psychological reality of these basic syntactic units has been validated from various other sources. One of these is an experiment by Caplan (1972). Subjects listened to sentences of the following kinds.

(3) a) When the granite blocks are very **big**, cranes lift them.
    b) When the granite blocks are raised, **big** cranes lift them.

(Caplan 1972: 75)

After having heard the sentence, subjects were presented with a probe word and they had to decide if that word was part of the sentence they had heard or not. For the sentences under 3) the probe word would have been *big*. Note that *big* is the fourth word from the end of the sentence in both cases. But in the first case *big* is part of the first clause in the sentence, whereas in (3b) it is part of the second clause in the sentence. Caplan found significant differences in reaction times: subjects were more than 100 msec faster in identifying a probe word that occurred after the clause boundary, i.e. in the final clause, than before the clause boundary. That is, clauses have an effect on the recognition of words in such a way that it is easier to recognise words that are part of the clause heard immediately before the recognition task.

Further evidence for the psychological reality of clauses comes from research on the function of pauses in speech. Without going into detail, Reich (1980) finds that pauses facilitate speech perception if they are placed at the right position, i.e. between the clauses of a complex sentence: in that case, it is easier for subjects to recall the content of the sentence accurately than if pauses occur within the clauses. Again, we see that the clause is a unit that is relevant for the processing of language, a unit that is psychologically real.

An experiment by Jarvella (1971) suggests that sentence boundaries, too, have an effect on recall. He asked subjects to listen to a text that was interrupted at specific points. After each interruption, participants were asked to write down word-for-word as much as they could remember from the passage they had heard immediately before the interruption. The interruptions always occurred after a piece of text that contained exactly three clauses, as in the examples below (clause boundaries are indicated by slashes '/', sentence boundaries by double lines '||').

(4) a) The document had also blamed him for / **having failed to disprove the charges**. || Taylor was later fired by the President.
   b) The tone of the document was threatening. || **Having failed to disprove the charges**, / Taylor was later fired by the President. (cf. Jarvella 1971: 410)

The third clause is referred to as the immediate clause (i.e. immediately before the interruption). The second clause is the previous clause (previous to the immediate one) and the first one is the context clause. We can also distinguish immediate and previous sentences, depending on their position relative to the sentence boundary. As you can see, in (4a) the previous clause is part of the previous sentence, whereas in (4b) the previous clause is part of the immediate sentence. Jarvella (1971: 410) refers to this distinction as 'Long' and 'Short' conditions (the numbers in brackets indicate the length of the clause in number of words):

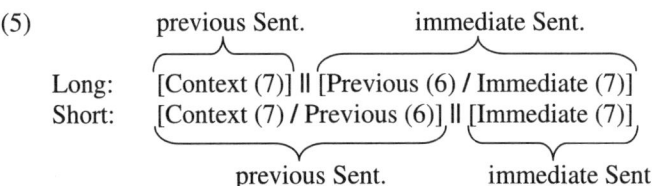

(5)   previous Sent.   immediate Sent.
       Long: [Context (7)] || [Previous (6) / Immediate (7)]
       Short: [Context (7) / Previous (6)] || [Immediate (7)]
                    previous Sent.   immediate Sent.

As to the results, Jarvella reports that the sum of the accurately recalled words was the same for both Long and Short condition. But he found that while immediate clauses were usually recalled completely correctly, subjects performed considerably poorer on the previous clauses and much worse on the context clauses. More interestingly, the results showed that the sentence boundary has a significant effect on recall. Clauses preceding the sentence boundary (as the first clause in 3b) were recalled accurately in only 15% of all cases, and pre-boundary sentences (as the first two clauses in 3a) only in 11% of all cases. In contrast, after a sentence boundary 69% of all clauses were recalled accurately and 67% of all sentences. This indicates that "the immediately heard sentence is an accessible syntactic unit in memory" (412). Another result that points at the relevance of the sentence is the fact that the previous clause was recalled correctly in 54.2% of all cases under the Long condition, i.e. if it was part of the immediate sentence. If it was part of the previous sentence, recall dropped to

19.8%: we seem to purge our memory from details of what we hear as soon as we recognise a sentence boundary.

On the whole, clauses as well as sentences not only seem to be units relevant for the description of language, but also psychologically real.

12.3 Parsing

The term 'parsing' refers to the analysis of sentences. This includes the hierarchical relations between the individual constituents as well as the functions that the constituents have, e.g. which is the subject, the direct and indirect object and so on, as well as semantic roles like 'agent', 'patient' or 'recipient'. Again, we can never really be sure about what is going on in the head of the language user when he or she analyses a sentence. What we are aiming at are models that account for observations that are made with regard to sentence processing. In particular, these observations concern the fact that some sentences seem particularly difficult to analyse and ambiguous sentences often show a tendency to be analysed in one particular direction.

Before we turn to the discussion of such experiments, a few remarks are in order here concerning the general nature of models of syntactic processing. A fundamental distinction is that between autonomous and interactive models (Harley ^{3}2008: 288): autonomous models claim that sentence processing is modular in that syntactic information is processed in isolation from possible other sources of information such as semantics and the context. In interactive models other kinds of information can influence the syntactic processing at any time of the parsing process. We will first take a look at autonomous models of parsing.

A first attempt in explaining parsing processes is Kimball (1973). He suggests seven principles of parsing that manage to account for a number of observations concerning sentence processing, such as the principle of end-weight and the preference for right-branching discussed in section 9.2.1 and 4.2.3, respectively. We will explore some of these principles by way of examples. One principle is called 'Right Association':

Right Association (Kimball 1973: 24)
Terminal symbols optimally associate to the lowest nonterminal node.

Kimball sees this principle at work in certain tendencies to interpret ambiguous sentences like the following.

(6) Joe figured that Susan wanted to take the cat out. (Kimball 1973: 24)

I assume that most of the readers of this book interpret this sentence to state that the cat is taken out, i.e. *out* is attached as particle to the verb *take* but not to the verb *figure* as in the modified version in (6a).

(6) a) Joe figured out that Susan wanted to take the cat.

Kimball's Right Association can account for this tendency. In those cases where a new word (a 'terminal symbol' in his diction) has to be attached to a phrase marker, the human parser will attach it to the lowest node possible. Consider Figure 12.2 below.

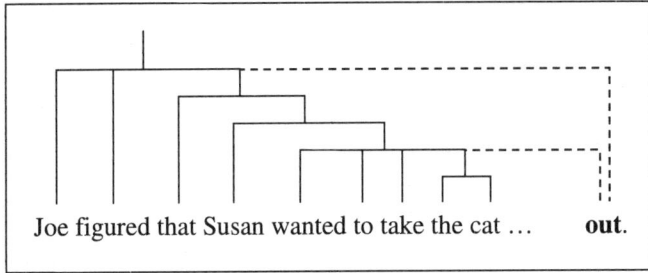

Figure 12.2: Parsing the sentence <u>Joe figured that Susan wanted to take the cat out</u>.

Having read all but the last word, the syntactic tree assigned to the string *Joe figured that Susan wanted to take the cat* might look like the solid part of Figure 12.2. On encountering the particle *out* the parser now has a choice of attaching it to the verb *take* or to the verb *figure*, as indicated by the two broken lines. Following Kimball's principle of Right Association, the parser is more inclined to attach the particle to the *take* node since that is the lowest possible node, which explains why we are more likely to interpret this ambiguous sentence as *take the cat out* rather than *figure out that*.

According to Kimball, this principle accounts for Heavy-NP shift:

> There seem to be grammatical mechanisms that avoid the generation of sentences that would be perceptually complex under [... Right Association], i.e. which would involve assigning terminals to other than the lowest, rightmost non-terminal. (Kimball 1973: 26)

Take a look at the non-shifted example under (7a) below.

(7) a) Many French politicians take a Europe in which France shares a lead for granted.
b) Many French politicians take for granted a Europe in which France shares a lead. (BNC-ABF:1495)

The lowest, rightmost non-terminal node to which the prepositional phrase *for granted* could be attached in accordance with syntactic rules would be the noun phrase *a lead* in (7a). However, it does not make any sense to attach the prepositional phrase *for granted* to that node. The only node we can really attach it to is the node for the verb form *take*, which, of course, is far away from the lowest and rightmost non-terminal node. In the case of (7b), the verbal node fulfils this requirement when the parser has reached the string *for granted* and created a tree fragment for the string *Many French politicians take*. The heavy-NP-shifted example in (7b) is in line with Right Association, (7a) is not.

Another principle manages to explain the difficulty that we usually have in processing what is called 'garden path sentences'. The term itself evokes a nice image: garden paths do not lead anywhere so you have to go back from where you started if you want to go somewhere. Something similar happens when processing this kind of sentences. We are lead to believe that the first analysis that we take is the correct one but find out towards the end of the sentence that it is not, and we have to redo the analysis. Consider the following (famous) example:

(8) The horse raced past the barn fell.

The first analysis of the sentence has the verb form *raced* as the main verb of the sentence (in the past tense). When our parser reaches the verb form *fell*, we find out that our previous analysis cannot be correct, because *fell* can only be the main verb. Going back to the verb form *raced* we now find that *raced* is the past participle form of the verb RACE and the whole clause *raced past the barn* is a reduced relative clause that postmodifies the head noun *horse*. That is, the whole sentence has to be understood as shown in (8a).

(8) a) The horse that was raced past the barn fell.

Kimball's 'Closure' principle manages to account for this phenomenon:

Closure
A phrase is closed as soon as possible, i.e. unless the next node parsed is an immediate constituent of that phrase. (Kimball 1973: 36)

We could paraphrase the Closure principle as follows: 'as soon as a syntactic analysis makes sense, go for that analysis'. This is exactly what happens in parsing the above sentence. The earliest possible phrase marker that makes sense, the earliest possible closure is to treat the string *The horse raced past the barn* as a complete sentence, as shown in Figure 12.3.

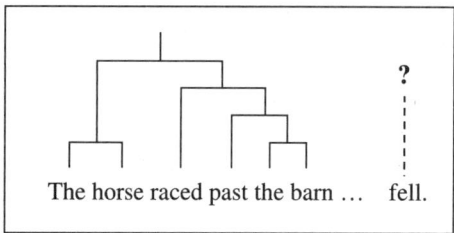

Figure 12.3: Parsing the sentence <u>The horse raced past the barn fell</u>.

Of course, as soon as we encounter the verb form *fell* we become aware that our first analysis cannot be the correct one, and the parser has to provide an alternative analysis, namely the one shown in (8a). Psycholinguistic experiments have shown that such processes (not surprisingly) take time. Kimball attributes this to a principle he calls 'Fixed Structure'..

Fixed Structure
When the last immediate constituent of a phrase has been formed, and the phrase E is closed, it is costly in terms of perceptual complexity ever to have to go back to reorganize the constituents of that phrase. (Kimball 1973: 37)

In Figure 12.3 we see that having processed *barn* a lot of structure, namely a complete sentence, has been closed. The correct analysis requires the parser to redo all structures related to *raced past the barn*, i.e. the only bits that can be retained are the two leftmost nodes. This re-analysis takes time, as is shown in experimental data. According to Kimball, the human parser, therefore, has lookahead capacities to prevent it from too frequent reanalyses. This seems plausible considering sentences like the ones below.

(9) a) Peter saw the man next to his wife Sarah read a book.
    b) Peter saw Tom read a book.

It appears that while we are lead along the garden path in (9a), where we are likely to first interpret *the man ...* as the direct object of the clause, we are not in (9b). In this case, the small number of constituents enables the look-ahead mechanism to prevent us from interpreting *Tom* as the direct object of the verb form *saw* and analyse it as the subject of a subordinate clause..

An elaboration of Kimball's principles is provided by Frazier and Fodor's (1978) 'sausage machine', a two-step model of parsing.

> The first step is to assign lexical and phrasal nodes to groups of words within the lexical string that is received; this is the work of what we will call the Preliminary Phrase Packager [PPP], affectionately known as the sausage machine. The second step is to combine these structured phrases into a complete phrase marker for the sentence by adding higher nonterminal nodes; the device which performs this we call the Sentence Structure Supervisor [SSS]. (Frazier & Fodor 1978: 291-292)

The first stage, the PPP or sausage machine, is supposed to make chunks out of a continuous string of lexical items, just as a sausage machine makes chunks of ground meat out of a continuous string of ground meat (hence the name). These 'lexical sausages' are then forwarded to the SSS for final analysis.

Both, PPP and SSS have limited capacity (around Miller's (1956) 7±2 items). As a consequence, the PPP can only work with about 6 words. Within this limited window, the PPP tries to accommodate any incoming word to the structure that it has already begun constructing. This, of course, only works within a 6-word window. Any relations between lexical items that are more than six words apart are therefore difficult to process, which explains the dependence of garden-path effects on the length of the sentence as in example (9). It also explains parsing preferences as in the examples below.

(10) a) Joe bought the book for Susan.
 b) Joe bought the book that I had been trying to obtain for Susan.
(Frazier & Fodor 1978: 299-300)

While the parser does not have any problems of assigning the prepositional phrase *for Susan* to the verb *bought* in (10a), it is more likely to analyse *for Susan* as a complement to the verb *obtain* in (10b). In the first case, the prepositional phrase is in the same 6-word window as the verb *bought*, whereas in the second case it is not, which leaves the parser only with the option to attach the prepositional phrase to *obtain*.

Let us consider (10b) is more detail. The first six words are *Joe bought the book that I*, and the parser does not have any chance of attributing a closed-off grammatical structure to the whole string. But it can attribute a structure like the following to the first four words (note that details are omitted):

(11)

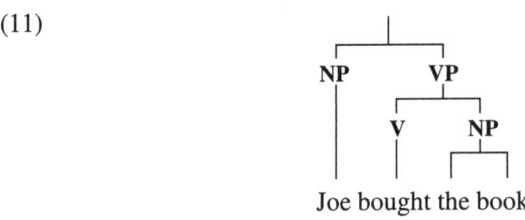

What also comes into play after having processed the first four words is a principle called 'New Nodes'. It is suggested by Kimball (1973: 29) and claims the "[t]he construction of a new node is signalled by the occurrence of a grammatical function word". Frazier and Fodor assume that the PPP follows this principle if it is close to reaching the limits of its capacity. That is, if a function word occurs, say, in position 5 or 6 the PPP will close off the package it is currently working on and it will transmit it to the SSS, as in the case above. The word form *that* in example (10b) signals a new phrase and the PPP will look at the next six-word string, i.e. *that I had been trying to*, to see if it can assign any structure to it. Again, the word form *to* introduces a new node, so that the PPP will come up with a structure for *that I had been trying*, as shown below (details omitted).

(12)

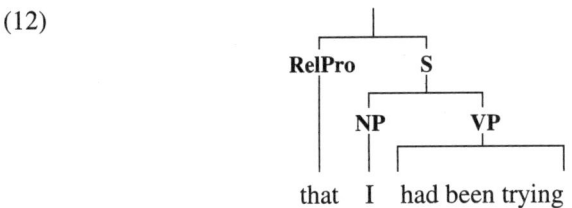

Finally, the string *to obtain for Susan* fits into the window of the PPP and it can assign a structure to this string as follows (details omitted).

(13)

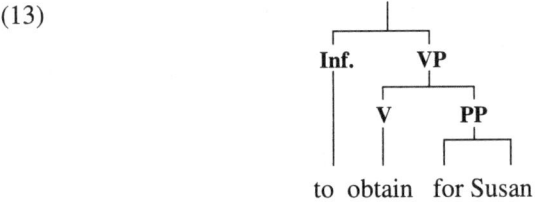

When the pre-packaged phrase under (13) has left the PPP, the SSS will start working on joining the three phrases together in one phrase marker for the whole sentence, which then yields the complete analysis..

These early models are autonomous, i.e. they work on syntactic information alone, disregarding frequencies or aspects of meaning and context. However, more recent research has shown that such aspects do come into play. As to the first, the garden-path effect with *The horse raced past the barn fell* might be explained by mere frequency effects. Harley (^{3}2008: 291) points to a study by McKoon and Ratcliff (2003) who show that reduced relative clauses with the verb RACE are highly unlikely to occur in natural language. That is, we have an extreme frequency bias towards analysing *raced* as the main verb of the clause.

Taraban and McClelland (1988) present findings which suggest that semantics come in during early stages of processing. They conducted a self-paced reading experiment, which means that subjects were presented with sentences, in which each letter was replaced by a dash. When the subjects pressed a switch, the first word was shown. Another press of the switch showed the second word and replaced the first word and so on. The sentence under (14a) was thus presented as under (14b), where each line shows what the subjects see after having pressed the switch.

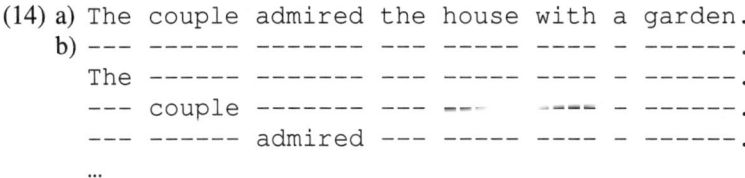

The authors tested reading times with sentence pairs like the following:

(15) a) The couple admired the house with a garden.
　　 b) The couple admired the house with a friend.
　　　　　　　　　　　　　　　(Taraban & McClelland 1988: 625)

It is important to note that the first sentence has a slightly more complex structure (if we measure complexity in terms of nodes in the syntactic tree). Compare the two phrase markers below.

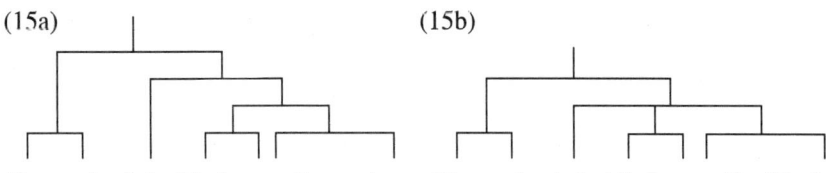

(15a) has seven nodes (including the S-node at the top) while (15b) only has six nodes. So, we would assume that (15a) should take longer to read than (15b). However, the experiments found that the reverse is true. As an explanation the authors suggest that the lexical context up to the final word in both sentences has built up expectations favouring (15a) instead of (15b). That is, it is more common for us to admire a house that has a garden than to admire a house together with a friend. So, we find that semantics comes into play during processing. The authors write:

> [A]ll our evidence is consistent with the view that subjects experience difficulty when their expectations are violated, and that these expectations are governed, at least in part, by content. Indeed it should be noted that the results we have reported cannot be accounted for by *any* syntactic principle of which we are aware – that is, by any principle that does not consider the content of the sentence, since our expectations effects occurred in sentences that differed in the content, and not in the syntactic constituents for the sentence frames. (Taraban & McClelland 1988: 611)

Expectations also seem to be raised by the main verb that occurs in a sentence. In another self-paced reading experiment by Trueswell et al. (1993), subjects were presented with sentences that contained main verbs which either had a strong bias to be followed by a direct object (NP-bias) or a complement clause (S-bias), as in (16a) and (16b), respectively.

(16) a) The student forgot the solution was in the back of the book. (NP-bias)
b) The student hoped the solution was in the back of the book. (S-bias)

The authors found

> clear syntactic misanalysis effects when a noun phrase that was a plausible object of an NP-bias verb turned out instead to be the subject of a sentence complement. However, no misanalysis effects obtained when the same noun phrase followed an S-bias verb. (Trueswell et al. 1993: 548)

It is important to emphasise that "subcategorization information becomes available almost immediately after a verb is recognized" (547). That is, the sentence is not processed first on the basis of syntactic heuristics only and then approved or rejected on the basis of semantic information. Instead, semantic information comes in at early stages in parsing, i.e. syntax and semantics go hand in hand during processing. On the whole, parsing does not seem to be autonomous, i.e. a process solely guided by abstract syntactic principles of the kinds described by Kimball (1973) or Frazier and Fodor (1978). Rather, the human parser seems to be biased by frequencies and semantic expectancies. Parsing proceeds word by word, and at each word the parser makes use of different kinds of information that this word provides.

12.4 Further reading

An accessible introduction to psycholinguistics is Prideaux (1984), who also offers a chapter on experimental syntax which gives a good overview of the early studies in that area.

A more recent and more comprehensive account is provided by Harley (^{3}2008), who also includes information on neurological findings on parsing and information on syntactic processing in aphasics.

12.5 Study questions

1) Describe in your own words the lesson that we can learn from the Texas A&M joke discussed in the beginning of this chapter.
2) Does it make sense, according to Noam Chomsky, to try and validate models of competence in experimental procedures?
3) Describe the main claim underlying the Derivational Theory of Complexity.
4) Why would it be premature to interpret the findings reported in Miller and McKean (1964) as evidence for the reality of a transformational component?
5) Is the clause a psychologically real unit? Can you describe psycholinguistic evidence that shows why or why not?
6) What is the rationale behind click-migration experiments, and what can they tell us about the psychological reality of clauses?
7) How can Kimball's (1973) principles explain the garden path effect in the following sentence?
   After the Martians invaded the town was evacuated
8) Give a short description of Frazier and Fodor's (1978) 'sausage machine'.
9) How would Kimball and how would Frazier and Fodor explain the parsing difficulties associated with the following sentence?
   Joe figured that Susan wanted to take the train to New York out.
10) Sketch the experimental findings presented in this chapter that indicate that parsing involves syntactic, semantic and frequency information.

References

Aarts, B. (1997): *English Syntax and Argumentation*. London: Macmillan
Aarts, B. (2007): *Syntactic Gradience: The Nature of Grammatical Indeterminacy*. Oxford: Oxford University Press.
Aarts, B., D. Denison, E. Keizer & G. Popova (eds.) (2004): *Fuzzy Grammar. A Reader*. Oxford: Oxford University Press.
Aarts, F. & J. Aarts (1982): *English Syntactic Structures: Functions and Categories in Sentence Analysis*. Oxford: Pergamon Press.
Altenberg, B. & M. Eeg-Olofsson (1990): "Phraseology in English: Presentation of a project", *Theory and Practice in Corpus Linguistics*, ed. J. Aarts & W. Meijs. Amsterdam: Rodopi.1-26.
Aristotle (1963 [c.330 BC]): *Categories and De Interpretatione*, transl. J. L. Ackrill. Oxford: Oxford University Press.
Armstrong, S.L., L. Gleitman & H. Gleitman (1983): "What some concepts might not be", *Cognition* 13, 263-308.
Ball, C. (1994): "Automated text analysis: Cautionary tales", *Literary and Linguistic Computing* 9, 295-302.
Behaghel, O. (1909): "Beziehungen zwischen Umfang und Reihenfolge von Satzgliedern", *Indogermanische Forschungen* 25, 110-142.
Behaghel, O. (1932): *Deutsche Syntax. Eine geschichtliche Darstellung. Band IV. Wortstellung. Periodenbau*. Heidelberg: Carl Winters Universitätsbuchhandlung
Biber, D., S. Johansson, G. Leech, S. Conrad & E. Finegan (1999): *Longman Grammar of Spoken and Written English*. Harlow: Pearson Education Limited.
Birner, B. & G.L. Ward (1998): *Information Status and Noncanonical Word Order in English*. Amsterdam: John Benjamins.
Bloomfield, L. (1933): *Language*. London: George Allen & Unwin.
Caplan, D. (1972): "Clause boundaries and recognition latencies for words in sentences", *Perception and Psychophysics* 12, 73-76.
Carter, R. & M. McCarthy (2006): *Cambridge Grammar of English: A Comprehensive Guide. Spoken and Written Grammar and Usage*. Cambridge: Cambridge University Press.
Chafe, W.L. (1982): "Integration and involvement in speaking, writing, and oral literature", *Spoken and Written Language: Exploring Orality and Literacy*, ed. D. Tannen. Norwood, NJ: Ablex. 35-53.
Chomsky, N. (1957): *Syntactic Structures*. The Hague: Mouton.
Chomsky, N. (1965): *Aspects of the Theory of Syntax*. Cambridge, MA: The M.I.T. Press.

Chomsky, N. (1970): "Remarks on nominalization", *Readings in English Transformational Grammar*, ed. Waltham, MA: Ginn. 184-221.
Clark, E.V. & H.H. Clark (1977): *Psychology and Language: An Introduction to Psycholinguistics*. New York: Harcourt, Brace, Jovanovich.
Clark, H.H. & S.E. Haviland (1977): "Comprehension and the given-new contract", *Discourse Production and Comprehension*, ed. R.O. Freedle. Norwood: Ablex. 1-40.
Croft, W. & D.A. Cruse (2004): *Cognitive Linguistics*. Cambridge: CUP.
Cruse, D.A. (1986): *Lexical Semantics*. Cambridge: Cambridge University Press.
Dabrowska, E. (2004): *Language, Mind and Brain: Some Psychological and Neurological Constraints on Theories of Grammar*. Edinburgh: Edinburgh University Press.
Daneš, F. (1964): "A three-level approach to syntax", *Traveaux du Cercle Linguistique de Prague* 1, 225-240.
Daneš, F. (1974): "Functional sentence perspective and the organization of the text", *Papers on Functional Sentence Perspective,* ed. F. Daneš. The Hague: Mouton. 106-128.
Dorgeloh, H. (1997): *Inversion in English: Form and Function*. Amsterdam: John Benjamins.
Drubig, H.B. (1988): "On the discourse function of subject verb inversion", *Essays on the English Language and Applied Linguistics on the Occasion of Gerhard Nickel's 60th Birthday*, ed. J.Klegraf & D.Nehls. Heidelberg: Groos. 83-95.
Esser, J. (1984): *Untersuchungen zum gesprochen English: Ein Beitrag zur strukturellen Pragmatik*. Tübingen: Gunter Narr.
Esser, J. (1988): *Comparing Reading and Speaking Intonation*. Amsterdam: Rodopi.
Esser, J. (1992): "Neuere Tendenzen in der Grammatikschreibung des Englischen", *Zeitschrift für Anglistik und Amerikanistik* 40, 112-123.
Esser, J. (1995): "Einzelaspekt: Wortstellung und Fokusstrukturen", *Handbuch Englisch als Fremdsprache (HEF)*, ed. R. Ahrens, W.-D. Bald & W. Hüllen. Berlin: Erich Schmidt. 151-154.
Esser, J. (1999): "Collocation, colligation, semantic preference and semantic prosody: new developments in the study of syntagmatic word relations", *Words, Lexeme, Concepts – Approaches to the Lexicon: Studies in Honour of Leonhard Lipka*, ed. W. Faulkner & H.-J. Schmid. Tübingen: Narr. 155-165.
Esser, J. (2000): "Corpus linguistics and the linguistic sign", *Corpus Linguistics and Linguistic Theory: Papers from the Twentieth International Conference on English Language Research on Computerized Corpora (ICAME 20)*, ed. C. Mair & M. Hundt. Amsterdam: Rodopi. 91-101.

Esser, J. (2006): *Presentation in Language: Rethinking Speech and Writing*. Tübingen: Gunter Narr.
Euler, B. (1991): *Strukturen Mündlichen Erzählens: Parasyntaktische und Sententielle Analysen am Beispiel des Englischen Witzes*. Tübingen: Narr.
Evans, V. & M. Green (2006): *Cognitive Linguistics: An Introduction*. Edinburgh: Edinburgh University Press.
Fillmore, C., P. Kay & M. C. O'Connor (1988): "Regularity and idiomaticity in grammatical constructions: the case of *let alone*", *Language* 64: 501-538.
Firth, J.R. (1968 [1957]): "A synopsis of linguistic theory, 1930 – 55", *Selected Papers of J.R. Firth 1952 – 59*, ed. F.R. Palmer. London: Longmans, Green and Co, 168-205.
Fodor, J.A. & T.G. Bever (1965): "The psychological reality of linguistic segments", *Journal of Verbal Learning and Verbal Behavior* 4, 414-420.
Francis, G. (1993): "A corpus-driven approach to grammar: principles, methods and examples", *Text and Technology: In Honour of John Sinclair*, ed. M. Baker, G. Francis & E. Tognini-Bonelli. Amsterdam: John Benjamins. 137-156.
Francis, G., S. Huston & E. Manning (1996): *Collins COBUILD Grammar Patterns 1: Verbs*. London: HarperCollins.
Francis, G., S. Huston & E. Manning (1998): *Collins COBUILD Grammar Patterns 2: Nouns and Adjectives*. London: HarperCollins.
Frazier, L. & J.D. Fodor (1978): "The sausage machine: a new two-stage parsing model", *Cognition* 6, 291-325.
Fries, C.C. (1952): *The Structure of English: An Introduction to the Construction of English Sentences*. New York: Harcourt, Brace and Company.
Gabelentz, v.d. G. (1901, 1972 2nd imprint): *Die Sprachwissenschaft, ihre Aufgaben, Methoden und Bisherigen Ergebnisse*. Tübingen: TBL.
Givón, T. (2009): *The Genesis of Syntactic Complexity: Diachrony, Ontogeny, Neurocognition, Evolution*. Amsterdam: John Benjamins.
Goldberg, A. (1995): *Constructions: A Construction Grammar Approach to Argument Structure*. Chicago: University of Chicago Press.
Goldberg, A. (2005): "Argument realization: the role of constructions, lexical semantics and discourse factors", *Construction Grammar: Cognitive Grounding and Theoretical Extensions*, ed. J.-O. Östman & M. Fried. Amsterdam: John Benjamins. 17-43.
Goldberg, A. (2006): *Constructions at Work: The Nature of Generalization in Language*. Oxford: Oxford University Press.
Greenbaum, S. (1996): *The Oxford English Grammar*. Oxford: Oxford University Press.
Haegeman, L. (^{2}1994; 1991): *Introduction to Government & Binding Theory*. Oxford: Blackwell.

Halford, B. (1996): *Talk Units: The Structure of Spoken Canadian English*. Tübingen: Narr.

Halliday, M.A.K. (1987): "Spoken and written modes of meaning", *Comprehending Oral and Written Language*, ed. R. Horowitz & S. Samuels. San Diego: Academic Press. 55-82.

Halliday, M.A.K. (1989): *Spoken and Written Language*. Oxford: Oxford University Press.

Halliday, M.A.K. (2001): "Literacy and linguistics: relationships between spoken and written language", *Analysing English in a Global Context: A Reader*, ed. A. Burns & C. Coffin. London: Routledge. 181-193.

Harley, T.A. (^{3}2008): *The Psychology of Language: From Data to Theory*. Hove: Psychology Press.

Haviland, S.E. & H.H. Clark (1974): "What's new? Acquiring new information as a process in comprehension", *Journal of Verbal Learning and Verbal Behaviour* 13, 512-521.

Hawkins, J.A. (1994): *A Performance Theory of Order and Constituency*. Cambridge: Cambridge University Press.

Hoey, M. (2005): *Lexical Priming: A New Theory of Words and Language*. London: Routledge.

Huddleston, R. & G.K. Pullum (2002): *The Cambridge Grammar of the English Language*. Cambridge: Cambridge University Press.

Hunston, S. & G. Francis (2000): *Pattern Grammar: A Corpus-Driven Approach to the Lexical Grammar of English*. Amsterdam: John Benjamins.

Jackendoff, R. (1977): *X' Syntax. A Study of Phrase Structure*. Cambridge, MA: The MIT Press.

Jarvella, R.J. (1971): "Syntactic processing of connected speech", *Journal of Verbal Learning and Verbal Behavior* 10, 409-416.

Katz, J.J. & J.A. Fodor (1963): "The structure of a semantic theory", *Language* 39, 170-210.

Kimball, J. (1973): "Seven principles of surface structure parsing in natural language", *Cognition* 2, 15-47.

Klenk, U. (2003): *Generative Syntax*. Tübingen: Narr.

Kreyer, R. (2006a): *Inversion in Modern Written English: Syntactic Complexity, Information Status and the Creative Writer*. Tübingen: Gunter Narr.

Kreyer, R. (2006b): "'Observer effect', 'eyewitness perspective', and 'imaginary guided tour': what is so natural about the way inversions represent spatial relations?", *Cahiers de Recherche* 9, 115-132.

Lamb, S.M. (2000): "Bidirectional processing in language and related cognitive systems", *Usage Based Models of Language*, ed. M. Barlow & S. Kemmer. Stanford: CSLI. 87-119.

Langacker, R.W. (1987): *Foundations of Cognitive Grammar, Volume 1: Theoretical Prerequisites*. Stanford: Stanford University Press.

Langacker, R.W. (1988): "An overview of cognitive grammar", *Topics in Cognitive Linguistics*, ed. B. Rudzka-Ostyn. Amsterdam: John Benjamins. 3-48.
Lipka, L. (2002): *English Lexicology: Lexical Structure, Word Semantics and Word-Formation*. Tübingen: Narr.
Longman Dictionary of Contemporary English (^{4}2003). Harlow: Pearson Educated Limited.
Louw, B. (1993): "Irony in the text or insincerity of the writer? The diagnostic potential of semantic prosodies", *Text and Technology: In Honour of John Sinclair*, ed. M. Baker, G. Franics & E. Tognini-Bonelli. Amsterdam: John Benjamins. 157-176.
Lyons, J. (1981): *Language and Linguistics. An Introduction*. Cambridge: CUP.
Marchand, H. (1969): *The Categories and Types of Present-Day English Word-Formation: A Synchronic-Diachronic Approach*. Wiesbaden: Harrassowitz.
Mathesius, V. (1975 [1961]): *A Functional Analysis of Present Day English on a General Linguistic Basis*, ed. J. Vachek. The Hague: Mouton.
Mathesius, V. (1929): "Zur Satzperspektive im modernen Englisch", *Archiv für das Studium der Neueren Sprachen und Literatur* 55, 202-210.
Matthews, P. H. (1981): *Syntax*. Cambridge: Cambridge University Press.
McKoon, G. & R. Ratcliff (2003): "Meaning through syntax: language comprehension and the reduced relative clause construction", *Psychological Review* 110, 490-525.
McRoberts, R. (1981): *Writing Workshop: A Student's Guide to the Craft of Writing*. South Melb., Vic.: Macmillan.
Miller, G A. & K.E. McKean (1964): "A chronometric study of some relations between sentences", *Quarterly Journal of Experimental Psychology* 16, 297-308.
Miller, G.A. (1956): "The magical number seven, plus or minus two: some limits on our capacity for processing information", *Psychological Review* 63, 81-97.
Miller, J. & R. Weinert (1998): *Spontaneous Spoken Language: Syntax and Discourse*. Oxford: Clarendon.
Mindt, D. (2000): *An Empirical Grammar of the English Verb System*. Berlin: Cornelsen.
Mukherjee, J. (2001): *Form and Function of Parasyntactic Presentation Structures: A Corpus-based Study of Talk Units in Spoken English*. Amsterdam: Rodopi.
Novak, V. (1996): *Form, Bedeutung und Funktion von Nomen-Nomen-Kombinationen*. Frankfurt a. M.: Peter Lang.
Ouhalla, J. (1996): *Introducing Transformational Grammar: From Rules to Principles and Parameters*. London: Arnold.

Palmer, F.R. (1976): *Semantics: A New Outline*. Cambridge: Cambridge University Press.
Partington, A. (1998): *Patterns and Meanings: Using Corpora for English Language Research and Teaching*. Amsterdam: John Benjamins.
Pilch, H. (1964): *Phonemtheorie*. Basel: Karger.
Pilch, H. (1990): "Syntax gesprochener Sprachen: die Fragestellung", *Syntax Gesprochener Sprachen*, ed. B.K. Halford & H. Pilch. Tübingen: Gunter Narr. 1-18.
Plag, I. (2003): *Word-formation in English*. Cambridge: Cambridge University Press.
Prideaux, G.D. (1984): *Psycholinguistics: The Experimental Study of Language*. London: Croom Helm.
Quirk, R., J. Svartvik, G. Leech & S. Greenbaum (1985): *A Comprehensive Grammar of the English Language*. London: Longman.
Radford, A. (1997): *Syntactic Theory and the Structure of English: A Minimalist Approach*. Cambridge: Cambridge University Press.
Reich, S.S. (1980): "Significance of pauses for speech perception", *Journal of Psycholinguistic Research* 9, 379-389.
Robins, R.H. (^{3}1980; 1964): *General Linguistics. An Introductory Survey*. London: Longman.
Rosch, E. (1978): "Principles of Categorization", *Cognition and Categorization*, ed. E. Rosch & B.B. Lloyd. Hillsdale, NJ: Lawrence Earlbaum. 28-48.
Rosch, E., C.B. Mervis, W.D. Gray, D.M. Johnson & P. Boyes-Braem (1976): "Basic objects in natural categories", *Cognitive Psychology* 8, 382-439.
Sapir, E. (1921): *Language: An Introduction to the Study of Speech*. New York: Harcourt Brace.
Saussure, F. de (1959 [1916]): *Course in General Linguistics*. Transl. by W. Baskin. London: Peter Owen Limited.
Savin, H.B. & E. Perchonok (1965): "Grammatical structure and immediate recall of English sentences", *Journal of Verbal Learning and Verbal Behavior* 4, 348-353.
Schäpers, U. (2009): *Nominal versus Clausal Complexity in Spoken and Written English*. Frankfurt a. M.: Peter Lang.
Sinclair, J. (1996): "The search for units of meaning", *Textus* 9, 75-106.
Sinclair, J. (2004): *Trust the Text: Language, Corpus and Discourse*. London: Routledge.
Sinclair, J. (1991): *Corpus, Concordance, Collocation*. Oxford.
Taraban, R. & J.L. McClelland (1988): "Constituent attachment and thematic roles assignment in sentence processing: influences of content-based expectations", *Journal of Memory and Language* 27, 597-632.
Taylor, J.R. (1998): "Syntactic constructions as prototype categories", *The New Psychology of Language. Cognitive and Functional Approaches to Lan-*

guage Structure. Vol. 1. ed. M. Tomasello. Mahwah, NJ.: Lawrence Erlbaum. 177-202.
Ten Hacken, P. (2007): *Chomskyan Linguistics and its Competitors.* London: Equinox.
Tomasello, M. (2003): *Constructing a Language: A Usage-based Theory of Language Acquisition.* Cambridge, MA: Harvard University Press.
Tomasello, M. (1992). *First Verbs: A Case Study of Early Grammatical Development.* Cambridge; Cambridge University Press.
Trubetzkoy, N.S. (1939): *Grundzüge der Phonologie.* Prag: Cercle Linguistique de Prague.
Trueswell, J.C., M.K. Tanenhaus & C. Kello (1993): "Verb-specific constraints in sentence processing: separating effects of lexical preference from garden-paths", *Journal of Experimental Psychology: Learning, Memory, and Cognition* 19, 528-553.
Wasow, T. & J. Arnold (2003): "Post-verbal constituent ordering in English", *Determinants of Grammatical Variation in English*, ed. G. Rohdenburg & B. Mondorf. Berlin: Mouton de Gruyter. 119-154.
Weil, H. (1978 [1844]): *The Order of Words in the Ancient Languages Compared with that of the Modern Languages.* Amsterdam: John Benjamins.
Wingfield, A. & J.F. Klein (1971): "Syntactic structure and acoustic pattern in speech perception", *Perception and Psychophysics* 9, 23-25.

Index

Aboutness	108
Abstraction	19–22
Acceptability	3–4
Adjective	38–40
Adjective phrase	89–94
Adverb	40–43
Adverb phrase	94–97
Adverbial	
attitude stance ~	118
circumstantial ~	115–17
epistemic stance ~	117
linking ~	118–19
stance ~	117–18
style stance ~	118
Agent	107
Appositive clause	83–84
Aspect	55–56
perfect ~	55–56
progressive ~	56
Associative relations	*See* Paradigmatic relations
Auxiliary	43–44
Bias of traditional grammar	151
Categorical rules	190
Categorisation	18–23
Aristotelian ~	141
form vs. function	22–23
problems with ~	137–50
Caused-motion construction	203–4
Clause	105–30
~ elements	106–19
canonical patterns	120–23
non-canonical patterns	123–30
obligatory and optional elements	122
relation to word, phrase and sentence	105–6
secondary patterns	123–30
structure of ~	120–23
Clause complex	153
Cleft sentence	127–30
It-cleft	127
wh-cleft	128
Closure	239
Colligation	196–98
Collocation	193–96
Complement	113–15
object ~	113–15
subject ~	113–15
Concord	109
Conjunction	47–48
Constituent analysis	*See* Constituents
Constituents	7–18
conflicting analyses	16–18
Construction	200–205
basic structure	222
Construction Grammar	200–205, 221–25
Coordination test	12–13
Coordinator	47
Dative alternation	170
Deep structure	211–13
Derivational theory of complexity	229–32
Determiner	
as function	70–74
as word class	46–47
Disfluency	157–58
Dislocation	
left ~	165
right ~	164–65
Ditransitive construction	202–3

Early Immediate Constituents 173–76
Endocentric phrase 97
Existential-*there* sentence 125–26
Exocentric phrase 98

Fixed structure 240
Fragmentation 162
Fronting 124, 171
Fuzziness 141–47

Garden-path sentence 239
Generative Grammar 189–92, 207–21
   standard model 207–14
   X-bar theory 214–21
Given information 176–80
Given-before-new information 176–80
Given-new contract 176–80
Gradience 147–50
Grammatical *See* Well-formed
Grammatical intricacy 158–64

Head 67–69
Heavy NP shift 170

IC- analysis *See* Constituents
Idiom principle 192–200
   and open-choice principle 192
Ill-formed 1–3
Indeterminacy 137–50
Infinitive clause 86
Information status 176–80
Integration 162
Inversion 124, 171
I-phrase (IP) 219–21
It-extraposition 126–27

Kimball's principles of parsing 237–41

Let-alone construction 201–2
Lexeme 30–31
Lexical density 158–64
Lexical rules 190
Lexical unit 30–31

Modality 54–55
Movement test 13
Multiple analysis 138–40
Multiple prepositional phrases 170

New information 176–80
Noun phrase 67–88, 67–88
   postmod. by appositive clause 83–84
   postmod. by finite clause 82–84
   postmod. by infinitive clause 86
   postmod. by non-finite clause 85–86
   postmod. by participle clause 85–86
   postmod. by prepositional phrase 80–82
   postmod. by relative clause 82–83
   postmodification 80–86
   premod. by adjective phrase 74–76
   premod. by noun phrase 77–79
   premod. by participles 76–77
   premodification 74–80
   structure of ~ 87

Object
   direct ~ 111–13
   indirect ~ 111–13
Occam's razor 228
Online production
   'keep talking' 156
   'limited planning ahead' 156
   'qualification' 157
Operator 63–65

Paradigmatic relations 7–8

Index

Parsing	237–45
Closure	239
Fixed structure	240
Kimball's principles	237–41
models of ~	241–43
Right association	237–39
Participle clause	85
Passive	*See* Voice
Passive clause	124–25
Pattern grammar	196–98
Phrase structure rules	*See* Rewrite rules
Preposition	44–45
Prepositional phrase	97–99
Principle of End-weight	173–76
Pronoun	45–46
Prototype theory	142
Psycholinguistics	227–45
Question test	14
Recursion	208–9
Recursiveness	*See* Recursion
Relative clause	82–83
Replacement test	9–12
Rewrite rules	207–9
Right association	237–39
Sausage machine	241–43
Selectional restriction	210–11
Semantic preference	198–200
Semantic prosody	198–200
Sentence	
complex ~	130–31
compound ~	131
relation to word, phrase and clause	105–6
Spoken language	
interactive nature of ~	166–67
structure of ~	158–65
Spoken Syntax	151–68
Subcategorisation rules	210–11
Subject	107–11
Subordinator	47
Substitutional Relations	*See* Paradigmatic Relations
Surface structure	211–13
Syntactic complexity	173–76
Syntactic variation	169–88
and artistic concerns	180–84
and emphasis	180–84
and text structure	180–84
factors	173–86
information status	176–80
interaction of factors	184
kinds of ~	170–72
syntactic complexity	173–76
weight	173–76
Syntagmatic relations	7–8
Syntax	
and meaning	189–205
and other disciplines	1–3
and psycholinguistics	227–45
and psychological reality	233–37
definition of ~	1
spoken vs. written ~	151–68
Talk unit	153–54
Tense	52–54
and time	52–54
Tone unit	152–53
'Toothpaste problem'	227–28
Transformation	211–14
and psychological reality	229–32
Turn	155
Ungrammatical	*See* Ill-formed
Variation	
according to use	169
according to user	169
Verb	
and clause patterns	121
as clause element	106

as word class	36–38, 43–44
auxiliary	44
complex transitive	120
copular ~	120
ditransitive	120
intransitive~	120
main	36–38
modal	43–44
montransitive ~	120
primary	43–44
transitive ~	120
Verb phrase	51–66
finite ~	51–63
finite, gramm. categories in ~	51–63
finite, structure of ~	62
non-finite ~	65
non-finite, kinds of ~	65
Voice	56–58
Weight	173–76
Well-formed	1–3
Word	29–31
as lexeme	30–31
as lexical unit	30–31
as word form	30–31
problems in defining ~	29–31
Word classes	31–48
closed ~	43–48
open ~	31–43
X-bar theory	214–21
X-phrase (XP)	216–17

Textbooks in English Language and Linguistics (TELL)

Edited by Magnus Huber and Joybrato Mukherjee

Band 1   Ulrike Gut: Introduction to English Phonetics and Phonology. 2009.
Band 2   Jürgen Esser: Introduction to English Text-linguistics. 2009.
Band 3   Rolf Kreyer: Introduction to English Syntax. 2010.

www.peterlang.de

Slávka Janigová

Syntax of -ing Forms in Legal English

Frankfurt am Main, Berlin, Bern, Bruxelles, New York, Oxford, Wien, 2008.
153 pp., num. tab.
European University Studies: Series 14, Anglo-Saxon Language and Literature.
Vol. 439
ISBN 978-3-631-57470-6 · pb. € 36,20*

The study is concerned with the issue of -ing forms in both the theoretical aspect (morpho-syntactic delimitation of the scalar range of -ing forms) and practical aspect (survey of their occurrence in a legal English corpus). The research concentrates on the syntactic analysis of -ing verbal nouns, gerunds and -ing participles, and is aimed to reveal the conditioning factors that influence the selection of a particular type of the nominalisations under analysis.

Contents: Degrees of nominalisation, complex condensation · Ing-forms in the projection of time (a diachronic approach) · Inflectional versus derivational nature of the -ing affix (a synchronic approach) · Status of respective types of -ing forms in terms of word-class assignment · Syntactic analysis of a legal English corpus · Summary of the factors conditioning the selection of a particular type

Frankfurt am Main · Berlin · Bern · Bruxelles · New York · Oxford · Wien
Distribution: Verlag Peter Lang AG
Moosstr. 1, CH-2542 Pieterlen
Telefax 00 41 (0) 32 / 376 17 27

*The €-price includes German tax rate
Prices are subject to change without notice
Homepage http://www.peterlang.de